Breakfast with Jesus

This **Billy Graham Library Selection** edition
is published by the Billy Graham Evangelistic Association
with permission from Tyndale House Publishers, Inc.

BREAKFAST
with
JESUS

Greg Laurie

Tyndale House Publishers, Inc.

Wheaton, Illinois

Breakfast with Jesus

Library of Congress Cataloging-in-Publication Data

Laurie, Greg.
  Breakfast with Jesus / Greg Laurie.
    p. cm.
Includes bibliographical references.
  ISBN: 1-59328-012-2
  Previous ISBN: 0-8423-5328-3 (sc)
  1. Jesus Christ—Biography—Devotional literature. I. Title.

Printed in the United States of America

CONTENTS

ACKNOWLEDGMENTS

Special thanks to Ron Beers, Mark Taylor, and their great team at Tyndale House Publishers. Thanks also to Steve Halliday and Mark Ferjulian for their help in making this book a reality.

Walking with the Savior

A little boy, frightened by a thunderous lightning storm, called out one dark night, "Daddy, come here. I'm scared!"

"Son," his father replied, "God loves you and He'll take care of you."

"I know God loves me," the boy answered, "but right now I want somebody who has skin on!"

That's a perfect description of Jesus. He was "God with skin on."

Many of us wish we could have walked the dusty streets of Jerusalem with Jesus while He ministered on this earth, or sat at the table with Him when He broke bread and blessed it. But we can't.

Or can we?

The apostle John, who personally walked and talked with Jesus, says that we *can* know Him. No, we cannot reach out and touch Him right now, but He is here just as powerfully as He was with His disciples some two thousand years ago. He wants to speak to us, guide us, protect us, and develop a close friendship with us.

"That which was from the beginning," John writes, "which we have heard, which we have seen with our eyes, which we have looked upon, and our hands have handled, concerning the Word of life . . . that which we have seen and heard we declare to you, that you also may have fellowship with us; and truly our fellowship is with the Father and with His Son Jesus Christ" (1 John 1:1-3). The phrase translated "seen with our eyes" could more literally be rendered "to view attentively, to contemplate, to gaze upon as a spectacle." Imagine what it must have been like to *see God* in human form, to be able to *hear* His voice with our own ears!

People often ask, "What did Jesus look like?" John spent several years with Him yet never mentioned His appearance—not once, even in passing. Yes, John spent hours gazing at Jesus, but not because of the Lord's striking physical appearance. It seems that Jesus was rather ordinary in the way He looked.

The two disciples on the road to Emmaus took the resurrected Christ to be an ordinary man. In the garden, Mary mistook Him for the gardener. Certainly no Bible passage tells us He wore a permanent halo. Judas told the enemies of Jesus that they could identify the Master when he would kiss Him on the cheek. Now, if the Lord looked as striking as we might imagine Him to look, He would have been easily identified—without a kiss from His betrayer. "He's the guy who looks like a king or a leader," Judas could have said. But he didn't.

As a Jew at this time in history, it seems likely that Jesus would have had dark skin and hair. Certainly He was not a fair-skinned Anglo-Saxon with blond hair. Why doesn't Scripture give us a physical description of Jesus? Because it isn't important.

Though He looked ordinary in outward appearance, John and the others had never met *anyone* like Him. The disciples spent practically every waking hour in the presence of Jesus, enthralled (and sometimes unnerved). Scripture tells us that John would often lean his head on the chest of Jesus so as not to miss anything (see John 13:23); he could hear even a whisper. All of the disciples watched carefully, hung on Jesus' every word, and scrutinized His every move.

And John is saying that *this* Jesus can be known today!

We might not be able to walk and talk and eat with Jesus in person as the disciples did, but we can fellowship with Him nonetheless. Jesus Himself said, "If anyone hears My voice and opens the door, I will come in to him and dine with him, and he with Me" (Revelation 3:20).

This book was created to help you do just that. I've designed the devotions in the first part, "The Person of Jesus," to allow you to come to know Jesus through the eyes of the disciples who lived and ministered with Him. The second part, "The Teaching of Jesus," introduces you to some of the main spiritual lessons the Savior entrusted to His followers. And the third part, "The Promises of Jesus," focuses on the delightful (and sometimes sobering!) promises that Jesus gives to everyone who chooses to walk with Him.

Are you ready to walk with the Savior? Are you hungry for the food He has prepared for you? Are you anxious to spend some quality time with Him, listening to His counsel and committing yourself to His plan for you? Then I invite you to join me as together we begin each day in fellowship with Jesus, walking with Him and listening to Him as the disciples did: "As soon as they had come to land, they saw a fire of coals there, and fish laid on it, and bread. . . . Jesus said to them, 'Come and eat breakfast'" (John 21:9, 12).

PART ONE

the person
of jesus

CHAPTER 1

He Must Increase

Then Jesus came from Galilee to John at the Jordan to be baptized by him. Matthew 3:13

Before Jesus officially began His public ministry, He had to take a couple of very important steps. The first was to be baptized.

Sometimes that troubles people. *Why should Jesus have to be baptized?* The idea certainly bothered John the Baptist. Matthew tells us that when Jesus came to be baptized, "John tried to prevent Him, saying, 'I need to be baptized by You, and are You coming to me?'" (Matthew 3:14).

In one way, it's really not so hard to understand why some don't understand Jesus' baptism. The Gospel of Luke tells us that John preached "a baptism of repentance for the remission of sins" (Luke 3:3). Since Jesus never committed any sin and therefore never had to repent of anything (see 2 Corinthians 5:21; Hebrews 4:15), what purpose would His baptism serve? Why should someone who never sinned undergo a baptism for the repentance of sins? John knew of Jesus' spotless character (see John 1:29), and so at first he opposed Jesus' request.

So why *did* Jesus ask John to baptize Him?

Before suggesting an answer, perhaps it would help if we recall something of John's background and importance.

The Gospel of Luke tells us that Jesus and John were cousins. By his early thirties, John had emerged as a major national figure. It's worth noting that Josephus, the renowned Jewish historian, wrote more about John than he did about Jesus. Why? Since the death of the prophet Malachi—a period of some four hundred years—Israel had not heard from a genuine prophet of God.

Until John.

John shook a nation with his bold words and unusual actions, drawing huge crowds eager to hear him preach. He was a radical, a revolutionary who proclaimed an uncompromising message of repentance and faith in the Messiah. John came at a strategic time in human history when the old covenant was about to roll into a new one and when all the law and sacrifices were to be fulfilled in the life and ministry of one man—a man like no other who had ever walked the earth (or will again). That man was Jesus. Yet at this point, John's notoriety and fame were greater.

But John had no desire to toot his own horn. He clearly knew his role. He was to pave the way and point people to Jesus.

John humbly accepted his role as the forerunner of the Messiah (see John 1:27). His motto in life was, "He must increase, but I must decrease" (John 3:30). He felt content to speak as a herald of the coming King.

When John clearly understood Jesus to be the Messiah, he directed even his own disciples to start following the Lord (see John 1:36-37). Once he did that, he was ready to fade into obscurity. His role was to point people to Jesus and then step aside.

For all these reasons, Jesus proclaimed John to be the greatest prophet who ever lived. "I say to you," Jesus declared, "among those born of women there is not a greater prophet than John the Baptist" (Luke 7:28).

None greater? How can that be? We know of no miracles that John performed. Unlike Moses, he never turned the Nile to blood. Unlike Elijah, he never called fire down from heaven. He never stopped the rain or raised a single person from the dead. He left behind no written record, unlike Isaiah and Jeremiah and even "minor prophets" like Malachi and Micah.

So why would Jesus call him the greatest of prophets?

Only one reason: his nearness and connection to Jesus. As God's appointed herald of the Messiah, John had no peer among the prophets.

How many of us think of greatness in terms like these? Too many of us wonder how God can enrich our lives, make us feel better about ourselves, or help us achieve success in business. We ask what God can do for *us* to make us greater and better.

John had a very different attitude. He constantly asked himself, "What can I do to prepare people for the coming of the Messiah? How can I direct them to Him? How can I decrease and He increase?"

John's godly character and unique mission help us to understand why Jesus came to His cousin to be baptized. For a long time, John had been preparing the people to receive the coming Messiah; at the baptism of Jesus, he would publicly identify the Lord as God's Anointed One.

Jesus also was baptized because He had come into the world to identify with the human race. So it was that He who was without sin submitted to a baptism designed for sinners. "Permit it to be so now," He told John, "for thus it is fitting for us to fulfill all righteousness" (Matthew 3:15).

When the day finally came for Jesus to make His very public stand, John welcomed Him into the waters of the Jordan River. As Jesus prayed, "the heaven was opened. And the Holy Spirit descended in bodily form like a dove upon Him, and a voice came from heaven which said, 'You are My beloved Son; in You I am well pleased'" (Luke 3:21-22).

In this way, John found true greatness with God and with all humanity. His life stands as an example to us of what it takes to shake a nation.

May we adopt John's philosophy of life as well!

May Christ increase, and may we decrease.

If we really lived like that, who knows how it would affect others for their good?

Like John, we must prepare men and women to get ready for the kingdom of God. May the Word of God burn in our hearts as we, too, prepare the way for the Lord.

CHAPTER **2**

How to Resist Temptation

Then Jesus, being filled with the Holy Spirit, returned
from the Jordan and was led by the Spirit into the
wilderness, being tempted for forty days by the devil.

Luke 4:1-2

Have you ever had one of those times when God blessed you in a wonderful way and then right afterwards you were tempted to do something wrong? It might have been after a wonderful worship service at church or a time of personal enrichment through Bible study, when suddenly an evil thought came knocking on the door of your imagination.

Have you ever wondered why that is?

Know this: you are not the first one this has happened to, nor will you be the last. And do not despair; it doesn't indicate that you are failing spiritually.

The fact is, it indicates that you are on the right track. You might be surprised to learn that it even happened to Jesus.

After the dove came the devil.

After the blessing came the trial.

Immediately following His baptism, Jesus marched into the wilderness to be tempted. Yet Jesus, as our champion and representative, met Satan face-to-face—and won. We can both share in His victory and follow His example.

The way that Jesus dealt with waves of spiritual attack gives us a model to follow, a template to apply, in our own times of testing and temptation.

FIRST TEMPTATION: MEET YOUR PHYSICAL NEEDS

Satan first tempted Jesus by suggesting that He turn a stone into bread (see Luke 4:3). It's as if he said, "Jesus, I just happened to be listening around the corner at your baptism. I heard Your Father say that You are His beloved Son. So, seeing as You are who You are, command these stones to become bread. Don't worry about the long-term repercussions. Just enjoy the moment. Satisfy Yourself. Play now, pay later."

Jesus replied, "It is written, 'Man shall not live by bread alone, but by every word of God'" (Luke 4:4). In essence He told the devil, "I'm not here to deal with you today as God—that day will come when you are cast into the bottomless pit. I'm dealing with you now as a man, on humanity's behalf."

Jesus stood on ground that we can occupy. Our Lord used the Word of God as His primary weapon against temptation. He did not use "executive privilege," but instead gave us a model for winning our own spiritual battles. We are to follow His example.

SECOND TEMPTATION: TAKE A SHORTCUT

Next, the devil tempted Jesus to take a shortcut to His objective: "Taking Him up on a high mountain, [the devil] showed Him all the kingdoms of the world in a moment of time. And the devil said to Him, 'All this authority I will give You, and their glory; for this has been delivered to me, and I give it to whomever I wish. Therefore, if You will worship before me, all will be Yours'" (Luke 4:5-7).

Note that Jesus did not refute Satan's claim. The Bible calls Satan "the god of this age" (2 Corinthians 4:4) and "the prince of the power of the air" (Ephesians 2:2). Satan was offering Jesus an opportunity to bypass the cross and rule anyway. How? Just by giving Satan the momentary satisfaction of worshiping him.

That's really all the devil has wanted all along: the top job. He lost his once-exalted place in heaven because he wanted to be God (see Ezekiel 28). Now he was saying to Jesus, "Just bow once; look at all You'll gain!"

But Jesus answered, "Get behind Me, Satan! For it is written, 'You shall worship the Lord your God, and Him only you shall serve'" (Luke 4:8). Notice that Satan had said nothing about *serving*—he wanted only a moment's *worship*. But Jesus recognized that a moment of worship can mean a lifetime of service.

It always starts with that first time. Just once. You'll know when to stop. When you get this one thing, this one possession, this one experience, this one win at the gambling table. But "just once" never satisfies. It's never enough. Give Satan an inch and he'll take a mile.

To Jesus, Satan offered "all the kingdoms of the world." Others sell out far cheaper. Esau sold his birthright for a bowl of beans (see Genesis 25). Married men and women sell out their spouses and children for a one-night fling that leads to a lifetime of regret. Judas sold his soul for thirty pieces of silver (see Matthew 26:15). Achan lost his life for a Babylonian garment (see Joshua 7).

The problem with the father of lies is that even when he *does* deliver on his promises, you still lose out. Just a moment at the altar of greed can lead to a lifetime of regret. That "one time" can lead to a ruined marriage, a destroyed reputation, a devastated family. And too late you discover that all that glitters is the point of a dagger.

THIRD TEMPTATION: MISUSE GOD'S PROMISES

Last, Satan set Jesus on the pinnacle of the temple and said to Him, "If You are the Son of God, throw Yourself down from here. For it is written: 'He shall give His angels charge over you, to keep you,' and, 'In their hands they shall bear you up, lest you dash your foot against a stone'" (Luke 4:9-11).

Satan quoted Scripture—yet note that he left out a crucial part. Psalm 91:11-12 actually says, "He shall give His angels charge over you, to keep you *in all your ways.* In their hands they shall bear you up, lest you dash your foot against a stone" (emphasis added).

That Satan omitted "in all your ways" shows us the importance of those words. In the context of Satan speaking to Jesus, "your ways" refers to *God's* ways, not to whatever path we might choose. Leave that out and we void the promise. We cannot violate God's Word and yet expect His blessing and protection.

None of us enjoys temptation, yet it is a reality of the Christian life. But temptation can have a positive effect. Martin Luther once quipped, "One Christian who has been tempted is worth a thousand who haven't." And it has been said, "Christians are a lot like teabags. You don't know what they're made of until you put them in hot water."

Follow Jesus' example the next time you're faced with temptation. Remember what you know of God's Word, then ask God to help you fight the battle. And guess what? You're on the winning side!

CHAPTER 3

Safer with Him

Then He arose and rebuked the wind and the raging of the water. And they ceased, and there was a calm. But He said to them, "Where is your faith?" And they were afraid, and marveled, saying to one another, "Who can this be? For He commands even the winds and water, and they obey Him!" Luke 8:24-25

Storms are quite common on the Sea of Galilee. Although the lake stretches only five miles wide and thirteen miles long, its perils are infamous. The reason? Its unique geography.

The lake lies at an incredible distance below sea level and stares up at mountains creased with deep ravines. The ravines serve as gigantic funnels that bring winds whirling down upon the lake without notice. A thermal buildup in the extremely low valley sucks cold air violently downward, often strengthening these gales.

One of those very violent storms engulfed the disciples one day after Jesus told them, "Let us cross over to the other side of the lake" (Luke 8:22). Soon after they launched, Jesus fell asleep. A windstorm quickly swept down on the lake and began to swamp their boat. The panicky disciples shook Jesus awake and shouted, "Master, Master, we are perishing!" (verse 24).

It's interesting to note that although the fury of the storm did not awaken the Lord, the frightened cries of His disciples did. In one sense, Jesus had fallen fast asleep, but in another sense, He had not. For God does not "sleep on the job." He is ever vigilant, watching over His beloved children. "Behold, He who keeps Israel shall neither slumber nor sleep," says the psalmist (Psalm 121:4).

Once awakened, Jesus stood and rebuked the wind and the raging waters. "Peace, be still!" He commanded (Mark 4:39).

That's a pretty unusual way to deal with a storm, don't you think?

But the fact is, Jesus recognized that this particular storm came from the devil himself. So Jesus was rebuking the one behind the storm.

A better translation of Jesus' phrase "Be still!" would be "Be muzzled!"

Like a wild animal, Satan was trying to stop Jesus and the disciples from reaching the other side and continuing His ministry.

So the Lord muzzled him, and he failed.

As the lake's waters grew calm and placid, Jesus turned to His quaking men and said, "Where is your faith?" Immediately their fear of the storm morphed into fear of *Him.* "Who can this be?" they asked one another, amazed. "For He commands even the winds and water, and they obey Him!" (Luke 8:25).

Can you identify with the disciples' alarm? Are you being pummeled by a storm right now? You thought you were headed in the right direction, when, without warning, a tempest hit. Your boat began filling with water, and you wondered, *Is Jesus sleeping? I'm going to drown!*

I have the privilege of serving on the board of directors of the Billy Graham Evangelistic Association. One year during a team retreat, Bible teacher Warren Wiersbe was the featured speaker. He spoke one morning on the "storms of life" and pointed out that there are three types of "storms" that may blow into our lives: correcting storms, protecting storms, and perfecting storms.

CORRECTING STORMS

Jonah faced this kind of storm when he disobeyed God and tried to run from the task God had assigned to him. A great storm overtook his ship. Through that storm the Lord took hold of His reluctant prophet and put him back on course (see the book of Jonah).

A correcting storm is entirely the result of disobedience to God and His call. Maybe you steal something and get caught. Maybe you're caught in a lie or found cheating on a test. When God allows you to reap the consequences of your actions, that is a "correcting storm."

The question is whether you will learn from your mistakes and change your behavior. When Jonah finally admitted his folly and repented, the storm stopped. Sometimes, however, we make the storm worse by our failure to respond properly. Liars and cheats may continue in their course. In that case, they have learned nothing, and the storm will surely grow worse.

PROTECTING STORMS

Some storms are designed to protect us from something far worse.

When God instructed Abraham, "Take now your son, your only son Isaac, whom you love," and sacrifice him atop Mount Moriah, He sent the patriarch into a howling storm. Why did God command such a thing? The Bible tells us it was a test to see if Abraham would place his love for his son on a higher plane than his love for the Lord (see Genesis 22:1-14). In other words, the great man of faith ran the risk of making his son an idol. When it was all said and done, Abraham passed the test beautifully, and God prevented him from taking his son's life. So the storm ended, and Abraham's faith and love for the Lord grew even stronger. Protecting storms may cause us a great deal of alarm and discomfort, but they shield us from something far worse.

PERFECTING STORMS

Joseph endured this kind of storm. God used hardship and disappointment to turn a promising young boy into a seasoned man of God. While we never get the sense that Joseph enjoyed the storms, we know he appreciated what they accomplished, for he could say to those who mistreated him, "You meant evil against me; but God meant it for good" (Genesis 50:20).

God used the storm on the Sea of Galilee to both protect and perfect Jesus' disciples. They really had no reason to panic. After all, Jesus had said to them, "Let us cross over to the other side of the lake." Had He said, "Let's go drown together," they would have had reason to worry. Jesus did not promise a smooth voyage, but He did say they would make it. And He Himself was on board!

When will *we* learn that we are safer with Jesus on a stormy sea than we are without Him even on the most placid lake? Better to be with Jesus, in any circumstance, than to be *anywhere* else without Him.

CHAPTER 4

No Match for Jesus

Now in the synagogue there was a man who had a spirit of an unclean demon. And he cried out with a loud voice, saying, "Let us alone! What have we to do with you, Jesus of Nazareth? Did You come to destroy us? I know who You are—the Holy One of God!" Luke 4:33-34

Make no mistake about it, demons are real. The Bible pictures them as powerful, malevolent, evil spirits who oppose God and His holy work. Scripture uses the word *unclean* to refer to their wicked, vile nature.

The New Testament records many accounts of demons inhabiting the bodies of unbelievers and causing all sorts of serious problems, such as making people mute (see Luke 11:14), epileptic (see Matthew 17:15; Mark 9:18), and self-destructive (see Mark 5:5). Satan is the leader of the demons, and they do his bidding (see Matthew 12:24).

The Bible also makes it clear that Jesus Christ and Satan are enemies. After Adam and Eve sinned, God put Satan on notice that One was coming who would crush him: "And I will put enmity between you and the woman, and between your seed and her Seed; He shall bruise your head, and you shall bruise His heel" (Genesis 3:15). Ever since, war has raged between God and Satan, good and evil, light and darkness—and also between their followers.

Know this: When you are God's friend, you are Satan's enemy (and vice versa). There will be no compromise, no negotiation.

Jesus will never turn from His purpose to crush Satan's head, and Satan will never turn from his lust to bruise Jesus' heel.

Frequently throughout His earthly ministry, Jesus demonstrated His superiority over the demonic realm. Once when the Lord cast a demon out of a man, the crowds who watched the incident "were all amazed and spoke among themselves, saying, 'What a word this is! For with authority and power He commands the unclean spirits, and they come out'" (Luke 4:36).

All demons greatly respect and fear Jesus Christ. In fact, whenever they met Jesus when He was on earth, they affirmed His authority. Mark writes, "And the unclean spirits, whenever they saw Him, fell down before Him and cried out, saying, 'You are the Son of God'" (Mark 3:11). Curiously, however, Jesus never welcomed these demonic endorsements. More than once we are told that He commanded the demons to be quiet, "for they knew that He was the Christ" (Luke 4:41; see also Mark 1:34).

It should not surprise us, then, to realize that the demons—and even the devil himself—are neither atheists nor agnostics. They believe in the existence of God. They believe in the deity of Jesus Christ. They believe that the Bible is the very Word of God. They believe Jesus is coming back again. In fact, in a very limited sense, you could say that demons and the devil are quite orthodox in their beliefs.

Yet they are far from followers of Jesus!

James tells us that the demons believe and "tremble" (2:19). This verb, occurring only here in the New Testament, means "to bristle" and pictures what happens when some unspeakable horror causes one's hair to stand on end. Why do the demons tremble? Because they not only believe in the person of Christ, they also recognize His power and authority.

When I was a young Christian, I remember someone saying, "Let's pray for Satan's conversion." Even as someone with a thimbleful of Bible knowledge, I knew this was crazy. The devil will never turn to God. Scripture is clear about his origin, agenda, and destiny. He recognizes Christ's power over him, but his "faith" does not transform his character or improve his conduct. He and his demons are headed for everlasting destruction.

More than that, Satan and his demons know their day of judgment is coming. When Jesus was about to cast some demons out of a man, the demons cried out, "Have You come here to torment us before the time?" (Matthew 8:29). Luke adds that the evil spirits "begged Him that He would not command them to go out into the abyss" (Luke 8:31).

What is this "abyss"? It may be the place mentioned in 2 Peter 2:4, where the apostle writes, "God did not spare the angels who sinned, but cast them down to hell and delivered them into chains of darkness, to be reserved for judgment." Some demons apparently committed such heinous offenses that God threw them into a special "holding tank" until the final Day of Judgment. The word translated "hell" in this verse is the Greek word *tartarus,* a term describing a place lower than hades where divine punishment is meted out.

The devil knows and fears the divine judgment awaiting him—but he does *not* fear mere humans. The book of Acts tells us about seven young "sons of Sceva" (Acts 19:13-16). These fellows ran around trying to cast out demons. One day they encountered a demon-possessed man and said to him, "We exorcise you by the Jesus whom Paul preaches." The evil spirit answered, "Jesus I know, and Paul I know; but who are you?" The possessed man then beat the men up, forcing them to flee "naked and wounded" (verse 16).

This shows us the considerable supernatural power of demons and the absolute futility of trying to fight them in our own strength. I once heard an evangelist say to a church he was visiting, "I am here to fight the devil." How foolish!

As Warren Wiersbe has said, "The Christian life is not a playground, but a battlefield." And from the day you committed yourself to follow Christ, you entered that battle. So you need to put on your armor!

In Ephesians 6, the apostle Paul tells us about the various pieces of armor we need to survive and even win in the spiritual battle, including the helmet of salvation, the breastplate of righteousness, the sword of the Spirit, etc. But before he tells us about suiting up for spiritual battle, he reminds us to "be strong in the Lord and in the power of His might" (Ephesians 6:10).

As believers, we need a healthy respect for our adversary, the devil. But more importantly, we need a total dependence on our God. We want to stay as close to Jesus as possible. When Satan comes knocking at *my* door, I ask Jesus to answer. I am no match for the devil. Neither are you.

CHAPTER 5

Satan, Society, and the Savior

When He stepped out on the land, there met Him a certain man from the city who had demons for a long time. And he wore no clothes, nor did he live in a house but in the tombs. Luke 8:27

Does a graveyard seem like an odd place to witness the power and love of Jesus? Maybe, but one tortured, suicidal, miserable, lonely shell of a man discovered how fabulous it can be to become such a witness. For a very long time, this man had been trapped in a hopeless situation—until Jesus came along.

Luke describes three forces at work in this remarkable story: Satan, society, and the Savior. What did each do for this man?

As the story begins, we find a man completely taken over by the power of Satan. He was possessed, not by one but by many demons. He hung around in a graveyard and cut himself with sharp rocks. *The Amplified Bible* says, "Night and day among the tombs, and on the mountains he was always shrieking and screaming, and beating and bruising and cutting himself with stones" (Mark 5:5).

Here was a pathetic, demented man, a mass of bleeding lacerations, scabs, and infections. The man possessed superhuman strength and could break chains with his bare hands. No doubt the townspeople avoided his hangout, especially at night! Superstitious individuals would have said this was a place for ghosts and goblins.

This dangerous and frightening individual furnishes a picture of Satan's ultimate goal, his "finished product." What steps led to this state we can only imagine, but here we see "the package deal"—sin, Satan, and death working together. The power of Satan was so intertwined with this man that most observers could not see the hurting soul deep inside. When they looked at him, they saw only a crazed, suicidal maniac roaming the graveyard.

Satan's goal was to destroy this man.

What did society do for him? It chained him up. "Civilization" kept the man "under guard, bound with chains and shackles; and he broke the bonds and was driven by the demon into the wilderness" (Luke 8:29). Once the forces of Satan removed the man from "polite company," society took no more notice of him, other than to avoid contact with him.

When it comes to demonic influences, society lacks the tools to win the battle. We see this even in our own society. A wave of violent crime is sweeping across our nation, with perpetrators getting younger and younger. Our police are understaffed, many of our courts and judges give out lenient sentences, and violent gangs are growing and spreading. Sadly, the family continues to fall apart at an unprecedented rate. Meanwhile, our schools teach "situation ethics." Students are often taught that there is no right and wrong, no black and white—only shades of gray. With all its wonderful scientific and technological achievements, society still cannot cope with the problems caused by Satan and sin. Nor could the society of Jesus' day.

No one could help this demon-possessed man. His situation appeared utterly hopeless. But underneath that dark exterior lived a truly tortured soul, and in his eerie cries Jesus heard a desperate man who wanted His help.

That brings us to the third force in the story: the Savior!

Jesus *had* to reach this man. He simply would not be stopped. He had work to do and nothing would deter Him from accomplishing it. Just as He went out of His way to meet and bring spiritual healing to the immoral woman of Samaria (see John 4) and to little Zacchaeus in Jericho (see Luke 19), He also determined to minister to this pathetic, demon-plagued, wild man.

And what did Jesus do for the man? He sought him out in his spooky little graveyard and offered him hope. What the chains could not do, Jesus did—with one word. Luke says simply that Jesus "commanded the unclean spirit to come out of the man" (Luke 8:29). In fact, "many demons had entered" the man (verse 30), yet even working together they were no match for Jesus. Apparently these demons preferred inhabiting something instead of nothing, so they begged Jesus to allow them to enter a herd of swine rather than to be sent to "the abyss." Jesus agreed to their request and sent them into the pigs, which promptly stampeded over a cliff.

And what happened to the man? Luke says the Lord "healed" him (verse 36) and gave him some clothes. Now "in his right mind" (verse 35), the man sat at the feet of Jesus, humbly and gratefully listening to whatever the Lord had to say.

What a change! Jesus came to this poor, tortured man and made him into an altogether different person.

Jesus is still in the people-changing business. It thrills me to look at some Christians and know how different they are now from what they once were. Strangers could never guess their dark and unsavory backgrounds. If you want proof of the existence of God, just look at the Christians around you!

None of us has the power to overcome Satan in our own strength. Neither can we count on society to give us the help we need. But if we cry out to Jesus, He can step in and transform us—no matter what kind or how many "demons" may torment us.

CHAPTER **6**

Bad for Business

> *Then the whole multitude of the surrounding region of the Gadarenes asked Him to depart from them, for they were seized with great fear.* Luke 8:37

Jesus just might be bad for business.

We Christians tend to remember nostalgically the famous phrase from the book of Acts that the early church "turned the world upside down" (Acts 17:6), but we forget that the words were first spoken in bitter complaint. The gospel upset so many in Thessalonica that they started a riot, forcing the apostle Paul to flee the city.

Jesus Himself experienced such hostility more than once. Luke tells us that when He was preparing to cast a flock of demons out of one tormented man, the demons "begged Him that He would permit them to enter" a herd of swine feeding near a bluff (Luke 8:32). Jesus permitted them to do so, and the terrified pigs stampeded over the cliff and drowned in the lake below. (Could we say that this was the first case of "deviled ham"?)

Some residents of the town of Gadara saw what had happened, ran into the city, and spread the news. The townspeople immediately turned out to see for themselves. When they observed the formerly demon-possessed man "sitting at the feet of Jesus, clothed and in his right mind," they quickly made up their minds: Jesus had to go (Luke 8:35-37).

You would think that these people would rejoice in the dramatic transformation that had taken place in this poor man's life. But there was another issue at stake here: making money.

And in this case, Jesus was bad for business.

Hogs were big business on this side of the Sea of Galilee. Two thousand hogs is a lot of "the other white meat," and now they all lay dead at the bottom of the lake. Their owner was, quite literally, not going to be bringing home the bacon. And clearly, if Jesus stuck around, it didn't bode well for the bottom line. It might be nice that a man recovered his soul, but the people couldn't stand the economic loss. So they asked Jesus to leave.

Might there also have been other reasons the Gadarenes sent Jesus away? Perhaps. If He could so radically change the life of one man, might He not want to do the same thing to *them?* Some worried that He would require something of them and decided it would be best for Jesus to sail away.

Then again, there was their own guilt. The presence of Jesus Christ always produces a deep sense of guilt in those who have not been washed clean by His blood. Remember how Peter felt during one of his first encounters with the Savior? "Go away from me, Lord; I am a sinful man!" (Luke 5:8, NIV). Perhaps these Gadarenes could see in Jesus' eyes that He knew everything about them, that He could read them like an open book. Perhaps He seemed able to look straight through them and see their deepest thoughts, and they felt themselves withering in His presence. So they asked Jesus to leave.

Will you do the same?

When you get down to it, all of mankind reacts to Jesus Christ in one of two ways. It's either "Away with Him" or "Be with Him." All of us belong in one of those two camps.

You might protest, "I admit that I have not made a commitment to Christ. I have not declared that I want to be with Him. But neither have I said, 'Away with Him.' I simply have not yet made up my mind."

But Jesus said that whoever is not for Him is against Him

(see Matthew 12:30). We either pray for Him to go away, or we pray to be near Him.

Which is it for you?

I've noticed at least three ways in which people today say, "Away with Him."

For some, it happens in church. The Spirit of God begins to work on their hearts, and they realize that the message of Christ is both true and what they need. Some even feel real joy in making this discovery. Yet because of concern over what their friends might think, or out of fear of being mocked, they resist the Spirit and shake off His influence. They vow never to return to church, saying in essence, "Away with Jesus!"

For others, the rejection happens not at church but through a chosen lifestyle. God has clearly shown them in His Word what is right and wrong, but they decide to do what pleases them. They determine to divorce their husband or wife, whether they have biblical grounds or not; they want out, and that's that. Or maybe they choose to continue in a sexual relationship with a person to whom they are not married. *God will forgive me,* they think. Or perhaps they decide to continue abusing drugs or alcohol, despite what God has spoken to their hearts through their conscience, friends, or His Word. All those who consciously choose an ungodly lifestyle are in effect saying, "Away with Jesus!"

Still others reject Christ simply by getting busy with other things. For them, it's nothing so blatant as deliberately breaking God's commandants. They just consume themselves with work, with recreation, with home life—with anything and everything but Jesus. By their actions, these folks also cry out, "Away with Jesus!"

I admit that Jesus may be bad for business, but He's *great* for the soul. He can deliver you from anything—not only from a miserable past but also from present sins, whatever they may be. He can and will do that, unless you do what the Gadarenes did and send Him away.

Tell Jesus to leave you alone, and He will. Tell Him often enough, and the time will come when you've run out of opportunities to repent.

But today you still have time.

So which is it for you? "Away with Jesus"? Or "Lord, take all of my life"?

If Jesus is bad for your business, it's time for a new line of work.

CHAPTER 7

God's Tests

> *There came a man named Jairus, and he was a ruler*
> *of the synagogue. And he fell down at Jesus' feet and*
> *begged Him to come to his house, for he had an only*
> *daughter about twelve years of age, and she was dying.*
> Luke 8:41-42

The daughter of a wealthy and well-connected man named Jairus suddenly fell ill. As an only child, she was "daddy's girl" and the light of his life.

Jairus realized he was in a race against time as soon as he saw that his daughter was dying. Humanly speaking, her case appeared hopeless. In his desperate hour, Jairus sought out Jesus. We don't know if he was even a believer, but as a last resort, he begged the Lord to come home with him immediately to lay hands on his daughter.

Once Jairus made his request, he did nothing but stay close to Jesus. He placed himself in the Lord's hands, without reservation. Hope blossomed in his heart as the Master made his way to the house—but then a woman with a desperate need of her own appeared out of nowhere and delayed the procession (see Luke 8:43-48).

How easily Jairus could have resented this intrusion! He could have said, "Hey, I was here first! No cuts!" He could have pointed out that, according to the Law, this woman was ceremonially unclean. He could have added that he was a leader of a synagogue with connections and resources, while this wretched woman had nothing.

Yet Jairus did no such thing. Why not? It may be that he had heard about Jesus and His special love for underdogs.

Whatever the case, this turned out to be a test in Jairus's life. You ask, "A test?" That's right. God gives us tests, although He rarely, if ever, announces them ahead of time. They just come.

When I was in school, my heart always sank when my teacher would say, "We're having a surprise test today, so put your textbooks away and take out a sheet of paper and a pencil." I got that sinking feeling because usually I had not learned the material.

Well, God gives surprise tests, too.

The Gospels tell the story of the Gentile woman who came to Jesus, asking Him to heal her demon-possessed daughter. Jesus said to her, "It is not good to take the children's bread and throw it to the little dogs" (Matthew 15:26).

"Yes, Lord," she responded, "yet even the little dogs eat the crumbs which fall from their master's table" (verse 27).

She passed the test. Jesus turned to her and essentially said, "Whatever you want, I will give to you."

God uses tests to determine whether we have learned what He's been teaching us. We tend to think we know certain truths so well. We love to tell others "how to do it." But through a test, the Lord says to us, "Let's see how well you've been listening."

Do you think God does this because He is cruel? Quite the contrary! He wants us to learn so we can advance in our faith. He doesn't want us to stay in "spiritual kindergarten" forever.

Consider the way a mother eagle teaches her eaglets to fly. When the time comes for the babies to soar (a time the mother knows instinctively), the mother bird pushes her young out of the nest. She lets her frightened fledglings drop a distance of ninety feet or more before she swoops under them to carry them back to safety. She repeats the process about every fifteen minutes until the eaglets begin to fly on their own.

To us, the adult bird may seem very cruel. Yet if the babies weren't shoved out, they would feel content to remain in the nest. In that case we could classify them as "twenty-something" eagles. I can imagine Mama saying, *"When* are you going to learn how to fly? All you do is sit around the nest all day long and sleep!"

God uses tests to kick *us* out of the "nest" so we can learn how to fly. He wants us to trust Him even when we don't understand Him. He wants us to be patient with Him even when He doesn't work according to our schedules. He wants us to grow up and be strong spiritually.

"When all kinds of trials and temptations crowd into your lives . . . ," James tells us, "don't resent them as intruders, but welcome them as friends! Realise that they come to test your faith and to produce in you the quality of endurance. But let the process go on until that endurance is fully developed, and you will find you have become men of mature character, men of integrity with no weak spots" (1:2-4, Phillips).

Had Jairus failed his test, who knows what would have happened? But he did not fail; he passed with flying colors. He accepted not only Jesus but His timing.

This is just where a lot of us have trouble with God. We grow impatient with Him.

"When are You going to open the door of ministry for me?"

"When are You going to provide me with a husband or a wife?"

"How long are You going to let that person get away with that sin?"

In our impatience, sometimes we take things into our own hands. We get tired of waiting for that "right" guy or girl or refuse to wait for God to bring judgment. But Jesus does not ask us to understand His ways and timing. He asks only for our trust.

From Jairus, He got it. What about from you?

CHAPTER **8**

Does God Heal Today?

Now a woman, having a flow of blood for twelve years,
who had spent all her livelihood on physicians and
could not be healed by any, came from behind and
touched the border of His garment. And immediately
her flow of blood stopped. Luke 8:43-44

The unfortunate woman described here had some kind of hemorrhage that caused continual bleeding for twelve painful years. In that culture, the stigma and humiliation of such a thing came second only to leprosy.

Her hemorrhage made her ceremonially unclean and so barred her from the synagogue. As the synagogue had by then become the center of Jewish spiritual and social life, she was isolated and alone.

To make things worse, she had spent her last cent on medical care, yet without any improvement. Mark tells us, "She had suffered a great deal under the care of many doctors and had spent all she had, yet instead of getting better she grew worse" (Mark 5:26, NIV).

Much of the so-called medicine of the first century left much to be desired. One traditional "remedy" directed such a woman to carry the ashes of an ostrich egg in a linen bag in summer and in a cotton bag in winter. Another "cure" involved carrying around a barleycorn kernel from the dung of a white female donkey. So this woman had probably been extorted by the quack doctors of her day.

Yet, in the midst of her years of disappointment and rejection, this woman came to believe that God could and would touch her. She had heard about Jesus and His ministry and concluded that if she could just touch the hem of His garment, she would be healed.

Her day finally came.

Jesus was passing through her town. As the crowd pushed and pulled and jostled all around Him, this persistent woman managed to get her hand through and touch the edge of His robe. Immediately God's healing power shot through her.

What a glorious day this was for her!

Her case makes us wonder: Can we expect God to heal *us?*

First, we need to remember that disease and death were never a part of God's original plan; they both came as a result of sin. Romans 5:12 says, "Therefore, just as sin entered the world through one man, and death through sin, and in this way death came to all men, because all sinned" (NIV). Sometimes we get sick merely because we live in a sin-sick world.

At other times, however, we fall ill because of our own personal sin. When Jesus healed a paralytic in Bethesda, He said, "See, you are well again. Stop sinning or something worse may happen to you" (John 5:14, NIV). Paul wrote that some members of the Corinthian church had become ill and even died because of their sin (see 1 Corinthians 11:30).

On the other hand, God may allow sickness to teach a believer some important lessons. Paul called his own physical affliction a "thorn in the flesh" (2 Corinthians 12:7) and three times asked God to remove it. The Lord refused and told the apostle, "My grace is sufficient for you, for My strength is made perfect in weakness" (verse 9). This suggests that God may allow sickness to keep us humble, to teach us, or to bring us back to Him. The psalmist wrote, "Before I was afflicted I went astray, but now I keep Your word" (Psalm 119:67).

Finally, at still other times God really may want to heal us. James tells us, "Is anyone among you sick? Let him call for the elders of the church, and let them pray over him, anointing him with oil in the name of the Lord. And the prayer of faith will save the sick, and the Lord will raise him up" (5:14-15).

So why are some of us still sick?

One reason is a simple lack of asking: "You do not have because you do not ask" (James 4:2). That was not the problem of the woman in Luke 8! Clearly, she took hold of what God had for her. To the best of her ability, with as much faith as she could muster, she touched the Lord and was healed.

Some fault those who are not healed, claiming that they lack the necessary faith. It is true that a lack of faith can keep the Lord from providing His healing touch (see Mark 6:5-6), yet it is not always so. Many times Jesus responded not to the faith of the sick, but to the faith of others (see Matthew 8:10; 9:2; 15:28). And sometimes Jesus healed in the presence of no discernible faith at all (see Matthew 17:17-18; Luke 22:50-51; Acts 3:6).

Yes, sometimes God heals, and other times He allows the natural cycle of life to unfold. There is "a time to be born, and a time to die," says Ecclesiastes 3:2. It's only a matter of time until all of us pass into eternity. Whether we live to be 10 or 110, we're still only "a vapor that appears for a little time and then vanishes away" (James 4:14).

The point is, God heals the sick when *He* wants to. When it is His will, God can and will heal us. Our part is to reach out with as much faith as we can muster.

Perhaps you say, "I would love to have Jesus touch me, but I don't feel His touch." Then be like this woman. If you're not feeling Jesus' touch upon you, then reach out and touch *Him.*

Have you made the effort to press through the crowd of unbelief, of busyness, of activities? Have you pushed through whatever blocks you from getting to Jesus? If not, press through today and say like the woman, "I want to touch the hem of His garment. I know if I can just touch Him, I'll be helped."

CHAPTER **9**

Still Trusting

"Do not be afraid; only believe, and she will be made well." Luke 8:50

When Jesus healed the woman of her longtime blood flow, Jairus's heart probably leapt for joy. This miracle proved Christ's power to do the amazing—and the Teacher was now on His way to touch Jairus's sick little girl!

But then came the worst news imaginable. "Your daughter is dead," someone told Jairus. "Do not trouble the Teacher" (Luke 8:49).

On two occasions I have been with fathers who received this very news. You cannot imagine the devastation; it's as if their world has collapsed. Most fathers feel a special bond with their daughters. They want to protect and provide for them; their little girls feel safe and secure in daddy's presence.

I'm sure Jairus felt personally responsible for what happened (most dads do). I can imagine him berating himself, "I should have dragged Jesus here faster!" He could so easily have accused Jesus of making a mistake, of neglecting him in his hour of need.

But he did not.

He *still* trusted. He humbled himself and bet his whole future on Jesus of Nazareth.

Jesus always stands ready and willing to receive and bless those who come to Him humbly and in faith. He has said, "The one who comes to Me I will by no means cast out" (John 6:37) and "Come to Me, all you who labor and are heavy laden, and I will give you rest" (Matthew 11:28).

To those who admit their weakness, He will bend over backwards to help. But those who come in pride or with no real interest in spiritual things will find and hear nothing.

Remember King Herod? He had a great fascination with Jesus. He hoped that the Lord might do some dramatic miracle or sign to impress him, or perhaps give some impassioned speech to plead why "the great Herod" should spare His life. But Herod got nothing from Jesus but silence. The Lord spoke not a single word to the king, for he was not a true seeker (Luke 23:8-11).

But to Jairus, a genuine seeker, Jesus revealed Himself. "Do not be afraid," He said, "only believe, and she will be made well" (Luke 8:50). It's as if Jesus had said, "Jairus, you had a certain amount of faith when you came to me. Your faith grew stronger when you saw what I did for that woman. Don't quit now! Keep on believing!"

What a perfect picture of the Christian life.

When we place our faith in Christ, we cease to struggle so fiercely with many of the problems that once plagued us. Gone is the guilty conscience. Beaten is the terrible fear of death. For some time things go well—but one day we stumble. The devil dangles some temptation in front of us and we bite. And Satan whispers, "That's it for you! Give up. You have sinned too greatly this time, sunk too low to ever get out of the pit."

But then our Savior steps in! Jesus speaks up and reminds us, "You've made it this far. Don't quit. Keep on believing!"

That's exactly what Jairus did. He kept on believing and kept on moving ahead with the Lord. Yet when they reached his home, they found a house in uproar—a scene wholly hostile to faith.

In contrast to the modern western world, funerals in ancient Israel were not occasions for quiet whispers and soothing music. Instead, loud wailing and the harsh sounds of various musical instruments filled the air. Families hired "professional wailers" who loudly shouted the name of the dead. Even the poorest of families would hire two minstrels, two flute players, and a screamer. The wealthier you were, the more mourners you hired. Since Jairus was *very* wealthy, perhaps fifty to a hundred wailers descended upon his home. Jesus, Jairus, and the disciples had arrived to a macabre circus.

Jesus could not tolerate such a raucous environment, so He announced that all was well, that the child merely slept.

And they laughed Him to scorn. How quickly they moved from so-called "grief" to full-scale mockery!

So Jesus responded decisively; He evicted them all. Unbelief and mockery hinder God from doing what He wants do in our lives, and Jesus will have none of it.

Even today, the devil and his forces constantly try to bring us down. He tries to discourage our faith at every opportunity. And the fact is, we would stand no chance against his dark forces unless Jesus contended with them on our behalf. The Bible tells us to "be strong in the Lord and in the power of His might" (Ephesians 6:10) and reminds us that Jesus "always lives to make intercession" for us (Hebrews 7:25).

That's just what the Lord did for Jairus. Jesus took his little girl by the hand and said softly, "Little girl, arise"—and immediately she woke up (Luke 8:54-55). Jesus gave her back to her parents, directed that she be given something to eat, and left Jairus and his wife in a happy state of shock.

Do you need a touch from Jesus today? If so, will you come to Him as Jairus did? Will you approach the Lord in humility and faith, regardless of the bad news you may have just received?

That's the surest way to a touch from God.

CHAPTER 10

But It's Impossible!

Then He took the five loaves and the two fish, and looking up to heaven, He blessed and broke them, and gave them to the disciples to set before the multitude. So they all ate and were filled. Luke 9:16-17

Have you ever looked in the cupboards and found nothing to eat? Or realized you had no money to pay your bills?

I have.

Yet I can testify that, after walking with the Lord for thirty-one years, He has always met my needs. I have learned the truth of Philippians 4:19: "My God shall supply all your need according to His riches in glory by Christ Jesus."

Are you in a desperate situation right now? Do you find yourself backed up against a wall with nowhere to look but up? If so, cheer up. God is still in the miracle-working business!

King Jehoshaphat made that discovery when his enemies, who already greatly outnumbered him, joined forces with several other large armies. Now they were on their way to destroy him and his people. When he heard the news, his heart sank. His situation looked utterly hopeless.

If you were Jehoshaphat, what would you have done? Does the Bible say, "Jehoshaphat totally freaked out and threw a mighty temper tantrum before the LORD and screamed, 'What about *my* needs?'"

No, that's not what happened. The Bible tells us he "set himself to seek the Lord, and proclaimed a fast throughout all Judah" (2 Chronicles 20:3). The king scheduled a national prayer meeting and publicly petitioned the Lord: "O our God, will you not judge them? For we have no power to face this vast army that is attacking us. We do not know what to do, but our eyes are upon you" (verse 12, NIV)

And you know what? God decisively delivered His people.

The disciples faced their own crisis in a remote place not far from Capernaum. While it certainly wasn't as dramatic as the one that faced Jehoshaphat, nor as urgent as the one that confronted Moses at the Red Sea, nevertheless it rose to the level of crisis. A huge crowd of five thousand men (and an uncounted number of women and children) had followed Jesus into an isolated spot, far from food and drink. It was getting late, the crowd had grown hungry, and the disciples urged Jesus to send the people away.

And Jesus told them, "*You* feed them."

When the disciples picked up their jaws from the grassy turf, they protested. "We have no more than five loaves and two fish, unless we go and buy food for all these people" (Luke 9:13).

It never occurred to them that just maybe, Jesus could miraculously feed everyone present.

Why hadn't the thought entered their minds? Already they had seen Jesus perform a number of dramatic miracles. He had healed a crippled man, cured a blind man, and raised a dead girl to life. They'd also seen Him turn water into wine. Did they think the feeding of these people too trivial? Or too big?

Scripture rejects both ideas. "Is anything too hard for the Lord?" it asks (Genesis 18:14). Nothing is too big for God. At the same time, the Lord is interested in even the smallest matters. "You keep track of all my sorrows," David writes in Psalm 56:8-9 (NLT). "You have collected all my tears in your bottle. You have recorded each one in your book. On the very day I call to you for help, my enemies will retreat."

The disciples should have known that the power of God was present with them. To prove the point, Jesus determined to show them that *nothing* was too big or too small for Him to do. As the disciples stuttered and made excuses, Jesus asked for the five loaves and the two fish. Taking them in hand, He looked up to heaven, blessed and broke them, and gave them to His men to hand out to the multitude.

This isn't the only way Jesus could have performed the miracle, of course. He could have materialized the food out of nothing. He could have done "special orders"—surf for her, turf for him. Or He could have caused manna to fall on the ground, as it did for ancient Israel. Instead, He asked His disciples for what they had, regardless of how little it seemed.

We see an important spiritual principle here: God *wants* but does not *need* our participation in His work. Acts 17:25 reminds us, "He is not served by human hands, as if he needed anything, because he himself gives all men life and breath and everything else" (NIV). God can do much with little.

God used a young boy with a slingshot to slay Goliath and send the Philistine army running.

God used a poverty-stricken widow to sustain Elijah, and a young girl to lead the leprous Namaan to Elisha.

God used Balaam's donkey to teach His truth, and the jawbone of another donkey to slay a thousand men.

God used a little child to teach Jesus' disciples humility.

You can never be too small for God to use, only too big.

Do you believe that Jesus can meet your needs, even when it seems impossible? As we use the gifts God has given us—no matter how feeble or small they seem—it may be that God will develop and multiply them. God wants us to realize that all we have comes from Him and that He delights in meeting our needs.

All of them.

CHAPTER **11**

Even for the Unworthy

And when Jesus went out He saw a great multitude; and He was moved with compassion for them.

Matthew 14:14

Jesus' fame was growing by the minute. The crowds swelled wherever He went and multitudes anxiously followed Him. John's Gospel tells us, "A huge crowd kept following him wherever he went" (John 6:2, NLT).

Many churches today would consider such huge crowds an unqualified success. They don't much care why the people come as long as they come. They tend to see church as a big numbers game.

But motive and purpose were everything to Jesus. He didn't want big crowds so much as committed disciples. That is why several times during His ministry He intentionally pared down the size of the crowds that followed Him. Periodically He said "hard things" to thin out the ranks.

Luke reports how "while the crowds were thickly gathered together," Jesus declared to them, "This is an evil generation. It seeks a sign, and no sign will be given to it except the sign of Jonah the prophet" (Luke 11:29). Not exactly the sort of thing one says to gain an adoring crowd! John tells of another incident in Capernaum when literally boatloads of fans followed Jesus across the Sea of Galilee. He took note of their swelling numbers and said several things like, "Unless you eat the flesh of the Son of Man and drink His blood, you have no life in you"

(John 6:53). Many complained about His teaching and grumbled, "This is a hard saying; who can understand it?" (verse 60). When Jesus sensed their discomfort, He said a few more things to add to it. The result? "From that time many of His disciples went back and walked with Him no more" (verse 66).

Why did Jesus do such a thing? John gives us a hint when he writes, "While he was in Jerusalem at the Passover Feast, many people saw the miraculous signs he was doing and believed in his name. But Jesus would not entrust himself to them, for he knew all men. He did not need man's testimony about man, for he knew what was in a man" (John 2:23-25, NIV).

Though these people "believed in Him," Jesus didn't "believe in them." Though many "trusted" in Him, He didn't "trust" in them. Why not? Because He knew what was in them. Jesus sees us for who and what we are. There are no secrets from Him. He is the searcher of hearts (Romans 8:27). And the Bible tells us "the heart is deceitful above all things, and desperately wicked" (Jeremiah 17:9).

Jesus didn't want big crowds at all costs. He's not after followers who seek Him because it makes them feel better about themselves or because they want a little religion in their lives. God wants followers who love Him and want to know Him.

Why did many in the crowds follow Jesus? Jesus Himself said that it was "not because [they] saw the signs, but because [they] ate of the loaves and were filled" (John 6:26). Many of these people were nothing more than thrill seekers and free-lunch enthusiasts.

And yet . . .

According to Matthew's Gospel, as Jesus surveyed one massive crowd, numbering as high as ten thousand—and in spite of knowing their true motives—He still "was moved with compassion" for them (Matthew 14:14). Even though these shallow people wanted nothing more than a few thrills and a free dinner, Jesus felt deeply moved as He observed them. He knew their fickleness. He knew that soon many of them would reject and scorn Him. Yet His loving heart burned for them nonetheless.

If I had been in Jesus' sandals, knowing what He knew, I probably would have let those people go hungry. I might even have eaten in front of them! If I knew that some of the very people for whom I was performing a miracle of provision would shortly join the crowds jeering, "Crucify Him!" I wouldn't have given them the time of day.

Not so with Jesus. When He found Himself surrounded by growing crowds and saw they were hungry, He fed them. Fickle or not. Selfish or not. Thrill seeking or not.

In His life and death, Jesus embodied the grace of God. He came to this earth and lived among us—not because we deserved it, but because He loved us. He died for us, not when we were righteous, but when we were sinners (Romans 5:6, 8).

As God told the people of Israel through Moses, "The Lord did not set His love on you nor choose you because you were more in number than any other people, for you were the least of all peoples." Then why did He love them and choose them? Moses answers simply, "because the Lord loves you" (Deuteronomy 7:7-8).

That's the sort of Lord we have. None of us deserves Him. None of us has earned His favor. None of us is worthy of Him. Yet He loves us.

What can we do but say, "Praise You and thank You, Lord!"

CHAPTER 12

We Have to Ask

The boat was in the middle of the sea; and He was alone on the land. Then He saw them straining at rowing.

Mark 6:47-48

The multitudes reveled in how Jesus had fed them so well in such a remote location with so few apparent resources. John says they were so impressed that "they were about to come and take Him by force to make Him king." Since this didn't fit with Jesus' plans, "He departed again to the mountain by Himself alone" (John 6:15).

Before He left, however, Matthew says, "Jesus *made* His disciples get into the boat" (Matthew 14:22, emphasis added). This strongly suggests that they went reluctantly. The disciples probably did not want to leave. They had seen Jesus provide for their temporal needs and had witnessed a surge of goodwill from the crowd. Perhaps they felt much like kids who are having a great time—and then their parents order them to get in the car.

Still, they complied. They got in the boat and started rowing for the other shore while Jesus stayed behind to pray. By the time evening fell, the disciples had managed to row to the middle of the lake, battling a strong headwind all the way.

Meanwhile, Jesus was praying and keeping a watchful eye on His disciples. He never lost sight of them, though He sat on the mountain while they labored on the lake. Mark says, "He saw them straining at rowing" (Mark 6:48). They may have lost sight of Him, but He never lost sight of them.

Jesus remained on the mountain for several hours. Not until "the fourth watch of the night"—the time just before dawn—did He go to His men (Matthew 14:25). This meant the disciples had spent at least nine hours at sea. They must have been exhausted.

Has it ever seemed to you as if God left you all alone in a storm, hidden from Him? It seemed as if you had been straining at the oars forever, yet you made little headway. *Where is God?* you wondered.

Especially at such times, we have to remember that nothing escapes God's attention. "The eyes of the Lord are in every place, keeping watch on the evil and the good," says Proverbs 15:3. We may lose sight of God, but He never loses sight of us.

Why did Jesus wait so long before He intervened? Why did He send His men into a howling gale, knowing the difficulties they'd face? Probably because He knew that it takes a while for us to exhaust our resources. Only when we get to the end of ourselves do we reach out for Him.

The great preacher Alexander Maclaren once warned his congregation that they should not be surprised that God seems to wait until the last second to intervene. "That is God's way always," he said. "Up to the very edge we are driven, before He puts out His hand to help us. It is best for us that we should be brought to desperation, to say, 'My foot slips' and then, just as our toes feel the ice, help comes and His mercy holds us up. At the last moment—never before it, never until we have discovered how much we need it, and never too late—comes the Helper."[1]

God's delays are not necessarily God's denials.

Any lifeguard knows the danger of taking hold of a drowning person. The drowning person is so panicked that his flailing could drown both him and the one trying to save him. Often it is safe for the lifeguard to intervene only when the person reaches a point of exhaustion. Only then can the lifeguard safely help a panicky swimmer.

Mark tells us Jesus began walking on the water toward His disciples and "would have passed them by" (Mark 6:48). It's as if the Lord waited for their invitation before intervening. He did something very similar after His resurrection, when He walked with two disciples on the road to Emmaus. After speaking to them for some time, "Jesus acted as if he were going farther" (Luke 24:28, NIV). He waited for their invitation before He accompanied them home.

In the same way, if you want Jesus to intervene in your life, you have to ask. He will not likely intercede without your invitation. Once you recognize your plight and ask for His help, however, He will be there for you, touching you in your hour of need.

A few years ago, during a Harvest Crusade in Anaheim, California, a man was in the vicinity looking for a liquor store to rob. He saw the bright lights of the stadium and out of curiosity drove over to check it out. (He thought he might find some people to rob.) He came in to the crusade, heard the gospel message, and realized he was a sinner who had broken God's laws. He ended up going forward to receive Christ.

Not until that moment did the man see his true need and ask Jesus to intervene in his life. The whole time the Lord had fixed His eyes on the man—but not until he cried out did Jesus come to him and bring him home, safely out of the storm.

We must follow that man's example. If we want Jesus to intervene, we have to ask. His eye is upon us and He's ready to help, but He waits to hear our call.

And remember, if you are going through a "storm of life" right now, Jesus has His watchful eye on you. No, you can't see Him, but He sure can see you!

CHAPTER 13

Glorious Sonshine

> *He took Peter, John, and James and went up on the mountain to pray. As He prayed, the appearance of His face was altered, and His robe became white and glistening.* Luke 9:28-29

The remarkable event we call the Transfiguration marked the halfway point on a very difficult journey. From it, Jesus looked backward to the cradle and forward to the cross.

Just a few days before, Peter had recoiled when the Lord announced that He would be rejected, beaten, crucified, and raised from the dead. The big fisherman repeatedly rebuked Jesus, saying, "Far be it from You, Lord; this shall not happen to You!" (Matthew 16:22). In other words, "What are you talking about?" Peter simply didn't understand. He was looking out for what he considered Jesus' best interests, not realizing that he had become a mouthpiece for Satan himself (verse 23).

Yet Peter also had correctly identified Jesus as "the Christ, the Son of the living God" (verse 16), and Jesus apparently sensed the time was right for His disciples—specifically, Peter, James, and John—to enjoy a greater glimpse of His glory. That's why the four trudged to the top of the mountain and as Jesus prayed, "the appearance of His face was altered, and His robe became white and glistening" (Luke 9:29). In that moment, God granted the "terrific trio" the privilege of seeing Jesus shine like the sun. Who would not be dazzled by such a display?

We might think the great miracle was that Jesus' appearance was altered into its true, glorious state. But that was not the miracle. The real wonder was what happened all the other days when Jesus did *not* shine like the sun.

Have you ever tried to hide light? It doesn't work very well; light has a tendency to "leak out." Paul tells us that Jesus "took the form of a bondservant . . . and became obedient to the point of death, even the death of the cross" (Philippians 2:7-8). A literal translation is that He "emptied himself." That's the only way Jesus' brilliant light wouldn't continually "leak out." The great miracle of Jesus was that, on a daily basis, He veiled His glory.

Yet on the Mount of Transfiguration, the Light of the World gave His disciples a fleeting glimpse of His brilliance. The Son shone in splendor that day!

To add to the drama, two Old Testament celebrities showed up in person. Moses and Elijah suddenly appeared and spoke to Jesus—noteworthy appearances because Moses and Elijah occupy unique positions in the Old Testament. We associate Moses with the giving of the Law, while we know Elijah as the great miracle-working prophet. The phrase "the law and the prophets" was a shorthand way of referring to the entire Old Testament. And both the law and the prophets prepared the way for the Messiah.

Have you ever wondered how the disciples recognized Moses and Elijah? No pictures or statues existed of either man. Neither had lived or ministered in Israel for centuries. So how did the disciples know that the two men speaking with Jesus were in fact Moses and Elijah?

The Bible does not directly answer, but the incident suggests that we will instantly recognize each other in glory. We won't need name tags in heaven. Someone once asked the great English preacher Charles Spurgeon if Christians would be able to recognize one another in heaven. "Do you think we will be bigger fools up there then we are down here?" he asked.

What an amazing sight this must have been! There stood Jesus—luminous, radiating, shining—talking with Moses, who had been dead for more than 1,400 years, and Elijah, who been gone for about 900.

What were they talking about?

Luke says they "spoke of His decease which He was about to accomplish at Jerusalem" (Luke 9:31). The Greek word translated "decease" is really the term "exodus." And who better to discuss an exodus than Moses, who led Israel out of Egypt? But here the men discussed a new kind of exodus, one that would take place through Jesus' death, resurrection, and ascension. This would be a worldwide exodus in which God's people would be freed from the bondage of Satan and sin and led into the streets of heaven.

No doubt it was a bittersweet meeting. Moses and Elijah, great as they were, now stood in the presence of their Creator—a privilege of the highest order. If the still-learning disciples had not yet grasped Jesus' full significance, these two champions of the Old Testament certainly had.

Perhaps the pair thanked Jesus on behalf of all those who would benefit eternally from His sacrifice. This was the very thing Jesus had just revealed to His disciples, and they could not handle it.

Whatever the specifics of their conversation, what Moses and Elijah discussed with Jesus involved *you!* For it was through His death on the cross that you can be forgiven of your sin. It was because He went to Calvary that you can come to God.

Against all odds (and Peter's advice), Jesus chose to suffer and die on Golgotha. How ironic that on that darkest of days, He would shine even brighter than He did on the Mount of Transfiguration.

CHAPTER **14**

On the Mountaintop
with Jesus

Then it happened, as they were parting from Him, that Peter said to Jesus, "Master, it is good for us to be here; and let us make three tabernacles: one for You, one for Moses, and one for Elijah." Luke 9:33

Have you ever had a "mountaintop experience" with God? A moment in worship or prayer where God's presence felt so near you could practically touch it? A moment when the spiritual seemed more real than the physical? Our natural inclination is to want to hold on to such an experience, to freeze it and never lose it.

That's what Peter wanted when he awoke from deep slumber to find Jesus standing on the mountain with Moses and Elijah. He should have taken it all in and remained completely silent, but instead he decided to say a few words. Mark tells us he "did not know what to say," he was so frightened (Mark 9:6). Ironically, this happened just as Moses and Elijah were about to depart.

Peter wanted the party to go on!

"Master," Peter said to Jesus as the Old Testament heroes were leaving, "it is good for us to be here; and let us make three tabernacles: one for You, one for Moses, and one for Elijah" (Luke 9:33).

The operative word for Peter was "here." It is good for us to be *here.* "This is where we belong, Lord. Up here with Moses and Elijah, basking in Your glory—not going down to Jerusalem

47

to die. This is how we want to see You, Jesus, hanging out with the prophets, shining before us. Forget this insane idea of death."

Peter liked bathing in divine glory on top of the mountain. He liked associating with famous heroes of the faith. He was all for staying where he was and forgetting any needs waiting at the bottom of the mountain.

We have a tendency to do the same thing, don't we? As the world grows darker, we want to withdraw into our own subculture, concentrate on our own needs and problems, and forget about anyone else. So we enroll our kids in Christian schools and listen to Christian radio as we drive in the car we bought from a Christian dealer to go to a Christian meeting with Christian friends.

Don't get me wrong. I thank God for the many resources and opportunities Christians enjoy today. And I am all for giving some of our business to other believers—but I am also for evangelism! It is vital for people in the world to see what real Christians are like. If they don't see the genuine article in us, their only impression of believers may come from some psycho preacher on TV. How are we going to evangelize those with whom we have no contact?

"But I don't want to be polluted by contact with unbelievers," someone says. Paul has a word for us about that: "When I wrote to you before, I told you not to associate with people who indulge in sexual sin. But I wasn't talking about unbelievers who indulge in sexual sin, or who are greedy or are swindlers or idol worshipers. You would have to leave this world to avoid people like that" (1 Corinthians 5:9-10, NLT).

And that's exactly what some Christians would like to do: "leave this world." They ask, "What if we could create a 'Christian city'?"

I'm sure such a thing would work—so long as no one lived in it. Fallen humans tend to spoil everything. We'll have to wait for the millennial kingdom for that kind of thing. Jesus always sends us down the mountain into the real world to carry out the mission God has given to us.

As if to remind Peter of his priorities, God the Father broke the apostle's dreamy reverie with a command: "This is My beloved Son. Hear Him!" (Luke 9:35). In effect, the Father was saying, "If my Son tells you He must go to Jerusalem to suffer and die, then believe Him. If He tells you to take up your cross and follow Him, then that is what you must do."

Peter never forgot this day. Many years later, just before he was to "put off [his] tent" (2 Peter 1:14) and die in service to his Lord, he reflected on the mountaintop scene. "We did not follow cleverly invented stories when we told you about the power and coming of our Lord Jesus Christ, but we were eyewitnesses of his majesty," he wrote. "For he received honor and glory from God the Father when the voice came to him from the Majestic Glory, saying, 'This is my Son, whom I love; with him I am well pleased.' We ourselves heard this voice that came from heaven when we were with him on the sacred mountain" (verses 16-18, NIV).

We, like Peter, may want to live continually on the mountaintop. But the Bible tells us the great lessons of life and the crucial missions of God await us in the "valleys of experience." It's not more "mountaintop experiences" we need, but more day-to-day obedience that empowers us to walk by faith, not by feelings.

Peter and the disciples learned that we can't always have mountaintop experiences. And even when God gives them to us, He means for them to prepare us for living in the valleys. God never allows His people to build their tabernacles in the place of glory while the world still needs to hear about the Savior.

CHAPTER **15**

Waiting in the Valley

> *Now it happened on the next day, when they had come down from the mountain, that a great multitude met Him.* Luke 9:37

All of us have "mountaintop experiences," but we cannot live off of them exclusively. At the bottom of most mountains lies a valley, perhaps even an enemy seeking to ambush us.

When Adolf Hitler invaded his European neighbors during the early days of World War II, in almost every case he attacked on a weekend. Hitler knew the various national parliaments would not be in session, making it more difficult to react swiftly to an invasion.

In the same way, our enemy the devil waits for an opportune time to attack—and it may be when we think we are the strongest. As Paul reminds us, "Let him who thinks he stands take heed lest he fall" (1 Corinthians 10:12).

The disciples learned this lesson the day after coming down from the Mount of Transfiguration. In the valley they encountered a poor, desperate father whose son suffered greatly under the power and control of the devil. This distraught man had brought his boy to the other nine disciples who had not gone up on the mountain, but their weak faith prevented them from giving much help.

How sad—and yet, how very much like us. Just moments after a moving worship experience, our hearts can quickly drift from God. We pray, and the next words out of our mouths hurt and sting. On the way home from church we get into an argument with our spouse or we find ourselves gossiping.

Our problem? Jesus identified it as "the littleness of your faith" (Matthew 17:20, NASB). Like the disciples, we have faith—just not much of it.

Faith is a lot like a muscle. You have to use it to make it grow. Some individuals spend hours in the gym pumping iron to get massive, but they don't do anything with it. They just wear tight clothes and flex a lot.

We need to *use* our faith. What good is it to have something we don't use? The other day I read about a lottery prize of twenty-five million dollars that went unclaimed. Someone bought the winning ticket at a Los Angeles area 7-Eleven store, but because no one claimed the prize in the allotted time, the state kept the money. You gotta use it or lose it!

The world desperately needs Jesus. We need to exercise our faith and, on behalf of others, claim God's unlimited power. We need to do what we can to help those under the power of the devil.

Closer to home, some of those who are under the power of the devil live under our own roofs. How many of us can relate to the situation of this father? He could represent many Christian parents who want to see their kids set free from Satan's power, whether the devil holds them through immorality, drugs, alcohol, or peer pressure. They have tried everything they know to free them, and nothing has worked. They've tried therapy, Ritalin, interventions, counselors, and even ministers.

But have they brought their children to Jesus?

That's what this father did with his son, and that's why the boy was healed: "Jesus rebuked the unclean spirit, healed the child, and gave him back to his father" (Luke 9:42).

While we can't physically bring our loved ones to Jesus, we can start by bringing them with us to church, even if they object. Notice that I didn't say drop them off and leave. We have to come *with* them and bring them to hear the Word of God.

Second, we can bring them to Jesus through prayer. Do we regularly pray for our children? We correct them, discipline them, nag them—but what about praying for them? They can escape our presence, but not our prayers.

In Mark's version of this story, the perplexed disciples asked Jesus why they could not drive out the demon. Jesus replied, "This kind can come out only by prayer" (Mark 9:29, NIV). Prayer is one of the most potent weapons in the Christian's arsenal. So bring your loved ones every day to the Lord in prayer. Get your friends and family members to pray for them, too.

Don't be surprised, however, if you face aggressive resistance from the devil. Notice what happened when this father brought his son close to Jesus: "As he was still coming, the demon threw him down and convulsed him" (Luke 9:42).

Oh no! the father probably thought. *Don't do this now!*

This is the typical pattern throughout Scripture. So long as a nonbeliever remains where Satan wants him, all seems at peace. But the second that nonbeliever takes a step toward Jesus, all hell breaks loose.

Don't be shocked by this; anticipate it and be ready for it. When a nonbeliever accepts a long-offered invitation to church or starts asking spiritually significant questions, you'd better put on your spiritual armor and get ready to rumble. The devil won't let that person go without a fight.

Once Jesus gets involved, however, the fight quickly turns into a rout. So make sure you don't try to rumble without Him.

CHAPTER **16**

The Stronger Man

> *"When a stronger than he comes upon him and overcomes him, he takes from him all his armor in which he trusted, and divides his spoils."* Luke 11:22

Do not be misled: Satan is strong in power and cunning. He has laid low some of God's choicest servants because they underestimated him and overestimated themselves. Even Samson with all his strength was no match for Satan. Nor was Solomon with all his wisdom.

Though Christians sleep, the devil never does. He is always on duty. He doesn't rest, night or day. The Bible says he is like "a roaring lion, seeking whom he may devour" (1 Peter 5:8). He has open access to this planet and roams about freely.

Before their conversion, every person is to some degree under the power of Satan. The body is his palace (Ephesians 2:1-3). Without Christ, we are all held captive by the devil (2 Timothy 2:26). He has us where he wants us, and there is nothing we can do about it. We do not even resist him; we have accepted the arrangement.

Worse yet, people can be and still are possessed by demons, though it may not be as common as some claim. One guy on TV holds regular "exorcism services" in which he allegedly casts out demons. I have watched this and thought, *Great, another positive presentation of Christianity for the world to mock!*

Still, demon possession is real. So confident are demons about those directly under their control that they may "take a vacation" (Luke 11:24-26). When a demon returns to his "house," however, he may find the place a little different. Maybe the person has undergone some kind of moral change. His house looks clean, swept, tidy, and the door is locked.

No problem for the demon! He still has the key (and he knows the alarm code, too). He calls out, "Is anybody home?" He checks around—no sign of blood on the doorposts. Maybe a few religious relics here and there, but nothing alarming. So he has a good laugh and invites in seven friends worse than he is. Luke's phrase "and they enter and dwell there" (verse 26) carries the idea of settling down. Paul uses the same verb in praying for the Ephesians: "that Christ may *dwell* in your hearts through faith" (Ephesians 3:17, emphasis added). Where Jesus Christ does not live, demons are free to dwell.

Such a home is empty, like a model home. It may look lived in, but it's vacant. The stereo is nothing but cardboard. The computer is plastic. The air conditioning is set on one temperature. The knickknacks are glued to the tables. The food on the plates is made of wax. The fireplace has ashes, but no flame.

Such is the life without Christ. The house may look occupied, but it's empty. Some who seem to have "found Christ" have the Christian jargon down pat. They immediately write their life story or give their testimony on Christian radio or TV. Their house has been swept, but not cleaned.

Sweeping merely moves around loose dirt; only a complete washing can remove the filth. Satan's greatest ploy is to find a person who thinks he has escaped. The devil plays with him like a cat plays with a mouse. Although he may have made changes, they went only skin deep. He never really repented, never really turned from sin, never really desired to know God.

So how can you keep the devil and his buddies out of your "house"? How can you "clean the house" as opposed to merely "sweeping" it?

A man stronger than the one who controls you must deliver you.

That "stronger one" is not you, because you're the one, with all your strength, who got you into this mess. Only One qualifies as stronger than Satan: Jesus Christ.

The Lord once proved His irresistible strength when He delivered a man from a mute demon (Luke 11:14). The crowds "marveled" at this, and rightly so, for when the "stronger one" comes in, everything changes. In this case, the man who formerly could not utter a word now spoke freely.

A flame burned in his fireplace. Real fruit sat in the dish on the table. The faded picture of Jesus had vanished, replaced with Jesus Himself. Jesus did a real and thorough housecleaning, not a mere sweeping.

I want to make it clear that genuine Christians need not fear being possessed or controlled by demons; Jesus is not into a time-share program with Satan. The Bible tells us, "He who has been born of God keeps himself, and the wicked one does not touch him" (1 John 5:18).

Therefore, no one who truly comes to Christ needs to fear the devil's intrusion. Oh, Satan may knock on the doors and rattle the windows. He may threaten to "huff and puff and blow the house down." But he cannot enter because someone stronger has taken up residence. "Greater is He that is in you, than he that is in the world" (1 John 4:4, KJV).

Do you have this protection, or do you remain victim to your own passions? What is often called a demon is in reality our flesh, which we are to die to, not cast out. Unless Jesus Christ changes you from the inside, you can still fall into your old sins—or worse. Jesus is your only hope.

So—who is at home and settled down in your heart right now? Jesus or the devil?

CHAPTER **17**

Dead Man Walking

And it happened when He was in a certain city, that
behold, a man who was full of leprosy saw Jesus;
and he fell on his face and implored Him, saying,
"Lord, if You are willing, You can make me clean."

Luke 5:12

Have you ever hit bottom? Maybe you had certain goals and dreams, but life just didn't turn out the way you had hoped.

Some of your dreams even turned into nightmares. The very things you thought would fulfill you made you miserable. You may have turned to drugs or alcohol—something to numb the pain—and too late you found yourself bound by some addiction from which you could not escape.

The leper depicted in Luke 5 probably felt much like that. Luke, the physician, describes the man as "full of leprosy" (verse 12). The illness had nearly run its course with this man, and in Bible times no medical cure existed.

Today this terrible affliction is called Hansen's disease. Once it was thought to cause limbs to rot and fall off, but research has proven that disfigurement occurs when the illness destroys the body's ability to feel pain. A victim can wash his or her face with scalding water and not know it or cut a finger or burn a foot and feel no pain. In Third World countries, vermin sometimes chew on sleeping lepers without them even realizing it.

In ancient Israel, lepers had to cry out, "Unclean! Unclean!"

when they were in the vicinity of the healthy. If a leper stuck his head inside a house, the house was declared unclean. No one could greet a leper. One Jewish historian said that lepers were treated as if they were dead men; they were completely ostracized.

You probably don't have this horrible disease, but you do have another that's far worse. It's called sin. Sin disfigures the soul like leprosy disfigures the body. You may change your looks, job, friends, location, or vocabulary, but the spiritual disease of sin still can destroy you—and in the most ugly, horrible ways. No cure exists apart from the forgiveness of God.

Fortunately for us, the story of the leper provides a model for how to reach out to God and receive His healing touch.

First, the leper honestly admitted his condition. "Lord, if You are willing," he said, "You can make me clean" (verse 12). This poor man not only *said* he was unclean, he *knew* it. Everybody else probably had given up on him; he was just waiting to die. His only hope lay in Jesus.

In a spiritual sense, this is true of all of us. We are all "dead in trespasses and sins" (Ephesians 2:1). We have no hope in human religion or good works. We can do nothing to change our condition, try as we may. Like this leper, our only hope is Jesus.

So long as you rationalize your behavior or condition, you will not heal. God does not come to the aid of those who think they have no needs or who imagine they can make it on their own. He comes only to those who see their desperate situation. He comes only to those who, like this leper, are willing to cry out, "Unclean! Unclean!" He will not come if we insist on saying, "Only partly unclean!" or "Okay, so I'm a leper—but I'm not as unclean as that guy over there!"

Second, the story of the leper teaches us that Jesus will touch only those who come reverently and in desperation. When the leper saw Jesus, he fell to the ground and knelt before Him (Mark 1:40). The basic meaning of the Greek word translated "kneel" is "to kiss," as in kissing the ground while lying prostrate.

This is not some casual, "Yo, God—whassup?" This is total, reverent, complete dependence. God's healing touch comes to the person who sees God for who He is, and himself for who he is.

Third, Jesus acts on behalf of those who put their faith in Him. Mark's Gospel reports that the leper made his request a number of times. This guy just would not give up! The man was saying, "Jesus, you've done it for others; now do it for *me!*" He had faith that Jesus could and would do what he asked.

Jesus felt deeply touched by the man's display of faith and was "moved with compassion" (verse 41). In response, He reached out and touched the untouchable leper. Remember, it may have been twenty or thirty years since any healthy hand had touched this man's skin. Once he may have known the touch of a beloved wife or the embrace of his darling children. But for years no one had touched him even once.

And Jesus did not lightly brush a finger against the man. Luke tells us, "Then He put out His hand and touched him" (Luke 5:13). At the very least, Jesus placed His whole hand firmly on the leper—and at that moment, healing flowed through the man's body. Toes and fingers grew back. Skin took on a healthy flesh color. His sense of touch returned. His very *life* returned!

What Jesus did for the leper on the physical plane, He wants to do for you on the spiritual plane. Perhaps you have tried everything else. You have seen how Jesus has transformed others—and now you want the same to happen to you. It can and will if you come to Him as did the leper: honestly, reverently, and in faith.

CHAPTER **18**

The Heart of the Problem

When He saw their faith, He said to him, "Man, your sins are forgiven you." Luke 5:20

It was quite an event to have Jesus in town. Imagine if your pastor announced, "Folks, next week Jesus Christ will be here for one night!" Imagine the excitement, the buzz. Everyone would show up!

That's exactly what happened one day in Capernaum. Jesus began teaching there in someone's house, and people came to hear Him from "every town of Galilee, Judea, and Jerusalem" (Luke 5:17). This was a mega-event and everyone showed up.

A paralyzed man also wanted to come, but since he was unable to walk, four of his friends offered to take him. They rallied together and each took a corner of his cot. Yet when these four men and their friend got to the door of the meeting house, they found the place packed, with no room even to get near the door.

Fortunately, they believed that the business of bringing others to Jesus was so important that when it seemed they couldn't find a way, they made one. It would have been great had they been able just to come through a door, but since that was not an option, they looked for another. These guys had daring faith and believed that if being conventional doesn't succeed, try being original.

In those days, the roof of a Palestinian house was flat; in hot weather it served as a place for sleeping, while year round it provided extra storage space. Most homes were simply built. Workers placed wooden beams, about two or three feet apart, across a stone structure, packing brush tightly between those beams. Sun-dried mud cemented the whole thing together. Often an outside stairway leading to the roof completed the house.

Luke tells us that this man's friends "went up on the housetop and let him down with his bed through the tiling into the midst before Jesus" (verse 19). The friends dug through the dried-mud roof above where Jesus stood, and when they had scooped out an opening, they let down the mat with the paralyzed man on it.

It must have been a strange moment when dirt began falling on the heads of those in the house! Looking up, they saw the faces of some men holding ropes, silhouetted against the sky. When the light broke through the ceiling and landed on the mat, everyone could see a paralytic being lowered.

Jesus observed the man on the mat, but He took note of more than that. He focused His attention on the men still on the roof, faces poking through the thatch, eagerly anticipating their friend's miracle.

"When He saw their faith," Luke writes, "He said to him, 'Man, your sins are forgiven you'" (verse 20).

Jesus *saw* the faith of these faithful friends. In His mind's eye, perhaps, He had seen them working together to bring their friend to hear the Lord preach. He had seen them take the corners of the cot and struggle down the streets to the house. He had seen them unable to reach the doorway. And He had seen them as they climbed the stairs and dug through the roof.

Can He see *your* faith? When was the last time you went out of your way to bring someone to hear the gospel? It's a remarkable fact that *85 percent* of the unbelievers who come forward to receive Christ at a Harvest Crusade are brought by a friend. Many will never get to Jesus unless a friend tells them how.

Paul reminds us, "How can they hear about him unless someone tells them? And how will anyone go and tell them without being sent? That is what the Scriptures mean when they say, 'How beautiful are the feet of those who bring good news!'" (Romans 10:14-15, NLT).

These men had several admirable characteristics. First, they felt genuinely concerned about their friend and wanted him to get help. Second, they had faith to believe that Jesus could and would meet his need. They did more than just pray about the problem; they put feet to their prayers and *did* something. Third, they worked together and dared to do something different. Consider this: Capernaum had a lot of needy people in those days, but only this man was healed and forgiven. Why? Because his persistent friends brought him to Jesus.

The Lord not only healed the man's physical paralysis, He also healed his soul by forgiving him of his sin. Sometimes we come to Jesus as a last resort. We have grown weary of addiction to drugs, to alcohol, to you-name-it. The heart of the problem is the problem of the heart. It's our sin that we need forgiven, and we can do nothing to remedy that situation apart from Jesus. Sin leaves a stain we cannot wash out. Only Jesus can do that!

That's the life-changing lesson this man learned on a sunny day in Capernaum. He came to Jesus to get his body healed, but walked out of that house with a restored body and a renewed spirit. It is no wonder that Luke ends the story, "And they were all amazed, and they glorified God and were filled with fear, saying, 'We have seen strange things today!'" (verse 26).

CHAPTER **19**

The Squeaky Wheel

Jesus stood still and commanded him to be brought to Him. And when he had come near, He asked him, saying, "What do you want Me to do for you?" He said, "Lord, that I may receive my sight." Then Jesus said to him, "Receive your sight; your faith has made you well."

Luke 18:40-42

Jericho seemed alive with excitement. The famed Jesus of Nazareth had arrived! By this point in His ministry, Jesus had nearly reached the pinnacle of His popularity. In just a few short weeks, ecstatic crowds in Jerusalem would lay palm branches at His feet and shout, "Hosanna!"

On this day in Jericho, a solitary figure heard the noise of animated crowds but had no idea what so excited them. Every day he positioned himself as close to the front gate as he could get. He knew every cobbled stone and wall in the city, though he probably couldn't give a complete description of any of them. As a blind man, he would grope his way to his usual post, hoping for handouts from kind passersby.

But on this day, something unusual was happening. He heard a raucous crowd passing in front of him, but no one bothered to tell him what was up. Finally he asked someone to explain what was causing all the hubbub.

"Jesus of Nazareth has come!" the stranger said.

The blind man immediately recognized the opportunity of a lifetime and grabbed it.

"Jesus, Son of David," he cried, "have mercy on me!" (Luke 18:38).

Though this beggar could not see, he had great spiritual insight. In using the phrase "Son of David," he revealed his personal knowledge of Jesus' true identity. Clearly, he knew the Scriptures taught that the Messiah would come from the tribe of David. By calling Jesus the "Son of David," he proclaimed his belief that Jesus was indeed the Messiah of Israel and the Savior of the world.

Not bad insight for a blind man!

Someone once asked Helen Keller, who grew up both blind and deaf, "Isn't it terrible to be blind?"

"Better to be blind and see with your heart," she wisely responded, "than to have two good eyes and see nothing."

This man certainly "saw with his heart." So strongly did he believe that Jesus was the Messiah that he refused to stop calling out for the Lord, even though irritated members of the crowd told him to shut his mouth. In fact, the Gospel of Mark says that although "many warned him to be quiet," he "cried out all the more, 'Son of David, have mercy on me!'" (Mark 10:48).

He *would* be heard!

The beggar appeared to know instinctively that spiritual blessings belong to those who "go for it." Even in the spiritual realm, the squeaky wheel gets the oil; the halfhearted need not apply. But there was nothing halfhearted about this man.

God says, "You will seek Me and find Me when you search for Me *with all your heart*" (Jeremiah 29:13, emphasis added). And Jesus adds, "Blessed are those who hunger and thirst for righteousness, for they shall be filled" (Matthew 5:6).

When Jesus heard the man's insistent cries, He immediately stopped and commanded that the man be brought to Him.

"What do you want Me to do for you?" He asked (Luke 18:41).

Jesus' question puzzles some people. If He's really the Messiah, then why should He have to *ask* the man what he wanted? Wouldn't it be obvious? It doesn't take a medical doctor to identify a blind beggar who for years has been crawling around, seeking handouts. Why *did* Jesus ask, "What do you want Me to do for you?"

First, we should remember that God often asks us questions, not to gain information but to get us to admit our need. When Adam sinned in the Garden of Eden, the first thing God said to him was, "Where are you?" (Genesis 3:9). The passage makes it clear that God knew precisely where Adam was; it was *Adam* who had gotten himself lost through disobedience.

Jesus may have been doing something similar with the blind man. By asking him, "What do you want Me to do for you?" the Lord not only urged the beggar to admit his need but also encouraged him to declare his dependence upon Jesus to meet that need.

Second, the Bible makes it clear that while "all things are possible with God" (Mark 10:27, NIV), it reminds us that we can't expect to tap into His miracle-working power without explicit prayer. The Lord repeatedly tells us to make our requests specific. "You do not have because you do not ask," God says in James 4:2. "Let your requests be made known to God," Paul counsels in Philippians 4:6. If we want God to do something specific in our lives, we need to make our prayers specific.

So Jesus turns to this sightless man and asks, "What do you want Me to do for you?"

The man doesn't wait to respond. He knows his need. He believes he is speaking with Israel's long-promised Messiah. And so he says simply, "Lord, that I may receive my sight."

No doubt Jesus smiled broadly as He replied, "Receive your sight; your faith has made you well."

At that moment, the blind man required a different title. His eyes were opened, and for the first time in years, he saw clearly. And the One he first saw, he followed.

May we have the spiritual insight of the man *formerly* known as the blind beggar from Jericho!

CHAPTER 20

Up a Tree

When Jesus came to the place, He looked up and saw him, and said to him, "Zacchaeus, make haste and come down, for today I must stay at your house." Luke 19:5

As a chief tax collector, Zacchaeus headed up a lucrative tax-farming corporation. Judean taxes were collected at three places inland: Capernaum, Jerusalem, and Jericho. Zacchaeus had become the kingpin of the Jericho tax cartel, a Godfather-like figure, both feared and hated. His employees extorted money from the people, then paid Zacchaeus before he paid the Romans. Zacchaeus had it made in the shade.

Yet to be a member of this despised profession invited both personal isolation and social banishment. The countrymen of Zacchaeus considered him a traitor, a turncoat, and a collaborator with Rome. Thus while Zacchaeus had vast wealth, he had no one with whom to enjoy it. Most Jews hated him—but not Jesus.

Somehow, Zacchaeus learned of Jesus' visit to Jericho. How did the tax collector hear about the Lord? Who would have bothered to tell a man like him? Most people probably thought, *He'd never listen; he has everything in life!* But behind all the facades and masks, everyone who tries living without God ends up empty, lonely, guilty, and afraid to die. To outsiders it may have looked as if Zacchaeus had no needs, but he desperately needed God.

Perhaps Zacchaeus had learned of the conversion of Levi, a fellow tax collector, who was now one of Jesus' actual disciples. If so, this may have given him hope. Whatever the truth, by this point I'm sure he had begun to recognize the emptiness of a dishonest life. No doubt he found his wealth and opulent lifestyle deeply unsatisfying. In any case, when he heard about Jesus' Jericho visit, he knew he just *had* to see Him.

Undignified though it was, he ran to a spot on the road where he knew Jesus would pass. Yet as a short man, he couldn't see over the crowd. How could he get a glimpse of Jesus before the Teacher headed out of town? Immediately, an unconventional idea occurred to him: he'd climb a nearby tree!

Much to the amusement of the downtrodden populace, this powerful government official, this hated VIP, scampered up to a precarious perch on a handy sycamore. From there he tried to snatch a peek at Jesus.

The crowd hadn't expected *that,* but even less had they anticipated what happened next. Before even Zacchaeus knew what was happening, Jesus stopped directly below him, looked up in the tree . . . and spoke his name.

At that moment Zacchaeus may have worried that the Lord would reprove him, berate him, call him what he was: "You rotten little thief! How dare you rip off all these people?"

But that is not what Jesus said. Instead, with love and tenderness, He commanded, "Zacchaeus! . . . Quick, come down! For I must be a guest in your home today" (Luke 19:5, NLT)

This is the only instance in the Gospels where Jesus invites Himself to someone's home. He often visited other households—the homes of Mary and Martha, of Peter, of Simon the leper, of a synagogue leader, etc.—but always He came at their invitation. Why would He invite Himself to the home of Zacchaeus? Perhaps He knew that while Zacchaeus desperately wanted a visit, he was sure Jesus would turn him down. So Jesus invited Himself.

Zacchaeus shimmied down the tree and excitedly led the Lord to his home. No doubt everyone followed—watching with disapproval. Their cheers for Jesus quickly turned to jeers.

Luke says, "They *all* complained, saying, 'He has gone to be a guest with a man who is a sinner'" (Luke 19:7, emphasis added).

But none of that mattered to Jesus. He and Zacchaeus disappeared from the crowd. While we don't know exactly what happened or what was said during those unrecorded moments, one thing is clear: at some point Zacchaeus received a spiritual heart transplant. He was transformed, changed, saved, redeemed, converted. How do we know this? Because of his dramatic change in character.

"Look, Lord," he said, "I give half of my goods to the poor; and if I have taken anything from anyone by false accusation, I restore fourfold"(verse 8). That very day, Jesus became Zacchaeus's Savior and Lord. What brought about such a remarkable change? Interestingly, we know of no claims that Jesus made on Zacchaeus's life.

He just loved him.

In response, Zacchaeus promised to do far more than what the law required. He determined to go the extra mile. He had cheated many people, and now he intended to place his entire fortune in jeopardy in order to make restitution.

Our society has largely lost sight of restitution, but it's an integral part of a life lived to please God. Do you want a close walk with God? Then ask yourself: "Is there anyone to whom I need to make restitution?" If you have stolen something, return it. If you have slandered someone, go to those who heard your lies and tell them you were wrong, that the things you said are untrue.

May your repentance be as widely known as your sin! And may Jesus be able to say of you, as He did of Zacchaeus, "Today salvation has come to this house" (verse 9).

CHAPTER **21**

The King
Weeps

*They threw their own clothes on the colt, and they set
Jesus on him. And as He went, many spread their clothes
on the road.* Luke 19:35-36

Jesus had never done anything like this. Usually He withdrew
from the crowds when they clamored for Him. Once He hid
Himself from a crowd that wanted to make Him king. But now
He deliberately arranged to enter Jerusalem as King. On this,
His last visit to the city, He decided to enter in a way that
would draw attention to Himself.

In Rome, a conquering hero returning from war entered the
city in a great triumphal procession with people cheering him
along. No Roman would miss the meaning of this day.

Nor would its meaning be lost on the Jews. As Jesus entered
Jerusalem riding on a donkey, the Jews would remember the
prophecy of Zechariah 9:9: "Rejoice greatly, O daughter of
Zion! Shout, O daughter of Jerusalem! Behold, your king is
coming to you; He is just and having salvation, lowly and riding upon a donkey, a colt, the foal of a donkey."

Though Jesus had repeatedly said, "My hour has not yet
come," now the hour had at last come. He intended to fulfill
the prophecy of Malachi 3:1: "'The Lord you are seeking will
suddenly come to his Temple. The messenger of the covenant,
whom you look for so eagerly, is surely coming,' says the Lord
Almighty" (NLT). On this day He would leave no doubt that He
came as the Messiah.

Jesus knew He was a wanted man, yet He chose to publicize His arrival. The religious authorities had commanded anyone aware of His location to reveal the information (John 11:57), and yet here He was, coming forth publicly—not as a helpless victim unaware of what lay ahead, but as a powerful victor, marching bravely into battle.

As He entered the city, delirious throngs shouted, "Blessed is the King who comes in the name of the Lord!" (Luke 19:38). Others cried out, "Hosanna!" which means, "Save now!" (Matthew 21:9). The disciples' hearts must have leapt for joy as the masses celebrated what they already believed so earnestly: that Jesus was indeed the long-awaited Messiah.

Yet a great sadness also filled this day, for the cries of "Hosanna" came from ignorance of His true role. The people wanted Jesus on their own terms. They wanted a deliverer who conformed to their plans instead of they to His. They wanted Jesus to destroy Rome but leave untouched their cherished sins and superficial religion.

Little has changed in two thousand years. Many who love to celebrate Palm Sunday neglect Jesus the rest of the year. They'll celebrate His birth and arrival at Christmas but live as if He never came. They'll celebrate His resurrection at Easter but live as if He were dead.

Many of us will sing the praises of a Jesus we think will give us wealth, success, and happiness; we recoil, however, from one who requires obedience and commitment. We'll loudly acclaim Jesus as long as we believe He will satisfy our selfish desires. When He fails to deliver, however, we are quick to reject and denounce Him—as did the multitude celebrating His Triumphal Entry.

Jesus knew all this and it made Him weep (Luke 19:41). While the crowd whipped itself into a frenzy, Jesus cried. At the tomb of Lazarus, Jesus wept quietly. Here, however, He sobbed in the open. The word Luke uses to describe Christ's weeping signifies bitter anguish, as one mourning the dead.

One wonders: did a hush fall over the crowd? Or did the people continue to celebrate, never noticing the Lord's hot tears?

Why did Jesus weep? For one thing, He knew His ministry was almost over. He had healed their sick, raised their dead, cleansed their lepers, and fed their hungry—but He remained mostly alone and rejected. He also knew that one of His own would soon betray Him. He knew Caiaphas and Pilate would conspire against Him. He knew the same people crying "Hosanna" would in a few days change their cry to "Crucify!"

And He also knew their future. He foresaw the destruction of Jerusalem and knew that in less than forty years, the Romans would lay siege to the city, killing or capturing thousands. After the disaster happened in 70 A.D., the Jewish historian Josephus told how rivers of blood flowed through the gates of the city. He described how their beloved temple was burned to the ground and dismantled, stone by stone, to get at the melted gold—thus fulfilling the prophecy of Jesus that "not one stone shall be left here upon another" (Matthew 24:2).

All of this broke the heart of Jesus.

Unbelief and rejection always breaks God's heart, for He knows the consequences. The same God who placed the planets in orbit and made light shine out of darkness refuses to forcibly enter the door of the human heart. He will only knock. He knows the repercussions of turning Him away, and that breaks His heart.

So Jesus wept. But after His weeping would come His ultimate work. For despite His rejection, He would go to the cross and die for the sins of humankind.

For that was why He had come.

CHAPTER 22

When Temples Get Dirty

Then He went into the temple and began to drive out those who bought and sold in it, saying to them, "It is written, 'My house is a house of prayer,' but you have made it a 'den of thieves.'" Luke 19:45-46

The story of Jesus "cleansing" the temple surprises some of us. It seems to go against the image of a meek and mild Jesus to which we've grown accustomed. Mark says Jesus "went into the temple and began to drive out those who bought and sold in the temple, and overturned the tables of the money changers and the seats of those who sold doves" (Mark 11:15).

It's a violent act to overturn a table. We've seen it happen in a thousand Western movies, when the hero flips over the table and calls the other guy a cheater. The piano player always stops playing, and everyone freezes. Then they shoot it out.

But how does flipping tables square with our Lord's statement, "Take My yoke upon you, and learn of me; for I am meek and lowly in heart: and ye shall find rest unto your souls" (Matthew 11:29, KJV)?

First, we need to understand what meekness is. It is not weakness. Meekness has been defined as "strength under control" and "power under constraint." While meekness has the strength to *not* defend itself—as when Jesus freely chose to go to the cross—it *will* boldly defend others.

Jesus' outburst in the temple shows us what righteous indignation looks like. He grew furious because the priests and their associates were keeping people away from God—and that always makes God *very* angry.

A merchandising and scam operation was taking place outside of the temple proper in the area called the court of the Gentiles. In this area, Gentiles could come to worship God—except I can't imagine how much worshiping they could do in what had become a noisy marketplace where money changers and animal sellers did business. The priests required worshipers to pay the temple tax in special sanctuary half-shekels; regular currency had to be exchanged for the temple coin. In the exchange, some merchants jacked up the price and ripped off the people. Also, all animals brought for sacrifice had to be without spot or blemish. Often the priests found a blemish on worshipers' animals—so their animals would be rejected and they would have to buy "pre-inspected and priest-approved" animals from the temple merchants (again at jacked-up prices).

The fact that such a market even existed, filling up the place where the Gentiles were supposed to worship, and the fact that there was corruption there infuriated God. He welcomes all people to Himself, Jew and Gentile alike. When Jesus said, "My house is a house of prayer," He was really referring to Gentiles being able to freely approach God (Isaiah 56:6-8). But these Gentiles were being discriminated against.

The same error can happen today in the church. Suppose a nonbeliever comes to a service, tattooed, pierced, or wearing some strange T-shirt. Sometimes we look away in disgust or maybe even turn him away. This, too, makes God angry. The church should be a place for sinners to come and find God.

We should also remember that Jesus twice cleansed the temple, once at the beginning of His ministry and once toward the end (see John 2:13-17). For a while after the first cleansing, things at the temple ran well. But soon one man set up his table, the prices soared, and another joined him. In time, things got as bad as ever, so Jesus came back and did it again right before His death.

In a similar way, when we first come to Christ, Jesus "cleanses our temple." The Lord banishes filthy habits and gives us a new purpose. In time, however, some of the old things find their way back in, and soon we find our lives cluttered with junk that shouldn't be there. That's when Jesus needs to return for another "house cleaning."

What does your "temple" look like today? Could it use a little cleansing?

I've learned there is a right way and a wrong way to clean. In our house, we call these the Greg way and the Cathe way. I am basically a messy person; my wife Cathe is a cleaning fanatic. The Greg way is to never do today what you can put off until tomorrow. Just throw the shirt in the drawer if you don't know what else to do with it. Sweep the dust under the rug. Basically, the Greg way is the path of least resistance.

The Cathe way champions a very different path. Don't merely sweep, but mop the floor. Organize the drawer, don't just throw things into it. In other words, do whatever it takes to get the job done right. The Cathe way is the right way; mine is the wrong way.

We could make a similar application to our spiritual lives. Some take the Greg way to spiritual cleaning and make a few exterior changes without any significant change on the inside. Others go the Cathe way and get to the core of the problem, the source of the mess, and scrub until it shines.

Does your "temple" need cleansing today? Are there some sins, vices, or bad habits that have found their way back into your life? Perhaps you used to engage in these things before your conversion and now they've returned. Then again, they may be new problems, vices that never before troubled you. Are you, by your words or life, putting up obstacles to keep people from coming to Christ?

Then let Jesus "clean house." Ask the Lord to show you what needs cleaning, then cooperate with Him to wash away the dirt. And don't worry if a few tables get overturned in the process! Sometimes that's exactly what's needed.

CHAPTER 23

You Are the Reason

> *And He was withdrawn from them about a stone's throw, and He knelt down and prayed, saying, "Father, if it is Your will, take this cup away from Me; nevertheless not My will, but Yours, be done."*
>
> Luke 22:41-42

The devil came to Gethsemane in full force. We know that he had already "entered Judas" (Luke 22:3); even as Jesus knelt down to pray, Judas was in the garden and approaching.

The fact that Jesus interrupted His prayer three times to return to His sleeping disciples may suggest that He was facing waves of temptation similar to what He endured at the beginning of His ministry when Satan had offered Jesus a "shortcut" to glory—a kingdom without a cross (see Matthew 4:8-9).

But Jesus would have nothing to do with that—then or now. There was only one way to settle the sin issue. He *had* to "taste death for everyone" (Hebrews 2:9). He *had* to "drink the cup" (John 18:11). He *had* to go to the cross and die for our sins.

When the disciples finally awoke to find that an armed mob had arrived to arrest their Lord, Peter pulled out a sword and cut off the ear of the high priest's servant. Poor Peter just couldn't get it right. He was boasting when he should have been listening, sleeping when he should have been praying. Now he was fighting when he should have been surrendering.

Thanks to Peter's impulsive violence, the authorities could now claim they had a rebel uprising led by a fierce guerrilla leader. "Yes sir, this large man they call 'the Rock' pulled out a sword. He was cheered on by two others they call 'the Sons of Thunder'!"

In reality, Jesus needed no one to rescue Him. So He told Peter, "Do you think I cannot call on my Father, and he will at once put at my disposal more than twelve legions of angels?" (Matthew 26:53, NIV). A Roman legion numbered at least 6,000 troops; therefore something like 72,000 angels stood ready to aid Jesus on that terrible night. When you recall that a single angel killed 185,000 of ancient Israel's enemies in one night (2 Chronicles 32:21), you see how easily Jesus could have escaped.

Yet He steadfastly refused any route of flight. Why? He had come to this moment precisely to offer Himself to God as a sacrifice for us.

In the midst of this flurry of activity, very few noticed the last miracle of Jesus' earthly ministry, a wonder that showed His compassionate heart. He healed the ear of the man Peter had attacked. Jesus did not forget about one man's need, even a man who had come to take Him to His death.

Finally Jesus asked His enemies, "Am I leading a rebellion, that you have come with swords and clubs? Every day I was with you in the temple courts, and you did not lay a hand on me. But this is your hour—when darkness reigns" (Luke 22:52-53, NIV).

Notice the beautiful irony here. The fact is, *they* were the lawbreakers, not Him. They were the ones who came under the cover of night, breaking many laws in order to arrest Him. The physical darkness of the night covered a deeper spiritual and moral darkness. This was hell's hour. The devil was on something of a roll—or so it seemed.

Everything appeared to be lining up for Satan. He had his betrayer in Judas and loyal allies among both the religious and the civil authorities. He was personally energizing and directing the show. All his ducks appeared to be in a row.

Yet he had a problem. God also had *His* plans, and that made everything else irrelevant.

Amazingly, this was heaven's hour, too. Gethsemane was one of those very rare occurrences where, in one sense, both God and Satan were working toward the same goal. Satan's goal was to kill Jesus; by doing so, he intended to foil Christ's mission. God's goal also called for Jesus to die. Why? Because only through the death of Jesus could the sins of the world be forgiven.

Gethsemane marked a watershed moment for Jesus and His ministry. What caused Him to stick to heaven's plan, knowing that even the Father Himself would momentarily forsake Him as He took upon Himself the sins of the world? Hebrews tells us that Jesus, "for the joy that was set before Him endured the cross, despising the shame" (Hebrews 12:2).

And what is this "joy"? Our Lord provided a big clue in His story of a shepherd who went after a lost lamb. When the shepherd found his wandering sheep, he wrapped it around his shoulders and brought it back home. "I say to you that likewise there will be more joy in heaven over one sinner who repents," Jesus declared (Luke 15:7).

You are His joy!

"The kingdom of heaven is like treasure hidden in a field," Jesus said. "When a man found it, he hid it again, and then in his joy went and sold all he had and bought that field" (Matthew 13:44, NIV).

You are His treasure!

And *You* are the reason Jesus reaffirmed His decision in Gethsemane to go through the pain and agony of Calvary. With Paul, you and I can gratefully say, He "loved me and gave Himself for me" (Galatians 2:20).

CHAPTER **24**

God on Trial

Then they all said, "Are You then the Son of God?" So He said to them, "You rightly say that I am." Luke 22:70

No trial in history had greater ramifications than the trial of Jesus of Nazareth.

Though no reporters, computers, or satellite dishes beamed its proceedings to the four corners of the earth, it still shakes the planet. No *Court TV* interviewers talked to the plaintiffs or to the defendant, yet all heaven and hell watched as this drama of redemption unfolded.

It was quite literally the day *God* went on trial.

From a merely human perspective, the trial represented the worst miscarriage of justice imaginable. Yet even this fit into God's plan.

Rabbinical legal requirements of the day were supposed to guarantee a court's fairness and impartiality. An accused criminal had the right to a public trial, to defense counsel, and could be convicted only on the testimony of at least two reliable witnesses. Trials were to remain open to public scrutiny, and the defendant had the right to present evidence and witnesses on his own behalf.

To guard against deliberate false testimony, the law prescribed that witnesses who perjured themselves would suffer the very punishment meted out to the guilty (Deuteronomy 19:16-19). Anyone who knowingly gave false testimony in a trial involving capital punishment, for example, would be put to death. A strong deterrent to perjury!

The accused was always presumed innocent. If found not guilty, he or she was freed immediately; if convicted, the court did not pronounce sentence until two days later. Council members had to fast during the intervening day, and on the morning of the third day, the council reconvened. Each judge was then asked if he had changed his decision. If the judges reaffirmed a guilty verdict, an officer with a flag remained near the council while another officer, often mounted on horseback, escorted the prisoner to the place of execution. A herald preceded the slow-moving column, declaring in a loud voice, "This man is led to punishment for such and such crime. The witnesses who have sworn against him are such and such persons. If anyone has evidence to give in his favor, let him come forward quickly." If information that might exonerate the accused came to light at any time before the sentence was carried out—including the prisoner's recollection of something previously forgotten—one officer would signal the other and the prisoner would be returned to the council for reconsideration of the verdict. Note the governing principle in capital cases: The Sanhedrin was to save life, not destroy it.

No criminal trial could begin or continue at night. The property of an executed criminal could not be confiscated but had to be passed on to his heirs. And the council voted from the youngest member to the oldest, so that the latter could not influence the former.

Yet on the day Jesus was tried, Caiaphas and the Sanhedrin ignored every one of these principles. For example:

1. Jesus was tried illegally, without being charged with a crime.
2. Jesus was tried at night.
3. Jesus was tried in private.
4. Jesus was permitted no defense.
5. The witnesses against Jesus had been bribed to falsify their testimony.
6. Jesus was executed on the same day He was sentenced, so the judges had no opportunity to reconsider their verdict.

John's Gospel tells us that before Jesus arrived at Caiaphas's house, He was taken to the home of Annas, Caiaphas's father-in-law. Some twenty years earlier, Annas had served as high priest. Although long ago he had been replaced, he continued to wield great influence in temple affairs. Annas so controlled the temple money changers and "sacrifice sellers," for example, that sometimes residents called them the "bazaars of Annas." No temple merchant could operate without Annas's approval.

Jesus really got Annas's attention when He flipped over the tables and drove those religious hucksters out of the temple, accusing them of turning God's "house of prayer" into a "den of thieves." And remember that Jesus did this not once, but twice! Immediately after the second temple cleansing, His enemies "sought how they might destroy Him" (Mark 11:18). Jesus not only exposed the scam in the temple, He also exposed Annas as a greedy, power-hungry manipulator with no real interest in honoring God.

And now with Jesus' trial, Annas had a perfect opportunity for payback.

Annas closely questioned Jesus about His disciples and His teaching, searching for some technicality on which to hang Him. When he could find nothing, he and his companions settled for mocking and beating the Savior. At last Annas sent Jesus on to Caiaphas and the Jewish council for an official "trial."

In reality, the ones who stood in illegal judgment of Jesus were themselves on trial that day. In the end, the only conviction they could obtain came when Jesus agreed with their statement that He really was "the Son of God" (Luke 22:70-71).

Now, when you hear a confession like that, only two options remain. Either you bow before Jesus as Lord and Savior or you sentence Him to death as a blasphemer.

The Sanhedrin chose the latter option. What have you decided?

CHAPTER 25

Whose Voice Will You Hear?

> *They were insistent, demanding with loud voices that He be crucified. And the voices of these men and of the chief priests prevailed. So Pilate gave sentence that it should be as they requested.* Luke 23:23-24

Once they confirmed that Jesus did indeed claim to be the Messiah, the religious leaders of Jerusalem brought the Lord before the Roman governor, Pontius Pilate—who immediately landed on the horns of a dilemma.

It was the time of the Passover, and Jerusalem had swelled with thousands of Jews from all over the world who had traveled to the city for the festival. Things already felt tense, and Pilate wanted to avoid any kind of upheaval in the city. He had governed Judea for four or five years, a rule marked by several misjudgments that had made him highly unpopular with the Jews.

For example, he had deliberately offended the Jews by ordering his soldiers to carry into Jerusalem ensigns engraved with the likeness of Caesar. The Jews considered these standards idolatrous and sent a delegation to Pilate asking for their removal. Pilate responded by herding them into the amphitheater and threatening to cut off their heads. When they threw themselves to the ground and bowed their necks in a face-saving gesture, Pilate withdrew his threat (and his ensigns). A short while later, Pilate forcibly took money from the temple treasury to erect an aqueduct. When the Jews rioted,

Pilate sent soldiers disguised as civilians to slaughter many of the protesters. So by this time, major tensions had arisen between Rome and the Jews.

The governor already was walking on eggshells. He didn't need another problem, and he did not want to deal with either Jesus or the Jews. Anxious to stay uninvolved, Pilate said, "You take Him and judge Him according to your law" (John 18:31). In essence, the governor thus gave the Sanhedrin permission to kill Jesus; he knew that the Jews executed their most serious religious offenders. But while the chief priests wanted Jesus dead, they desired to avoid official responsibility for the deed (as well as possible reprisals from their own people). So they insisted that Pilate judge their enemy.

After Pilate examined Jesus and announced, "I find no fault in this Man," the crowd insisted, "He stirs up the people, teaching throughout all Judea, beginning from Galilee to this place" (Luke 23:4-5). It delighted Pilate to hear that Jesus came from Galilee, for that meant he could send Him to his rival, Herod, for judgment. This he quickly did—but a few hours later, Herod sent Him back, forcing Pilate once more to deal with Jesus.

Now what would he do? Just then Pilate remembered his custom to release a Jewish prisoner at Passover. Immediately he offered to release either Barabbas—an insurrectionist and murderer, largely hated—or Jesus, who still had His supporters. He figured this might get him off the hook.

He was wrong.

It is interesting to note that many self-proclaimed messiahs had arisen at this time in history, calling themselves Barabbas ("son of the father"). G. Campbell Morgan, in his commentary on Luke, points out that one or two old manuscripts list this man's name as "Jesus Barabbas," the very name and title of our Lord. Therefore, this Barabbas may have been calling himself the Messiah. That makes Pilate's choice all the more interesting.

The very form in which Pilate asks his central question—"Whom do you want me to release to you? Barabbas, or Jesus who is called Christ?" (Matthew 27:17)—suggests that Barabbas's first name *was* Jesus. He wanted to know which Jesus the crowd would choose: the one called Barabbas, or the one called Christ. Would they choose a murderer who had led a rebellion or a man against whom no charge of violence could be made?

But Pilate's plans failed once again. Instead of freeing the innocent Jesus, the people chose Barabbas. The multitude clearly wanted blood, not justice, and their vicious response must have chilled Pilate's blood, hardened pagan though he was. The irony is that the chief priests had falsely brought Jesus before Pilate on charges of insurrection but chose to free a man plainly guilty of that very thing.

In a pitiful attempt to absolve himself of responsibility, the governor finally washed his hands in public—a typically *Jewish* ceremony. But he couldn't wash his hands of Jesus. The moment he came into contact with Christ, he was found responsible.

Matthew's Gospel tells us one very important reason Pilate did not want to condemn Jesus: his wife had suffered a disturbing dream concerning Him. "Have nothing to do with that just Man," she warned (Matthew 27:19).

The governor heard many voices that day: the voice of his wife who warned him against condemning the innocent Jesus; the voice of the multitudes screaming "Crucify"; the voice of his own conscience wanting to release Jesus; and the voice of Jesus Himself.

Sadly, he listened to the wrong voice and made the wrong decision. In the end, he hardened his heart to the very voice of God.

History tells us that within seven years of his hand washing, Pontius Pilate, the great Roman governor, was removed from high office by his superior, the governor of Syria. He left

Judea broken, destitute, unwanted by Caesar, and all alone. One night shortly afterward, Pilate went out into the darkness and, like Judas, hung himself. A common workman found his body.

Pilate threw his life away because he cared more about what others thought than about what God thought—and his craving for popularity and power cost him everything.

We all know men and women like Pilate. We must help them to realize that they cannot "wash their hands" of Jesus. All people must decide which voice they will hear, and they must understand that the choice they make has eternal consequences.

The question before Pilate still confronts us today: Which Jesus do we want?

Some follow a Jesus of their own making, a Jesus who will not interfere with their plans or sins, a Jesus who smiles benignly at all they do and goes along with them as their "copilot." But this Jesus cannot save them because he does not exist.

Others choose to follow the real Jesus, the Jesus who died on the cross for us and who rose again from the dead three days later. He is the only Jesus who can save us.

Which Jesus have you chosen?

CHAPTER **26**

Are You Carrying the Cross?

> *As they led him away, they seized Simon from Cyrene, who was on his way in from the country, and put the cross on him and made him carry it behind Jesus.*
>
> Luke 23:26 NIV

Moments after Pilate pronounced sentence against Jesus, soldiers led our Lord away to an infamous spot known as "The Place of the Skull." Matthew's Gospel tells us that a "whole garrison" of soldiers surrounded Jesus (Matthew 27:27)— about six hundred armed men, each an elite legionnaire, the cream of the military crop, much like today's Navy Seals, Green Berets, or Delta Force.

But despite their special status, these soldiers behaved like swine.

One might think they would feel some sympathy toward Jesus. By this point, His face had swollen grotesquely from the beatings He had endured. He was bleeding profusely from terrible lacerations to His shoulder muscles, ligaments, blood vessels, and possibly even internal organs. Yet He had stood so strong under all this punishment that Pilate had exclaimed, "Behold the Man!" (John 19:5).

Without question, Jesus was a "man's man." You would think these legionnaires would have at least respected that much about Jesus.

But they showed no mercy. Instead, they wove a crown of thorns and pressed it into His head. It is worth noting that thorns were a part of the curse that God pronounced upon the earth after Adam and Eve sinned (Genesis 3:18). It seems only appropriate that Jesus, who "[became] a curse for us" (Galatians 3:13), would wear a symbol of the curse on His way to the cross.

The soldiers also gave Him a reed, in mockery of a royal scepter. Matthew tells us they used it to strike Jesus on the head (Matthew 27:30). They took a symbol of His royalty and beat Him with it as if to say, "Where is your royal army to defend you, *King?*"

When the time came for Jesus to begin His agonizing march to Calvary, He carried His own cross (John 19:17). It may only have been the crossbeam, but more likely it was the entire cross, weighing around three hundred pounds—a considerable weight for any man to carry, much less one who had been savagely beaten. Of course, Jesus was a carpenter, a man of about thirty-three, in the prime of life. He was accustomed to heavy lifting and certainly knew how to put His shoulder to a task. But by this point, He was in horrible shape. When He stumbled, the Romans forced an onlooker, a man named Simon, to carry His cross (Luke 23:26).

One might wonder, Where were the apostles? As Jesus' closest friends, wouldn't they have been around to support Him? After all, He had warned them that this would happen. If they had been close enough, couldn't one of them have said, "Hey, He's so weak. Let me carry the cross for Him!" Yet all of them had fled the scene. Only the women remained.

So it was that the Romans forced Simon, a stranger, to carry the cross of Jesus. What a testimony he must have had! To actually be able to say, "I carried the cross for Jesus"!

What if *you* had been given the opportunity to take that burden from your Savior, if even for a few steps? What if you could have carried Jesus' cross?

Maybe you still can.

Jesus said, "If anyone would come after me, he must deny himself and take up his cross *daily* and follow me" (Luke 9:23, emphasis added). He also said, "Whoever finds his life will lose it, and whoever loses his life for my sake will find it" (Matthew 10:39, NIV).

Are you bearing your cross for Jesus? Are you losing your life for Him, only to find it? To bear the cross of Jesus means that you take your plans, your aspirations—in fact, your entire life—and give it all to God. It means that you willingly choose His will over your own. Paul described such a life as being "crucified with Christ" (Galatians 2:20) and admitted, "I die daily" (1 Corinthians 15:31).

When was the last time you consciously chose to "die daily"?

We have hundreds of opportunities every day to "take up the cross." To take up the cross of Jesus means to love God more than anyone or anything else. It means that we willingly make any sacrifice He asks of us.

Does that sound depressing? It's really not. As Paul said, "I am crucified with Christ: nevertheless *I live*" (Galatians 2:20, KJV, emphasis added). Jesus promised that whoever *"loses* his life . . . will *find* it" (Matthew 10:39, emphasis added). To take up the cross of Jesus really means to live life to its fullest.

We can never talk about the cross too much or contemplate it too often. Yet to many of us, the cross is little more than a fashion accessory. We have sanitized the cross and stripped it of its original meaning.

A woman walked into a jewelry store to look for a cross. After examining various crucifixes, she asked, "Do you have any crosses without the little man on it?"

That's what people want today—a cross without Christ.

Forgiveness without repentance.

But according to the Bible, you cannot have one without the other.

Perhaps God would show you a way to "take up the cross" today.

It might be saying no to that temptation. It might be putting the needs of your husband, wife, or children above your own. It might be helping someone in need. It might be standing up for Jesus when it's not popular.

Ask God to show you how you can be a modern-day Simon of Cyrene.

CHAPTER **27**

Love Held Him There

And when they had come to the place called Calvary,
there they crucified Him. Luke 23:33

The dreaded moment had come.

Jesus' back, already shredded from scourging, was thrown against a rough wooden cross. Foul-mouthed Roman soldiers stretched out His arms and pounded spikes through His left and right wrists. They pressed His left foot backward against His right foot and drove another spike through the arches. With a bone-jarring jolt, they raised His crucified body high for all to see.

And then they waited for Him to die.

A fever soon set in, producing a burning thirst. The wounds in Jesus' back, hands, and feet grew increasingly inflamed. Virtually every vein in His body swelled to grotesque proportions, while blood congested His head, lungs, and heart.

So tragic.

No longer would the precious hands of Jesus reach out and touch the hurting and sick, for now they were nailed to a cross.

No longer would His feet allow Him to carry the gospel to the needy, for His feet, too, were fixed to the cross.

Crucifixion originated in Persia as a way to raise a condemned criminal above the earth so as not to defile it. Alexander the Great introduced the practice to Egypt and Carthage, and the Romans probably learned it from the Carthaginians. The Romans "perfected" crucifixion, designing it to produce a slow death with maximum pain and suffering. A crucified person usually lived at least twelve hours, sometimes even until the second or third day.

Normally the Romans reserved crucifixion for slaves, foreign revolutionaries, and the worst of criminals. Yet they did not shrink from putting it to use; they crucified people by the thousands. They often lined the main roads leading into a city with crucified men, a not-so-subtle warning to any who would dare to defy the power of Rome.

For all practical purposes, death by crucifixion amounted to death by suffocation. To prolong the agony of the condemned, the Romans attached a small footrest to the cross. The person on the cross could momentarily ease his pain by using the step to lift himself up for a breath. This explains why John reports that the religious leaders asked for the legs of the three men on the crosses to be broken (John 19:31). With their legs broken, those crucified could no longer lift themselves up to breathe. The result was quick suffocation.

So Jesus, with tongue swollen and body in excruciating pain, poured out His life on Calvary—for *us*.

Later in his famous sermon in Jerusalem, Peter declared how some of those listening to him speak had been personally involved in the crucifixion of Jesus Christ. When the guilty men heard Peter's words, "they were cut to the heart" and asked Peter and the rest of the apostles, "Men and brethren, what shall we do?" (Acts 2:36-37).

The phrase "cut to the heart" appears only here in the New Testament. It means "to pierce" or "to stab" and depicts something abrupt and unexpected. God used Peter's sermon to awaken these men to the awful realization that *they* were personally responsible for the death of their long-awaited Messiah.

Imagine! The One for whom they had longed for centuries, the One who gave hope to their nation, the One who offered them boundless joy—*that* One had finally come. But instead of welcoming Him, they had rejected Him and handed Him over for execution to their hated enemies. Can you imagine the crushing guilt they felt? Overwhelmed with remorse, they cried out, "What shall we do?"

Really, that ought to be the question for all of us. For in a very real sense, all of us are guilty. It was *our* sins that nailed Jesus to that cross.

We should have been hanging next to Jesus, along with the two criminals crucified on either side of him. It may be that these men were more than common thieves; perhaps they were revolutionaries, like Barabbas. If so, they had become vicious militants dedicated to the violent overthrow of Roman rule.

Whatever the case, they ended up on crosses for their personal crimes—but Jesus hung there for the crimes of all humanity. They were there against their will; He was there willingly. They could not have escaped; He could have left with a single word to heaven. They were held to their crosses by nails; Jesus was held to His cross by love.

It was *love* that drove Jesus to become our Savior. And it is that amazing love that continues to offer you life, whatever your offenses may be.

Almost two hundred years ago the creator of a new religion approached the great French diplomat-statesman Charles Maurice de Talleyrand to complain that he could not make any converts. "What would you suggest I do?" the man asked.

"I should recommend that you get yourself crucified, and then die, but be sure to rise again the third day," Talleyrand replied.

None of us needs a new religion. What we need is a Savior who loves us, a Redeemer who died for our sins and rose again from the grave to give us eternal life. And when we have that kind of loving Savior, we don't need anything else.

CHAPTER **28**

The Main Message

"For as Jonah was three days and three nights in the belly of the great fish, so will the Son of Man be three days and three nights in the heart of the earth."

Matthew 12:40

Sometimes we wonder what is the most powerful, convincing argument for the gospel.

Is it emphasizing how soon the Lord may return? We could show how Bible prophecies are being fulfilled before our very eyes and how the world is being prepared for Christ's return. But while Jesus is surely coming back—and perhaps very soon—that is not the essential gospel message.

We might emphasize that people feel empty inside and will remain that way until they put their faith in Christ. That, too, is very true; but neither is it the main message.

We could point out the great joy we have in Christ. We could say that anyone who wants to be truly happy needs to believe. That, too, is true—but still it is not the essential gospel.

Jesus said the main message, the essential sign, is this: "For as Jonah was three days and three nights in the belly of the great fish, so will the Son of Man be three days and three nights in the heart of the earth" (Matthew 12:40).

The main message of the Christian faith is that Jesus Christ, the Son of God, died on the cross for our sins and rose again from the dead. "For what I received I passed on to you *as of first importance,*" Paul wrote, "that Christ died for our sins according to the Scriptures, that he was buried, that he was raised on the third day according to the Scriptures" (1 Corinthians 15:3-4, NIV, emphasis added). When we believe the facts of the gospel story and place our faith in Jesus Christ, our living Savior, we begin a new life with God.

We must consciously remind ourselves of the tremendous power in the simple message of the life, words, death, and resurrection of Jesus Christ. Why? Because we often underestimate the raw might of the gospel in reaching even the most hardened heart.

During one Sunday evening service, a pastor asked an old childhood friend to say a few words. An elderly man stepped to the pulpit. "A father, his son, and a friend of his son were sailing off the Pacific Coast," he began, "when a fast-approaching storm blocked any attempt to return to shore. The waves were so high that even though the father was an experienced sailor, he could not keep the boat upright, and the three were swept into the ocean."

The old man hesitated for a moment and made eye contact with two teenagers who, for the first time since the service began, were looking somewhat interested in his story.

"Grabbing a rescue line, the father had to make the most excruciating decision of his life," he continued. "To which boy would he throw the other end of the line? He had only seconds to make his decision. The father knew that his son was a Christian, and he also knew that his son's friend was not. The agony of his decision could not be matched by the torrent of waves. As the father yelled out, 'I love you, Son!' he threw the line to his son's friend. By the time he pulled the boy back to the capsized boat, his son had disappeared beyond the raging swells into the black of night. His body was never recovered."

By this time, the two teenagers were both sitting up straight in the pew, waiting for the next words out of the old man's mouth. "The father," the man continued, "knew his son would step into eternity with Jesus, and he could not bear the thought of his son's friend stepping into an eternity without Jesus. Therefore, he sacrificed his son. How great is the love of God that He should do the same for us!"

With that, the old man turned, stepped away from the pulpit and sat down in his chair. Silence filled the room.

Moments after the service ended, the two teenagers raced to the old man's side. "That was a nice story," said one of the boys politely, "but I don't think it was very realistic for a father to give up his son's life in hopes that the other boy would become a Christian."

"Well, you've got a point there," replied the old man, glancing down at his worn Bible. A big smile broadened his narrow face, and he once again looked up at the boys. "It sure isn't very realistic, is it? But I'm standing here today to tell you that *that* story gives me a glimpse of what it must have been like for God to give up His Son for me. You see . . . I was the son's friend."

Time is short. The gospel message is not to be whispered in a corner but shouted aloud from the housetops.

Don't underestimate its appeal.

Don't be embarrassed by its simplicity.

Don't add to it or take away from it.

Just proclaim it, stand back, and watch what God will do.

PART TWO

the teaching of jesus

CHAPTER **29**

A Model of Forgiveness

"For if you forgive men their trespasses, your heavenly Father will also forgive you. But if you do not forgive men their trespasses, neither will your Father forgive your trespasses." Matthew 6:14-15

We live in a violent culture. Think about how many movies and TV programs you have seen where the basic premise amounts to this:

Good guy gets hurt by the bad guy.

Good guy regroups.

Good guy comes back to pulverize the bad guy.

When was the last time you saw a program where the good guy gets hurt and then *forgives* the bad guy? Are you kidding?

Our society does not like forgiveness. It exalts vengeance. Our culture firmly believes the adage "Don't get mad, get even!" I saw an actual bumper sticker on someone's car that read "If you love someone, set them free; if they are yours, they will come back to you. If they don't, hunt them down and *kill them!*"

I did not tailgate that car.

Violence seems to be everywhere in our culture. If you cut someone off on the freeway, you risk getting shot at. If you upset a neighbor, you don't work it out over the backyard fence; instead, you get sued and have to spend thousands defending yourself in court.

We are the most litigious society on the face of the earth. Did you know that about 80 percent of the world's attorneys live in the United States? More students will graduate from American law schools this year than from any other professional academic course in the country. Forget about forgiveness. Might as well sue and try to make some money from your trouble.

Unforgiveness is choosing to love hate, which produces bitterness, anger, rage, anxiety, and depression. It has been well said, "When you forgive someone, you set a prisoner free: yourself!" To withhold forgiveness usually ends up hurting *you*—not the other person. As you lie awake at night nursing your grudge, that person is sleeping like a baby and going on with his or her life. And the damage you do to yourself is not only spiritual but physical as well.

Time magazine recently ran a cover story headlined, "Should All Be Forgiven?" with the subtitle, "Giving up that grudge could be good for your health." The article described how researchers are pioneering a "science of redemption" based on an old form of grace. One of the researchers, Mitchell Wright, realized that there exists not only a religious impetus to forgive, but also therapeutic, social, and practical reasons. In the past two years, scientists and sociologists have transformed forgiveness into a subject of quantifiable research.

"The field is just exploding," says Virginia psychologist Everett Worthington, director of the Templeton Foundation Campaign for Forgiveness Research. A growing number of psychotherapists testify that there is nothing like forgiveness for dissipating anger, mending marriages, and banishing depression.

I'm glad the secular culture has finally come around to what Jesus taught all along. Jesus told us plainly, "If you forgive men their trespasses, your heavenly Father will also forgive you. But if you do not forgive men their trespasses, neither will your Father forgive your trespasses" (Matthew 6:14-15). An unforgiving Christian is an oxymoron, a contradiction in terms, like jumbo shrimp or working vacation.

Jesus constantly pressed the issue of forgiveness. His sermons, His parables, His private talks, and even His prayers overflow with powerful lessons about forgiving others. One would have to be blind to read the Bible and miss this continual emphasis.

This is what sets Christianity apart from every other belief system and philosophy. This is what sets Jesus Christ apart from all other gurus, teachers, and prophets. He stands ready to forgive, no matter the offense—and He directs us to do the same. As one commentator put it, "To return evil for good is devilish; to return good for good is human. To return good for evil is divine."

Jesus taught and lived forgiveness. He would have forgiven on the spot the very men who crucified Him if they had reached out. He would have forgiven even Judas Iscariot had the traitor repented. We might say that forgiveness is Jesus' middle name—and He asks us as His dearly loved children to willingly bear that same name. May God's Spirit fill us with His love as we seek to follow the model of forgiveness that Jesus gave us.

Christians should never take revenge. God says, "I will repay! Leave it up to me."

> Do not take revenge, my friends, but leave room for God's wrath, for it is written: "It is mine to avenge; I will repay," says the Lord. On the contrary: "If your enemy is hungry, feed him; if he is thirsty, give him something to drink. In doing this, you will heap burning coals on his head." Do not be overcome by evil, but overcome evil with good. Romans 12:19-21, NIV

We are to extend mercy and kindness rather than seek revenge. Why? Because God did that for us.

You might ask, "How can we possibly do this?" Only by the help of the Holy Spirit. But we must take that first step. Don't wait until you feel like it. Just do it.

Corrie ten Boom tells this true story in her classic book *The Hiding Place:*

> It was at a church service in Munich that I saw him, the former S.S. man who had stood guard at the shower room door in the processing center at Ravensbruck. He was the first of our actual jailers that I had seen since that time. And suddenly it was all there—the roomful of mocking men, the heaps of clothing, Betsie's pain-blanched face.
>
> He came up to me as the church was emptying, beaming and bowing. "How grateful I am for your message, *Fraulein,*" he said. "To think that, as you say, He has washed my sins away!"
>
> His hand was thrust out to shake mine. And I, who had preached so often to the people of Bloemendaal the need to forgive, kept my hand at my side.
>
> Even as the angry, vengeful thoughts boiled through me, I saw the sin of them. Jesus Christ had died for this man; was I going to ask for more? Lord Jesus, I prayed, forgive me and help me to forgive him.
>
> I tried to smile, I struggled to raise my hand. I could not. I felt nothing, not the slightest spark of warmth or charity. And so again I breathed a silent prayer. Jesus, I cannot forgive him. Give me Your forgiveness.
>
> As I took his hand the most incredible thing happened. From my shoulder along my arm and through my hand a current seemed to pass from me to him, while into my heart sprang a love for this stranger that almost overwhelmed me.
>
> And so I discovered that it is not on our forgiveness any more than on our goodness that the world's healing hinges, but on His. When He tells us to love our enemies, He gives, along with the command, the love itself.[2]

If Corrie ten Boom could forgive a man like that, surely we can forgive others, regardless of what they have done to us. Remember, it's good for your health, not only for your spiritual life.

CHAPTER **30**

Can Christians Defend Themselves?

> *"To him who strikes you on the one cheek, offer the other also. And from him who takes away your cloak, do not withhold your tunic either."* Luke 6:29

The words of Jesus about revenge and retaliation are both the most admired and resented of His teachings. Some ignore them altogether, citing their apparent impossibility. Others try to live by them to the letter and, in effect, have misunderstood and misinterpreted them.

For most of us, getting even comes naturally. If we're hit, we want to hit back. But Jesus gave a different teaching to His disciples, to new creations in Christ for whom "old things have passed away" (2 Corinthians 5:17). He calls us to live in an entirely new way.

Among the Jews, a slap in the face ranked among the most demeaning and contemptuous of acts. Even slaves would rather be struck on the back than on the face. But when Jesus speaks of turning the other cheek, He has in mind more than just this act; He was referring to mistreatment in general. Jesus wants to produce in us an attitude that does not immediately seek to strike back.

I will be honest with you; this does not come naturally to me. If someone cuts me off on the freeway, I want to do the same to them. I don't say this to excuse myself but to admit that I need God to help me.

Even the apostle Paul struggled with this issue. Once he stood before Ananias the high priest on trumped-up charges. The whole incident disgusted Paul, who knew it violated Scripture (having once been a Pharisee himself). "Brothers," Paul said, "I have always lived before God in all good conscience!" Instantly Ananias commanded that Paul be slapped on the mouth.

Now, according to these words of Jesus, Paul should have turned the other cheek. But instead, even the great apostle reacted in a very human way to his mistreatment. "God will slap you, you whitewashed wall!" Paul yelled at Ananias. "What kind of judge are you to break the law yourself by ordering me struck like that?"

"Is that the way to talk to God's high priest?" replied those nearby.

"I'm sorry, brothers," Paul answered. "I didn't realize he was the high priest, for the Scriptures say, 'Do not speak evil of anyone who rules over you'" (Acts 23:1-5, NLT).

I point this out only to emphasize that this is *not* one of the easier teachings of Jesus. Yet it is a biblical constant, as Paul himself taught: "Repay no one evil for evil. . . . do not avenge yourselves, but rather give place to wrath; for it is written, 'Vengeance is Mine, I will repay,' says the Lord. Therefore 'If your enemy is hungry, feed him; If he is thirsty, give him a drink; . . . Do not be overcome by evil, but overcome evil with good" (Romans 12:17-21).

This kind of action is so unusual in our world that it silences our critics and causes them to sit up and take notice. Though we could justifiably lash out, we instead decide to pray. By exhibiting self-control, we demonstrate our desire to win our opponents to Christ.

This does not come easily. In fact, if we wait for some feeling of love to suddenly overtake us and keep us from lashing out, it will *never* happen. We must begin to pray for our enemies even before we consciously love them. And we are to love them in an active way, not merely avoid lashing out against them. Of course, this is impossible apart from God's Holy Spirit.

Yet God makes it possible. Jesus prayed for His tormentors even while they drove iron spikes through His hands and feet. The Greek text suggests that our Lord kept praying this phrase, "Father, forgive them" (Luke 23:34). So if the cruel torture of crucifixion could not silence Jesus' prayer for His enemies, then what pain, prejudice, or unfair treatment could justify the silencing of ours?

So then, should a believer *never* resist evil? Hardly. Jesus Himself drove out the money changers from the temple, overturning their tables and chasing them out with a whip. Righteousness is confrontational by its very contrast with wickedness.

Neither does this teaching require that I stand by passively if some maniac attacks my family. If someone were to break into your house with the intent of killing you or your family, Scripture allows you to defend yourself: "If a thief is caught in the act of breaking into a house and is killed in the process, the person who killed the thief is not guilty" (Exodus 22:2, NLT). Jesus told the disciples to take a sword with them on their travels (Luke 22:36). Why? Self-defense.

Scripture also tells us that the military and police have been ordained to keep order. Romans 13:4 says of the king, "For he is God's servant to do you good. But if you do wrong, be afraid, for he does not bear the sword for nothing. He is God's servant, an agent of wrath to bring punishment on the wrongdoer" (NIV).

It is worth noting that the Lord Himself, in response to being struck unjustly, said, "If I have spoken evil, bear witness of the evil; but if well, why do you strike Me?" (John 18:23). It is clear that Jesus did not want to be unnecessarily injured.

Nevertheless, there is a time and place to turn the other cheek. We need to pray that God would show us when we ought to accept mistreatment and when to stand our ground. I am confident that God will show us what to do.

This is not weakness, mind you, but meekness! The Bible says, "Blessed are the meek" (Matthew 5:5). To be meek means you have the strength to strike back, but you choose not to do so. It's power under control.

Jesus had the power to speak His enemies out of existence, but instead He loved them. Stephen imitated the Lord's behavior when he prayed for those who stoned him: "Lord, do not hold this sin against them" (Acts 7:60, NIV). His prayer carried such power that ultimately even Saul of Tarsus was converted.

Who knows how the Lord may use our prayers for those who strike us?

CHAPTER **31**

Everyone's Favorite Verse

"Judge not, and you shall not be judged. Condemn not, and you shall not be condemned." Luke 6:37

How often have you heard someone quote Luke 6:37 to cover just about any bizarre or deviant behavior?

"Hey, who are you to judge *me? Are you* perfect? Doesn't the Bible say, 'Judge not lest you be judged'?"

Yes, it does—but what did Jesus mean when He said it?

Did He mean that we cannot make any evaluation of another Christian's behavior or actions because this is "judging"?

No, in fact, much to the contrary.

The Greek word for *judge* means to separate, choose, select, or determine. It may carry a dozen or more shades of meaning, determined by the context. In this passage, Jesus deals with *motives,* which no human being can know of another. Jesus is saying, "Don't try to judge a person's motives, especially not to pass final judgment."

Jesus rebukes the self-righteous—those who are hypercritical of others and who draw conclusions from their limited perspective of what someone else said or did (which can be enormously misleading). These individuals thrive on condemning others. They rarely know the facts; hearsay is enough, and the juicier the better. Without bothering to get the truth, they draw conclusions and pass judgments. The only exercise some Christians get is running others down and jumping to conclusions.

So then, if someone is openly sinning and we confront him about it, are we "condemning" him? No. In fact, if anything, we are seeking to spare him from the condemnation he will ultimately bring on himself if he continues in his sin. We should always judge and evaluate others with a view to their restoration, not their condemnation.

"Brothers," Paul wrote, "if someone is caught in a sin, you who are spiritual should restore him gently. But watch yourself, or you also may be tempted. Carry each other's burdens, and in this way you will fulfill the law of Christ" (Galatians 6:1, NIV).

When Jesus says "Judge not," He doesn't mean that we should offer no help to the brother with a splinter in his eye. He simply wants us to recognize the potential log in our own eye first and only then deal with our brother. So our Lord asks us, "Why do you look at the speck in your brother's eye, but do not perceive the plank in your own eye? . . . Hypocrite! First remove the plank from your own eye, and then you will see clearly to remove the speck that is in your brother's eye" (Luke 6:41-42). First we must confess our own sin, often that of self-righteousness and a condemning spirit. Then when we remove the telephone pole from our own eye, we will see our brother's sin—and we will want to restore, not destroy, him.

The words Jesus used here imply that the "speck" is of the same substance as the "plank"; the splinter I see in my brother's eye is of the same material as the beam in my own eye. That explains why I can spot certain sins in other people so easily. They're *my* sins!

Perhaps this describes you. You constantly criticize others but rarely yourself. Such individuals nitpick the tiniest flaws in others—and then one day we are shocked to hear that they have committed even grosser sin.

King David illustrates the principle. He committed adultery with Bathsheba and, for all practical purposes, had her husband executed. He hid his sin for about a year and thought he had pulled it off. But he had not bargained on one thing: there are no secrets with God!

One day the prophet Nathan paid David a visit. "King," he said, "I need your input on a problem in your kingdom. You see, there was this rich guy who owned a lot of sheep and cattle. He had a neighbor who owned only one little lamb that he had worked hard to buy. That lamb became a family pet and even ate from his plate; it was like one of his own children. Anyway, a guest came to visit the rich neighbor, who instead of killing one of his many sheep for a meal, took that poor man's lamb and butchered it."

David erupted. "Any man who would do such a thing deserves to die!"

Nathan pointed his finger at David and said, "You are the man!" (2 Samuel 12:7).

David could not tolerate the person Nathan described. In fact, he wanted to have the man executed—even though the law required only restitution. What made David so angry? The king had a plank in his eye. And we're always harshest on the sins lurking within our own hearts.

We must remind ourselves that since none of us knows another's motives, it's always foolish to judge. I heard of a lawyer who was trying to deliver an important paper to a man who was determined to avoid him.

Fourteen years passed and the man eventually wound up in the hospital, dying of cancer. One day the lawyer was wheeled in to him. The man laughed when he saw the attorney enter the room.

"It doesn't matter now—subpoena me if you want!" he said.

"Subpoena?" the lawyer asked. "I was trying to give you a document that proved you had inherited forty-five million dollars."

Let's leave the judgment of motives to God. We can't afford the alternative.

CHAPTER **32**

Bearing Fruit

"For a good tree does not bear bad fruit, nor does a bad tree bear good fruit. For every tree is known by its own fruit." Luke 6:43-44

Why did God put me on earth? What purpose does God have in mind for me now that I have received His Son into my life?

For many, the ultimate goal is to make big money as fast as possible. *The Los Angeles Times* recently ran an article headlined, "Fairy tale falls short for rich: Sudden Wealth Syndrome affects those who quickly make millions, therapists say." What causes this new syndrome?

This article described the misery of those who had come quickly into wealth. It said that "isolation and uncertainty replace euphoria" as those afflicted lose their sense of purpose.

Bay area clinical psychologist Steven Goldbart coined the term *Sudden Wealth Syndrome* after he noticed increasing psychological problems among newly minted multimillionaires. Although his clients' wealth brought them comfort beyond their wildest dreams, it also brought a sense of isolation, uncertainty, and imbalance—as if they had been teleported into an alien world that, while at times was very pleasant, still felt completely strange.

David Seuss, the chief executive of a search engine company, said it was as if a hurricane had picked him up from a life of ulcer-inducing drudgery and dropped him into a life of almost pointless ease. After buying all the toys and taking all the vacations, he still had to answer the question: "Okay, who do I really want to *be?*"

Life is our most precious possession. The Bible says we exist to know the God who made us (Revelation 4:11) and to glorify Him. And how do we do that? Jesus said, "By this My Father is glorified, that you bear much fruit" (John 15:8).

Scripture often uses the picture of fruit bearing to describe the results of a genuine relationship with Jesus Christ (Mark 4:20; Colossians 1:10). So what is this "fruit" God wants in our lives? What kind of "fruit" can we produce?

WHAT WE SAY IS "FRUIT."

"A good man out of the good treasure of his heart brings forth good; and an evil man out of the evil treasure of his heart brings forth evil," Jesus said. "For out of the abundance of the heart his mouth speaks" (Luke 6:45).

Some people don't even realize how much profanity they use. But new Christians discover that their vocabulary soon changes. Why? Because their heart does! Instead of cursing God, they praise Him. And nonbelievers take notice.

A pastor was doing some carpentry at his home one afternoon. As he pounded away with his hammer, he noticed a little kid carefully watching him. The boy didn't say a word, so the pastor kept on hammering, supposing the young child would eventually leave. *The little tyke is probably admiring my carpentry skills!* the pastor thought.

But after a long while, the boy still did not leave. Finally the pastor asked, "Well, son, trying to pick up some pointers on carpentry?"

"No," the boy replied. "I'm just waiting to hear what a preacher says when he hits his thumb with a hammer."

Watch what you say, Christian. People are watching and listening.

WINNING OTHERS TO CHRIST AND HELPING THEM GROW SPIRITUALLY IS "FRUIT."

Paul wrote to his friends at Rome, "I often planned to come to you . . . that I might have some fruit among you also, just as among the Gentiles" (Romans 1:13). And Proverbs 11:30 tells us, "The fruit of the righteous is a tree of life; and he that winneth souls is wise" (KJV).

Sometimes God gives us the privilege of personally leading someone to Christ; other times we simply sow a seed. Always it is God who gives the increase—but we certainly have a part to play.

PRAISING AND THANKING GOD IS "FRUIT."

The Bible says, "Let us continually offer the sacrifice of praise to God, that is, the fruit of our lips, giving thanks to His name" (Hebrews 13:15). This kind of fruit is especially succulent to the divine taste buds.

OUR CHANGE IN CONDUCT AND CHARACTER IS "FRUIT."

Paul writes, "The fruit of the Spirit is love, joy, peace, patience, kindness, goodness, faithfulness, gentleness and self-control" (Galatians 5:22-23, NIV). These traits should be found in the life of every follower of Jesus Christ. If the opposite is true—if instead of love there is hatred, if instead of joy there is gloom, if instead of peace there is turmoil, if instead of gentleness there is short temper, if instead of faith there is worry, if instead of meekness there is pride, if instead of self-control there are violent outbursts—then either we don't know God or we are living outside of fellowship with Him.

What is life about? When actress Meryl Streep turned fifty, she had only one request: "All my friends are having these big, elaborate parties," she said. "All I want is more time. That's what I want, and nobody can give me that as a present, all wrapped up with a ribbon."

Medical science is helping us to live longer through life-saving operations and miracle drugs. But while it can add years to life, it cannot add life to years. *That* only God can do, through the power of fruit bearing. May we say, as did Christian martyr Jim Elliot in his journal, "I seek not a long life but a full one, like you, Lord Jesus."

CHAPTER 33

Do What
He Says

*"But why do you call Me 'Lord, Lord,' and not do the
things which I say?"* Luke 6:46

Every person has a set of values by which to live—a group of beliefs, a philosophy, a moral foundation that provides guide-
lines for life.

Jesus informs us that we can build our life on one of two
foundations. One will hold us up not only in this life but in
eternity as well. And the other will crumble beneath our feet.

To a group professing an interest in spiritual things, our
Lord told a story about these differing foundations. Two men
built houses for their families. Perhaps they both wanted the
same thing. The houses stood near each other and we can
imagine that they were subjected to the same tests because
they looked nearly identical: same floor plan, same color,
same landscaping. Superficially they appeared indistinguishable. The only real difference was in their foundations. And
that difference became clear when a nasty storm hit.

The first man was in a hurry. He didn't have time for archi-
tects or instruction. He wanted it now, immediately—all the
benefits of the house without the sacrifice. He built as quickly
as he could, on a lot of sand. By contrast, the second man carefully laid the foundation of his home on solid rock. He didn't
want it quickly so much as he wanted it to last. And when a
storm slammed into these two houses, the first one collapsed
while the second stood firm.

Jesus' story describes the true believer and the pseudo-believer. They go to the same church, sit side by side in the same pews, hear the same sermons, even sing the same songs. Yet one is wise (the true believer) and the other foolish (the pseudobeliever).

Like the foolish man, many today look for the shortcut, the quick fix. They refuse to build their foundation on Jesus and obey His instructions. And so they get tossed to and fro by every wind of teaching or their own fluctuating emotions. These misguided folks want the blessing of God but not God Himself. They want happiness, but not holiness.

Why get married? Just have sex with whomever!

Why have integrity? Just lie if it will get you ahead!

Why live by God's standards? Just have fun!

These individuals are like the seed on rocky ground, without root; when trial or persecution comes for the gospel's sake, they wither (see Mark 4:1-20). They build their lives on the wrong foundation: crumbling sand! And when the storms descend, they disintegrate.

Contrast their fate with those who choose to follow Jesus and His Word. In so doing, they build on a solid foundation. They don't allow their emotions to control them. They desire deeper growth, more knowledge, richer wisdom. They're not know-it-alls but remain teachable and pliable in God's hands. Like Paul, they can say, "Not that I have already attained, or am already perfected; but I press on" (Philippians 3:12).

These believers are like the man whom a reporter found in the aftermath of Hurricane Andrew. Amid the devastation and debris, one house still stood firm on its foundation. The owner was cleaning up his yard when the reporter approached him.

"Sir, why is your house the only one still standing?" the reporter asked. "How did you manage to escape the severe damage of the hurricane?"

"I built this house myself," the man replied. "I built it according to the Florida state building code. When the code called for two-by-six roof trusses, I used two-by-six roof trusses. I was told that a house built according to code could withstand a hurricane. I did, and it did! I suppose no one else around here followed the code."

Are you following God's code? Are you committed to obeying the Lord? On what foundation is your life built?

The final test of our foundation comes in times of hardship. To whom or to what do we turn when life gets tough? It's true that into every life a little rain must fall. Sometimes it's a light drizzle and other times it's a hurricane!

How can you tell whether you're wise or foolish, a true believer or a pseudobeliever? How can you determine upon what foundation you have built your life? It comes down to the way you react when the storms hit.

If you have built on Jesus Christ and His teaching, you will stand. If you are not merely a hearer but a doer of His Word, you will endure. The true Christian—the one who has built his or her life on the right foundation—will stand the test. The pseudobeliever who has been playing religious games will fall.

It's not enough to say you are a Christian. If you are a true Christian, you will do what Jesus says. The apostle Paul said, "For to me, to live is Christ, and to die is gain" (Philippians 1:21). If you say, "For me, to live is money," then to die is to leave it all behind. If you say, "For me, to live is fame," then to die is to be forgotten. If you say, "For me, to live is power," then to die is to lose it all. But if you can say, "For me, to live is Christ," then to die is gain!

So again I ask: for what do *you* live?

CHAPTER 34

Dealing with Doubt

*And John, calling two of his disciples to him, sent them
to Jesus, saying, "Are You the Coming One, or do we look
for another?"* Luke 7:19

Has it ever seemed to you as if God has let you down? Has a difficult situation ever caused you to say, "Where is God?" Have you ever been plagued with doubt as to whether Jesus was *really* the Messiah? Has it ever seemed that God was intentionally dragging His feet or not paying attention to you?

It may surprise you that the greatest of all prophets—John the Baptist—had his own struggle with doubt. So if you've ever felt plagued with doubt (or are having some doubts right now), take heart! Consider this: Doubt is not always a sign that a person is turning away from the faith; it may simply be a sign that he or she is thinking.

What prompted John's doubt? At the beginning of Jesus' ministry, John baptized our Lord in the Jordan River and said, "He must increase, but I must decrease" (John 3:30). Without question, John had put it all on the line for Jesus.

But now hard times had come for the faithful prophet. King Herod had thrown him into prison. Instead of preaching in the open air under blue skies, John found himself trapped in a small, dark, damp dungeon, little more than a pit. Eighteen long, lonely months passed. Then John heard reports that Jesus was eating and drinking with sinners and tax collectors. This didn't make sense to John.

So John doubted. *Could this really be the Messiah? Could I have made a mistake? This isn't the kind of Messiah I expected.*

Let's not be too quick to criticize John. Sometimes we also misunderstand God and His Word. Sometimes Jesus isn't the kind of Messiah we expect. When tragedy hits a godly man or woman, we wonder, *Why?* When a child dies or someone we love gets cancer, we ask, *Why did God allow this? This isn't what I expected!*

Even the most spiritual people have days of doubt and uncertainty. It's important to realize that there's a difference between doubt and unbelief. Doubt is a matter of the *mind,* occurring when we cannot understand what God is doing and why He is doing it. Unbelief, by contrast, is a matter of the *will.* Unbelief happens when we refuse to believe God's Word and obey what it tells us to do. John's doubt was not willful unbelief; instead, it was prompted by physical and emotional strain combined with his inability to understand the way Jesus was working.

So how did Jesus respond to John's doubt? Our Lord instructed John's messengers to "go and tell John the things you have seen and heard: that the blind see, the lame walk, the lepers are cleansed, the deaf hear, the dead are raised, the poor have the gospel preached to them" (Luke 7:22). Jesus reported how He was fulfilling Old Testament prophecies of the Messiah that had been recorded by Isaiah. Essentially He said, "Go tell John that I am going in and out among the people and removing disabilities wherever I see them. I am bringing men and women into a right relationship with God, and when they are brought there, every other relationship changes. And I am doing this just as the Scriptures said I would."

Jesus used Scripture to combat John's doubt. And then He added, "And blessed is he who is not offended because of Me" (verse 23)—or more literally, "who is not hurt nor resentful nor annoyed nor repelled nor made to stumble, whatever may occur."

Jesus meant, "John, if you cannot understand My method, My ways, or My timing, I ask you to trust Me. And when you are unable to see why I am doing what I am doing or why I am not doing what you think I should be doing, all I ask is that you follow Me."

Jesus deals with our doubt in the same way he dealt with John's:

HE REFOCUSES OUR PRIORITIES.
John had unbiblical and unrealistic expectations of the ministry, purpose, and timing of Jesus. Jesus simply refocused him and brought his problems into perspective.

HE BRINGS US BACK TO THE SCRIPTURES.
As He did with John, Jesus reignited the listless hearts of the disciples on the road to Emmaus. "Did not our heart burn within us while He talked with us on the road . . . ?" they said (Luke 24:32). And how did Jesus do this? By opening to them the Scriptures.

HE CONTINUES WITH HIS PURPOSE AND ASKS US TO TRUST AND FOLLOW.
If you've been doubting God's purpose or timing in your life, remember how Jesus dealt with John. Don't be offended; don't stumble; just trust Him.

We may well arrive in heaven with many questions to ask God: Why this? Why that? But fifteen seconds after we pass through the pearly gates, we'll know. Right now "we see through a glass, darkly; but then face to face" (1 Corinthians 13:12, KJV). In the meantime, as we deal with our doubts, let us ask Jesus to refocus us, bring us back to His Word, and help us trust in Him.

CHAPTER **35**

Deny or Love Ourselves?

"If anyone desires to come after Me, let him deny himself." Luke 9:23

Many of us have "I" trouble.

You might say we bow at the altar of the unholy trinity: me, myself, and I.

It's all about how we feel about ourselves.

We live in a day that emphasizes self-love, self-worth, and self-esteem—not only in society but also in the church. Yet the Bible does not identify lack of self-esteem as our main problem. In fact, it points to our self-love as our greatest threat. The ultimate choice in life lies between pleasing ourselves or pleasing God.

"But God loves us," you might say, "so doesn't that prove our self-worth?"

Not really. Why does God love us? Because we are beautiful? No, because not all of us are. Because we are lovable? Again, some are, some aren't. He loves us not because of ourselves but in spite of ourselves. "While we were still sinners, Christ died for us" (Romans 5:8). Our value and worth come from what God is making us into. He has graciously put His divine treasure "in jars of clay" (2 Corinthians 4:7, NIV).

That's why Jesus does not tell us to love ourselves (we already do that very well). Instead, He tells us to *deny* ourselves.

I'm convinced that the greatest life possible is the Christian life when we're in fellowship with the God who made us and discovering His perfect plan, custom designed just for us. But the Christian life is more than simply praying a prayer and getting "fire insurance." It's following Jesus not only as Savior but as Lord. Jesus wants to be not only our friend but our God.

Unfortunately, many of us have lost sight of this. That is why the church has been so ineffective in impacting our culture. A recent article from pollster George Barna declared that Christians are having a minimal influence on those under the age of forty. Barna examined one hundred indicators of attitudes, beliefs, and behaviors, and discovered that the everyday behavior of Christians looks nearly indistinguishable from that of non-Christians.

Barna's findings reveal that many of us settle for an unbiblical brand of Christianity, one that embraces Jesus as Savior but neglects Him as Lord. It's big on self-esteem and small on self-denial—and because such a faith has not turned *us* upside down, neither is it turning our world upside down.

The men and women of the early church, on the other hand, *did* turn their world upside down (Acts 17:6). They experienced the Christian life as Christ offered it. How? They lived as disciples. I have dealt with this in depth in my book *The Upside-down Church* (Tyndale, 1999). In short, they were real disciples of Jesus Christ.

It's worth noting that the Gospels alone contain more than 250 references to disciples. But what is required to become a disciple?

Jesus gave us some clear answers to that question as He gathered His followers at Caesarea Philippi. This was a turning point in His ministry. His time in Galilee was coming to a close, and soon He would travel to Jerusalem to die on a cross. On the cross Jesus would pay the price for our sin. As Jesus spoke of His going to the cross, He segued to how His disciples must do the same. And the first thing required of a disciple, He said, is to deny oneself.

The word *deny* in the original Greek means "to repudiate, to disdain, to disown, to forfeit, to totally disregard." According to Jesus, the great barrier to discovering all that God has for you is self.

The English author C. S. Lewis discovered this to be true. "The real test of being in the presence of God," he wrote, "is that you either forget about yourself altogether or you see yourself as a small, dirty object. It is better to forget about yourself altogether."

Discipleship is a foundational issue. You have these choices in life:

- Will you live for yourself or deny yourself?
- Will you seek to save your life and ultimately lose it or invest your life and ultimately find it?
- Will you gain the world or forsake it?
- Will you share His reward or forfeit it?

It seems insane that anyone would choose death over life and emptiness over fullness, but sadly, most do. The truth is, anything short of true discipleship settles for less than what God desires. Jesus said, "Whoever loses his life for my sake will save it" (Luke 9:24). The Greek word *psuche* (soul life) refers to our will, ambition, goals, and desires. Jesus is therefore saying, "If you seek to be happy, you never will be." American philosopher Erick Hoffer apparently had it right when he wrote, "The search for happiness is one of the chief sources of unhappiness."

So how does one find happiness? According to Jesus, if you deny yourself and seek to be holy, happiness comes as a by-product.

God wants the Christian's life to be challenging and exciting, filled with purpose and direction. Does that describe your walk with God? Or is your Christian experience dull, unfulfilling, even boring? No ophthalmologist can solve our "I" trouble; only a trip to the cross can do that.

When we choose to live as disciples, we find life as God meant it to be lived. When we stop trying to seek life and instead seek God, He gives us what we wanted all along.

CHAPTER 36

Losers Are Keepers

"If anyone desires to come after Me, let him . . . take up his cross daily." Luke 9:23

The cross has lost most of its original meaning. Now shrouded in religiosity, the cross has become a symbol of many things, from a religious icon to an ornate piece of jewelry studded in diamonds or pearls.

Yet the real cross of history was a hated, despised, even scandalous emblem.

It pictured a very cruel death.

The Romans reserved the cross for executing and torturing the lowest of its criminals. The closest modern equivalent might be the electric chair or a hangman's noose, although both fall far short of the cross's dark significance. Still, we don't usually see anyone wearing a miniature electric chair or noose around his or her neck! Who wants a symbol of death, an emblem of shame, dangling from a pretty necklace?

Yet that's exactly what the cross was—a symbol of shame and death.

When a condemned man carried his cross on the streets of Jerusalem, people knew they were looking at a dead man. The convicted criminal would be marched outside the city, nailed to a cross, and set up in a very public location by the roadside. That way, everybody coming in and out of the city would see him in agony and would decide that obedience to Rome was by far the best way to go!

Why did Jesus use such an unsavory symbol to describe what He expected of His disciples? "If you desire to come after Me," He told His followers, "you must take up your cross *daily.*" Why did our Lord use such an offensive illustration? It appears that He intentionally chose such a radical symbol to get our attention.

A cross results from walking in Christ's steps. "Taking up the cross" speaks of the harassment and persecution we face because we hold to His standards and not this world's. It comes from living out the truths of what He teaches in the marketplace, in the community, in the family, in the world.

Taking up the cross flies in the face of conventional wisdom. As James Davison Hunter pointed out in his landmark study *Evangelicalism: The Coming Generation,* "Fascination with the self and with our own ways of seeing things has become a well-established cultural feature of evangelism. Self-focus is part of the modern Evangelical identity."

Hunter's insight helps to explain why our witness and testimony to this lost world have become so anemic and ineffective. We don't like to hear of bearing a cross. We would rather hear about how to be successful in business or how to overcome an eating disorder. We'd much prefer to get a nice pep talk in church.

So what does it mean today to bear the cross? Often we hear individuals say that they have a cross to bear. "My cross is my children," a woman might say. Or her children might declare, "Our cross is our mother." People tend to identify whatever problem or obstacle they face as their cross to bear.

But this is far from what the cross means. The cross symbolizes only one thing: identifying with Jesus by dying to self.

Remember that Jesus made this statement shortly after He announced His coming crucifixion and resurrection. In response, Peter took an authoritarian position over the Lord and rebuked Him, essentially telling Him, "Avoid the unpleasant, Lord. Don't do this!"

Jesus used the occasion to show us that we, too, must take up our crosses and follow Him. He calls us to die *every day* to our selfish plans, ambitions, and the pursuit of self-fulfillment. Instead, we are to say, "Not my will but Yours be done, Lord!"

Jesus says to us, "If you will get your priorities in order, deny yourself, and take up the cross, you will find the fulfillment you have wanted all along."

Notice: it is not misery to live like this; rather, we find life as it was meant to be lived in the will of God. That's why the apostle Paul could write, "I am crucified with Christ: nevertheless *I live*" (Galatians 2:20, KJV, emphasis added).

Scottish pastor and theologian Samuel Rutherford said in the seventeenth century, "The cross of Christ is the sweetest burden that I ever bore. It is a burden to me such as wings are to a bird or sails are to a ship, to carry me forward to my harbor."

Rutherford discovered four centuries ago what you, too, can know—that when you die to yourself, you find yourself. When you lay aside your personal goals, desires, and ambitions, then God will reveal the far better desires, ambitions, and goals that He has stored up for you.

We all remember the childhood saying, "Finders keepers, losers weepers." Jesus has a different version for us. He tells us, "Losers are keepers." It's certainly true that it costs to follow Jesus Christ—but it costs more *not* to.

A missionary at a religious festival in Brazil walked from booth to booth, examining various wares for sale. Above one booth he saw a sign: "Cheap Crosses." *That's what many Christians are looking for today, cheap crosses,* he thought. *But my Lord's cross was not cheap; why should mine be?*

It's an excellent question. How would you answer it?

CHAPTER **37**
Follow Me

> *"If anyone desires to come after Me, let him ... follow Me."* Luke 9:23

Of all the things the Lord could have said to Matthew, who would have expected *this?* The unscrupulous tax collector wouldn't have felt the least surprised had Jesus told him, "Get lost, creep!" He wouldn't have batted an eye had the Lord snapped, "You filthy sinner!" But that is not what Jesus said. Instead, as Matthew sat at his tax table, the Savior said to him:

"Follow Me" (Matthew 9:9).

No doubt Matthew lapsed into shock, for he was a hated agent of Rome. And yet there had been no mistake; Jesus had said to *him,* to Matthew the tax collector and sinner, "Follow Me"–just as he had said to the other disciples (Matthew 4:19; John 1:43).

In Greek, the phrase *follow me* comes from a term meaning "to walk the same road." The word appears here in the imperative mode, meaning that it is a command, not merely an invitation. The verb is also in the present tense, which means the one addressed is ordered to begin an action and to continue habitually in it. Jesus was saying to Matthew, "I command you to follow Me each and every day."

But there is more. The phrase also means "follow *with* me." These words of Jesus communicate a strong desire for companionship and friendship. It is as if the Lord had said, "Yes, I want obedience; but I also want friendship and companionship. Matthew, I want you to be my *friend!*"

Matthew knew a good deal when he saw one. "So he left all,

rose up, and followed Him" (Luke 5:28). Matthew quickly recognized the immense privilege being offered to him, and without hesitation he stood up and followed Jesus.

But he didn't act rashly or without thinking! Matthew knew that once he forsook his lucrative post, he could never return to it. He knew the cost—yet he willingly paid it. Of all the disciples, Matthew doubtlessly made the greatest sacrifice when it came to giving up material possessions and a position of power; yet he makes no mention of it in his Gospel. Apparently he felt, as did Paul, that "what things were gain to me, these I have counted loss for Christ" (Philippians 3:7).

Far from being depressed about what he left behind, Matthew's heart overflowed with joy. He lost a career but gained a destiny. He gave up his material possessions but won a spiritual fortune. He forfeited his temporal security but laid hold of eternal life. He exchanged his emptiness and loneliness for fulfillment and companionship. He gave away all that this world had to offer and found Jesus!

Did you know that Jesus is still looking for disciples? "If anyone desires to come after Me," Jesus says to us, "let him deny himself, and take up his cross daily, and *follow Me.*" When a person genuinely meets Jesus Christ, he or she cannot leave the old life fast enough. His old habits, standards, and practices no longer appeal to him. Her former desires come up seriously lacking, and she gladly leaves them behind. Matthew provides a model for all those who hear and obey Jesus' command.

Yet Jesus is unwilling to leave us with the bare command. He wraps up His famous teaching with a powerful statement: "For what profit is it to a man if he gains the whole world, and is himself destroyed or lost?" (Luke 9:25).

I can't help but think of Jim Carrey, one of the highest paid actors in the world (at last report, he earned about twenty million dollars per picture). In many ways, the comedian has gained the world. An interviewer recently said to him,

"There's a perception in show business that all comedians are really clowns crying on the inside"—and Carrey agreed. The reporter marveled, "There is something almost disarming about how up-front Carrey is about past bouts with depression, self-loathing therapy, and even his self-medication through marijuana."

Carrey himself elaborated on some of his bleaker moments. "You have to go through your periods where you cry and sob and scream," he said. "I've gone on little personal vacations where I'll go away all by myself and sit and curse at the TV for the whole weekend."

The actor's sad comments remind me of a distraught and unhappy man who went to a pastor, searching desperately for help and direction. After the minister evaluated the miserable condition of his visitor, he said, "Forget about all those things. Go and see the comedian who is performing at the local comedy club. I hear he is keeping everyone in stitches. Go listen to him and you will forget about all your troubles."

The young man said nothing for several long moments, then groaned, "I *am* that comedian."

Have you been trying to find happiness by chasing after fame or fortune? Have you attempted to find fulfillment through what this world offers? If so, Jesus has a word for you. He counsels you to deny yourself, take up your cross, and follow Him.

Jesus wants to be your friend. He wants you to bare your heart to Him, to tell Him your secrets, your fears, your hopes and dreams. And most of all, He wants you to be with Him. Forever.

I wonder, what would Jesus say to Jim Carrey? I'm sure He would say the same thing to him as He is saying to you right now:

"Follow Me!"

CHAPTER 38

Count the Cost

Then a certain scribe came and said to Him, "Teacher, I will follow You wherever You go." Matthew 8:19

Few things are more exciting than to see thousands of men and women come forward at a crusade to accept Jesus Christ. At the end of a message, I ask folks to make a public profession of their desire to commit their lives to Jesus Christ. I then ask them to leave their seats and stand in front of the platform. Last, I lead them in a prayer of commitment.

Many have asked what it feels like to stand on the platform and watch it all happen. Do I feel some incredible sense of euphoria or excitement? Is it an incredible ego trip?

No.

I sense that I am in a very real spiritual battle (because I am). I imagine that I am speaking to an individual, not to a huge crowd. I feel a great responsibility to properly represent God. And I know that not everyone who comes forward will really become a Christian.

Some come forward out of the impulse of the moment. Others come because their friends do. Still others come because they want to see what it's like.

This is nothing new. The Bible tells us of three men, all given the opportunity to know and follow Jesus. All expressed some interest, yet in the end each walked away. It's not enough to *come* forward; we must *go* forward with Christ.

The first man felt very impressed with Jesus. He may have

watched the Lord for some time as He healed the sick and cast out demons. No doubt he felt stirred to the depths of his heart by the Lord's teaching and challenge. Matthew tells us he was a scribe, an authority in Jewish law. These highly educated men made up the scholarly class of Jewish society. Normally they were teachers in their own right, not followers of other teachers.

Yet this scribe used the title "Teacher" to address Jesus. How astonishing that a man of such great stature would so address Jesus! Such a new disciple would be a "big fish," a "celebrity convert." If he came to Christ today, we would quickly ask him to give his testimony in our churches and appear on Christian TV and radio. No doubt he would also be writing a book.

The man had said to Jesus, "I will follow You wherever You go"—but the Lord does not encourage impulsive choices. He wants us to fully realize the implications of our words. "Foxes have holes and birds of the air have nests," replied Jesus, "but the Son of Man has nowhere to lay His head" (Luke 9:58). Jesus had no place of His own—no house or property, not even a tent. So would the scribe follow someone like that? It's easy in the emotion of the moment to make great vows; it's quite another to honor them.

The scribe probably enjoyed community respect and felt accustomed to an easy and comfortable life. Jesus is telling him, "Do you understand where I am going? Are you prepared to pay the price? I'm headed for the cross, for difficulty and rejection. If you follow Me, the same awaits you. I can't let anything or anyone deter Me or slow Me down from this purpose. I cannot let anything entangle or sidetrack Me. In the same way, if you truly want to be My disciple, you must detach yourself from everything that would entangle your own progress toward God."

It does not appear the man was quite *that* interested in Jesus. He refused to make such a sacrifice or take the next step—and we hear of him no more.

Do *we* count the cost to follow Jesus? Sometimes believers ask, "Can I do such and such and still be a Christian?" The Bible teaches us to avoid whatever relationships, friendships, habits, pleasures, or indulgences that entangle us or hinder our walk with God. Whenever we're tempted to ask, *Can I do this? Is it allowable?* we should ask ourselves the following questions:

DOES IT BUILD ME UP SPIRITUALLY?

The apostle Paul writes, "Everything is allowable! Yes but everything does not build up character" (1 Corinthians 10:23, TCNT). In other words, it's not just a matter of, Is it permissible? The bigger question is, Does it promote growth in our Christian character? As believers who want to stay strong spiritually, we must avoid things that tear us down by tearing us away from the people of God or by dulling our hunger for His Word.

DOES IT BRING ME UNDER ITS POWER?

You might have the freedom to do a certain thing, but does it bring you under its power? If you can't live without it, that is bondage, not freedom (1 Corinthians 6:12).

DO I HAVE AN UNEASY CONSCIENCE ABOUT IT?

"Whatever is not from faith is sin," says Romans 14:23. Or as the New Living Translation puts it, "If you do anything you believe is not right, you are sinning." If you are about to do this thing and have a sense that it displeases God, you should not do it. This sense is like a built-in warning system. The wise believer will learn to listen and respond to it.

"But so-and-so is doing it!" you protest. But you are not that person; you must obey God. What did your mother say when you told her, "But everyone is doing it"? She'd reply, "If everyone jumped off a cliff, would you do that, too?" Some are weaker in certain areas than others. Therefore what may cause a problem for one may not have the same effect on another.

COULD IT CAUSE SOMEONE TO STUMBLE?

Romans 14:15 says, in effect, don't do anything that will cause criticism against yourself, even though you know that what you're doing is all right. Because we don't live and die to ourselves alone. What we do has a direct effect on others, not only for life on this earth, but also for eternity.

Jesus came to earth to gather followers but not *blind* followers. He wants us to count the cost of following Him—and then to go where He leads with our eyes wide open.

CHAPTER **39**

Playing for Time

Then He said to another, "Follow Me." But he said,
"Lord, let me first go and bury my father." Luke 9:59

Not everyone responds positively when Jesus says, "Follow Me."

If riches and personal comfort held back a pampered scribe, then relationships held back a second man. It appears that this second fellow already had become a disciple. To some degree, at least, he had been following the Lord. One day Jesus challenged him to a deeper, closer relationship. And how did the man respond? "Lord, let me first go bury my father," he said.

What did he mean? Was the man on his way to his father's funeral? Not at all.

The phrase, a common Near Eastern figure of speech, referred to a son's responsibility to help his father in the family business until the father died. Such a commitment could involve a long period of time—thirty or forty years or more, if the father was relatively young. Apparently this man was playing for time, perhaps hoping that when his father eventually did grow old and die, Jesus would be long gone—and in that case he wouldn't have to worry about it.

Jesus knew that this man was about to settle for some second-best experience, and so He was deeply unsatisfied with his level of discipleship. Somewhere the man had suffered a spiritual breakdown; he had ceased to move forward.

How easily this can happen to us! We may not get entangled in a flagrant sin, but some subtle erosion has whittled away at our spiritual life. Perhaps it began with a disinterest in personal Bible study, a breakdown in prayer life, a laxness in fellowship with other believers. The Lord sees this and says to you and to me, "Follow Me."

In the parable of the talents (see Matthew 25:14-30), Jesus sketched out what He expects from His servants. Three servants in His story receive differing amounts to invest, "each according to his own ability" (verse 15). One receives five talents of gold, another two talents, and the last, one talent. Immediately after distributing his resources, the master goes on a journey.

Jesus' parable speaks of the talents that God places into each of our lives, the gifts of the Spirit we each receive as a result of committing our lives to Christ. God gives to us differing gifts, resources, and abilities. We are to use them for God's glory, not for our own selfish ambition.

And yet that's where we sometimes fall short.

A recent poll revealed that 61 percent of Americans agreed with the statement, "The main purpose of life is enjoyment and personal fulfillment." The same poll showed that 50 percent of those who call themselves born-again Christians also agreed with the statement. But is it true? Do we really exist only for personal enjoyment and self-satisfaction?

Not if we believe the Bible. Scripture says that we were created to bring glory to God. Through the prophet Isaiah, God speaks of "everyone who is called by my name, whom I created for my glory, whom I formed and made" (Isaiah 43:7, NIV). Isaiah declares that we were made to bring glory to God. The apostle Paul adds, "Because of Christ, we have received an inheritance from God, for he chose us from the beginning, and all things happen just as he decided long ago. God's purpose was that we who were the first to trust in Christ should praise our glorious God" (Ephesians 1:11-12, NLT). That's why we are to glorify the Lord in everything we do. As 1 Corinthians 10:31 teaches, "Whatever you do, do all to the glory of God."

Each of us has talents that we are to use for God's glory. Some can sing beautifully. Others have the ability to speak publicly. Others have incredible business acumen. Still others have great athletic skill. Our service to the Lord varies from person to person, but each of us is called to serve. Every man or woman who belongs to Christ should take his or her skills, abilities, and talents, and find a way to glorify God with them. That's what Jesus means when He tells us, "Follow Me."

"But I can't do that!" someone says. "I have so many bills to pay, so much fun to have, family to help, friends to enjoy. Maybe later?"

That is essentially what this man told Jesus. But time was of the essence and Jesus pressed the man to make a stand. "Let the dead bury their own dead," Jesus told him, "but you go and preach the kingdom of God" (Luke 9:60).

What "dead men walking" are keeping you from serving God as fully as you might? Perhaps God is calling you to bring His message to others, but so far you have been making excuses. You're just too busy; you have so many things to do. Or maybe God has been speaking to you about getting more involved at church. So far you have resisted; you don't want to leave your comfort zone.

"Follow Me!" Jesus says to you.

I know from personal experience that there exists no greater joy than serving the Lord. And I also know that if you keep waiting for a better time to become a believer, you're missing out on the best time of all.

CHAPTER 40

Beware the Unseized Moment

And another also said, "Lord, I will follow You, but let me first go and bid them farewell who are at my house."
Luke 9:61

At first glance, this man's request does not seem unreasonable. What could possibly be wrong with saying good-bye to friends and loved ones?

But Jesus knew the man's heart, and He saw a problem there. Jesus saw the man's weak motivation and his divided loyalties. He knew the man was not yet ready to give himself wholeheartedly to follow as Christ wanted. That's why the Master replied, "No one, having put his hand to the plow, and looking back, is fit for the kingdom of God" (Luke 9:62).

In Israel, almost no rain falls from May to October; the ground remains dry and hard. When the rains finally arrive, farmers must seize the moment and move decisively. It doesn't matter what time of the day it is or if they had something else planned. When that rain comes, it's the decisive moment to plant the crop.

Jesus is saying, "If you leave to say good-bye, you will never return. You must put your hand to the plow and move forward to follow Me *now!*"

Beware the tragedy of the unseized moment! God moves us to make a change in life, to break free from some binding habit or vice, to approach someone in spiritual need with the truth of Scripture—and we hesitate.

Please don't!

God calls you to follow Him *now* because He knows those days can turn into months, the months can turn into years, and the years can turn into a lifetime of waste.

The root of this man's problem can be found in the beginning of his statement: "Lord, I will follow You, *but . . .*" It matters little what follows; one excuse is as good as another.

My wife and I had gone out for dinner with some friends when the idea of ordering dessert came up. "Let's order it," I said, "but I'm going on a diet tomorrow." Everybody laughed—I guess because I say that a lot. It's a little lie we use to excuse what we are about to do. I think it would make a great title for a book: *I'm Going on a Diet Tomorrow (And Other Lies We Tell Ourselves).*

Maybe you would say, "I'll follow Jesus wholeheartedly, but not quite yet. Just a little later, when it's more convenient." But if you do that, you may never come.

Have you heard about the group of demons who were discussing strategies for keeping people from Jesus Christ? One demon said, "Why don't we tell them there is no God?"

"They won't believe that," the others responded. "They'll look around, see the glory of God's creation, and know there is a Creator."

Another demon suggested, "Let's tell them that Christianity is not true, that it's just a bunch of myths and fables."

"No" said the others. "They will see the changed lives of those who have been radically impacted by putting their faith in Jesus Christ."

Another devil said, "Let's tell them that God doesn't love them, that faith would never work in their lives."

"No" said the others. "Some Christian will remind them that the Bible says,

'For God so loved the world that He gave His only begotten Son . . .'"

After a short silence, one quiet demon finally piped up. "I know what we can tell them that will work for sure," he said.

"What?" asked the others.

"Tell them there is no hurry!"

Billy Graham said,

> The evangelistic harvest is always urgent. The destiny of
> men and of nations is always being decided. Every gener-
> ation is strategic. We are not responsible for the past
> generation, and we cannot bear full responsibility for the
> next one; but we do have our generation. God will hold us
> responsible as to how well we fulfill our responsibilities
> to this age and take advantage of our opportunities.

After preaching one Sunday night in Chicago, D. L. Moody allowed his hearers to leave the service without answering the question, "What will you do with Jesus?" The next morning—October
8, 1871—Chicago lay in ashes. To his dying day, Moody regretted
that he told the people to wait. "Since then, I have never dared to
give an audience a week to think of their salvation," he said. "If
they were lost they might rise up in judgment against me. I want
to tell you of one lesson I learned that night which I have never
forgotten; and that is when I preach, to press Christ upon the
people then and there, and try to bring them to a decision on the
spot. I would rather have that right hand cut off than to give an
audience a week now to decide what to do with Jesus."

Beware the unseized moment! This moment of opportunity
may never return. Jesus makes it clear that our commitment to
Him must be total, unreserved, and immediate, or it is no commitment at all.

What if Philip had not gone to the desert? What if Esther had
not spoken up? What if David had not visited his older brothers
at the Philistine battlefront?

Don't wait until tomorrow to follow Jesus wholeheartedly.
Don't tell Him that you'll follow Him, "*But . . .*" Follow Him *now,*
and keep on following.

CHAPTER 41

A Matter of Balance

And Jesus answered and said to her, "Martha, Martha, you are worried and troubled about many things. But one thing is needed, and Mary has chosen that good part, which will not be taken away from her."

Luke 10:41-42

When Martha saw Jesus making His way up the path to her home, she probably thought, *What He needs right now is a good meal!* So she frantically went to work preparing a feast fit for a king (because that is what He was).

Under normal circumstances, this might have been a good choice. Certainly Jesus enjoyed eating as much as the next guy. But storm clouds had gathered, and Jesus was making His way to Jerusalem to be crucified. He needed to share certain things with those He loved, and that included His dear friends Mary, Martha, and Lazarus.

While Martha busied herself preparing the meal, Mary recognized that the time had come to sit at the feet of her honored guest. She seemed to sense when Jesus wanted to speak intimately from His heart.

That's all fine and good, Martha may have thought, *but we just have to get these dishes prepared!* I can imagine her clanking pans, sighing loudly, and shooting severe looks at Mary (if looks could kill!). Martha no doubt caught snippets of Jesus' words as she banged away in the kitchen, but she probably considered the meal more important than the fellowship.

Martha failed to realize that at this critical time in Jesus' life, He would have preferred her company over her service. He wanted her fellowship and companionship more than her busy hands. Martha made the common mistake of offering activity instead of adoration, work instead of worship, perspiration instead of inspiration. Ironically, Martha received Jesus into her house, then neglected Him by preparing an elaborate meal that He neither needed nor wanted. And the result? She felt overwhelmed and overworked.

"Martha, Martha," Jesus said, "you are worried and troubled about many things. But one thing is needed, and Mary has chosen that good part, which will not be taken away from her" (verses 41-42). Certainly a meal was in order—but what we do *with* Christ is far more important than what we do *for* Christ. It is a matter of balance.

Many burn themselves out in God's service because they never learn this balance. They fail to realize they must find time for "sitting at His feet." If we make no time to take in, we will have nothing left to give out. We can't take people any farther than we ourselves have gone.

It's a great thing to serve the Lord, yet if we find ourselves burning out and complaining, then something is wrong. Though we can become weary *in* serving, we must never grow weary *of* it.

Mary found the right balance. She realized that there's a time to work and a time to worship, a time to stand and a time to sit, a time to move and a time to pray. Mary had an insight possessed by few others. Somehow she realized this was an important time to listen to Jesus. So she listened carefully to Him as she sat at His feet. And because she took time to sit at His feet, she enjoyed a kind of fellowship experienced by a select few.

You, like Mary, need to slow down and learn to sit at the feet of Jesus. If you don't, you're going to end up burned out and frustrated like Martha. You will find yourself running around in circles and going nowhere.

Remember the great irony of Martha. She was so busy *serv-ing* Jesus that she did not take time *for* Jesus. The house did not need to be spotless. Every little thing did not need to be in perfect order. Jesus wanted her fellowship.

Can you relate to Martha's problem? Could the Lord be saying to you, "I so appreciate your service to Me—but I would really rather have you spend a lot more time at My feet in fellowship with Me"?

A woman died, leaving behind her husband and one daughter. The little girl soon became the very apple of her daddy's eye. He loved to spend time with her, but because he had to work, they had only their evenings together. After dinner each night they would talk and play games; sometimes she sang for him. He treasured every moment.

One night the little girl announced, "Daddy, I need to go to my room early tonight. I have something I have to do!"

He felt very disappointed, but he let her go. She continued this pattern for a solid month. Finally, Christmas Day arrived, and early in the morning she burst in on her daddy and proudly displayed a pair of crude crocheted slippers she had made for him. It was this project that had taken her away from her father for every evening that month.

Her father thanked her warmly and gave her a big hug, but then he said, "Honey, I would rather have had you with me all those lonely evenings than to have these slippers, as beautiful and comfortable as they are."

In the same way, God wants our presence more than our slippers. He wants our devotion more than our work. It really is a matter of balance.

CHAPTER **42**

The Little Cell Phone That Could

> *"No one, when he has lit a lamp, puts it in a secret place or under a basket, but on a lampstand, that those who come in may see the light."* Luke 11:33

One night after an evening service, I went home to find that the power was out. My wife, Cathe, was at a women's retreat, my son, Jonathan, was staying at a buddy's house, and Christopher, my oldest, was gone. The dog had died a few months before—so there I sat, alone in the dark.

And when I say dark, I mean pitch black.

The phones didn't work, the lights wouldn't go on, the whole neighborhood lay under a shroud of darkness. I found myself in a very dark place, desperately in need of some light. So I took out my cell phone and used its pale, green light to search for a flashlight.

Even a little light helps to dispel the darkness!

That's the point Jesus made about His disciples living in this dark world. He wants them to provide some divine light. He thinks of them as beacons of light illuminating the darkness all around.

"No one, when he has lit a lamp," Jesus says, "puts it in a secret place or under a basket, but on a lampstand, that those who come in may see the light." In other words, Christians are to be different from those who do not know the Lord. Not different because of bizarre behavior or obnoxious antics but different by their godly priorities, outlook, and lifestyle. The apostle Peter says it this way: "But you are a chosen people, a royal priesthood, a holy nation, a people belonging to God, that you may declare the praises of him who called you out of darkness into his wonderful light" (1 Peter 2:9, NIV).

Jesus does not want us to pull away from others into some kind of Christian subculture. He does not call us to a new monasticism, where we avoid contact with nonbelievers. Instead, we are to be light, an influence for good in our society.

We believers are not called to isolate but to infiltrate!

In Matthew's version of this teaching, Jesus says, "You are the light of the world" (Matthew 5:14). The original language implies, "You *and you alone* are the light of the world." If observers do not see the light of God in you, His child, they will not see it at all.

Think of it this way. In what kind of world would we live if every Christian behaved just like you do? How many nonbelievers would be attracted (or turned off) to the gospel? What kind of opinion would the public have of Christianity if *you* were its sole representative?

We have a strategic and important part to play in God's plan of reaching this world. We are "light" that helps searching men and women find their way to God.

And how does this light shine? For one thing, it exposes the darkness. Have you ever been in a dark room when someone turned on a light? It's blinding! Things might have looked fine in the dark, but in the light problems are exposed.

The same thing happens in the spiritual realm. The more godly the person, the more obvious the ungodliness around him or her becomes. The believer doesn't even have to say a word. Just by being what he or she is, the ungodly grow ashamed of what they are doing.

But light does more than expose the problem; it also shows the way out. In the dark, we cannot see, much less find the door. But once the light gets switched on, we can find and walk through the door—if we so choose.

Some years ago a well-known skateboarder murdered his girlfriend. He had successfully covered it up and the police never would have discovered his crime. One day he heard me preaching on the radio about how God sees and knows everything and how His light exposes the darkness of sin. The young man came under major conviction and prayed to give his life to Christ.

At that point he wondered, *What should I do?* Should he tell God he was sorry for murdering his girlfriend? Did anyone else really need to know? He visited a local pastor, who gave him the right advice. The young man immediately turned himself in to the police and confessed his crime. He is now in prison.

"But that's not good, is it?" someone asks. Yes it is, because he did the right thing. He can't bring his girlfriend back, but he can pay his debt to society. He may be behind bars, but his conscience is clear. And who knows how God may choose to use his newfound light in the very dark place of prison?

God calls all of His children to shine the light of heaven into the darkness of a world shrouded in sin. Some of us, unfortunately, try to hide that light. We're glad that it has illumined the dark places of our soul, but we're not too sure we want others to see it. What if they make fun of it, mock it, or attack it? So we try to hide it under a basket or keep it confined to a secret place.

Jesus tells us, "Don't do that. I didn't give you the light so you could make it look dark. Besides, have you ever tried to hide light? Even if it's a tiny light, you see it far away. The darker the place, the brighter even the smallest light shines."

Our world is indeed a very dark place in need of some light; even a little would help. You may be just one person with a tiny light from a cell phone—but it's a start!

CHAPTER **43**
Double Vision

"The lamp of the body is the eye. Therefore, when your eye is good, your whole body also is full of light. But when your eye is bad, your body also is full of darkness. Therefore take heed that the light which is in you is not darkness." Luke 11:34-35

Several years ago I found my eyes getting tired after working on the computer. I chalked it up to sleepiness and ignored it. A couple of days later I got a headache and reached for a bottle of Tylenol. I couldn't remember how many pills to take, so I looked at the instructions on the side of the bottle. I could not read them. No matter how close or far away I held the bottle, I could not make out the words.

What is wrong with these people? I thought. *No one can read this!* To prove my point, I gave the bottle to my wife.

She could read the instructions easily.

Only then did I realize that my eyesight was beginning to fail. I had to break down and accept the fact that I had to wear glasses to read and work on the computer.

Sometimes it takes such an incident to remind us that clear vision is a priority in life—in the spiritual realm as well as in the physical.

Jesus tells us that our "spiritual eyesight" affects everything we do. "The lamp of the body is the eye," He said. "Therefore, when your eye is good, your whole body also is full of light. But when your eye is bad, your body also is full of darkness. Therefore take heed that the light which is in you is not darkness."

Scripture often uses the terms *eye* and *heart* as synonyms. To "set the heart" and to "fix the eye" frequently refer to the same thing. So Psalm 119:10 says, "With my whole heart I have sought You; Oh, let me not wander from Your commandments!" and later the psalmist writes, "I will fix my eyes on . . . thy ways" (Psalm 119:15, RSV).

Jesus seems to be saying, "Just as our physical eyesight affects our whole body, so our ambition—where we fix our spiritual eyes and heart—affects our whole life." In the same way that a fully functional eye gives light to the whole body, a single-minded ambition to serve God gives our lives purpose and direction.

A person determined to serve God with single-minded ambition does not suffer from double vision. He or she knows the difference between right and wrong and consistently acts on that knowledge. So David prayed, "Unite my heart to fear thy name" (Psalm 86:11, KJV). Paul also enjoyed this clear, singular aim. "This one thing I do," he wrote, "forgetting those things which are behind, and reaching forth unto those things which are before, I press toward the mark for the prize of the high calling of God in Christ Jesus" (Philippians 3:13-14, KJV).

No one moves ahead in the spiritual life without a singular, clear aim. Do you have such a focus? Or do you suffer from double vision?

I honestly don't understand people who want to live compromised lives. Don't they realize how empty and dead this world is? Those who grew up in church sometimes struggle terribly with this issue. They know what's right but the world seems so attractive to them. It feels alluring, seductive—mainly because they have never fully known its power and destructiveness. So they don't necessarily go for the world whole hog; they just flirt with it. They suffer from double vision.

Jesus says that such believers are salt with no saltiness (Matthew 5:13). They hide their light under a cover. They are like Coke without carbonation or coffee without caffeine. I recently accompanied a friend to Starbucks, where he ordered a decaf, low-fat latte. I said to him, "What's the point? No caffeine, no fat—all the fun's gone!"

Even more ridiculous is a "decaf disciple," an "uncarbonated Christian," a believer with no zing. Such believers are wasting their lives.

Elijah's challenge to ancient Israel still holds today: "How long will you falter between two opinions? If the Lord is God, follow him" (1 Kings 18:21). Jesus calls us to get a clear focus and purpose in life, and He warns us to stop trying to live in two worlds.

Is the Lord calling you out of your darkness? Realize that the more time you spend there, the more used to the dark you will become.

Back in 1789, a castle-like prison in Paris known as the Bastille was about to be destroyed. A prisoner who had been kept confined in a dark, dingy cell for many years gained his freedom. But instead of welcoming his liberation, he begged to be taken back in. It had been such a long time since he had seen the sunshine that his eyes could not endure its brightness. He desired only to die in the murky dungeon where for so long he had suffered as a captive.

Don't end up like this man. Don't get comfortable in the dark. Start living in the light! Without clear vision, you can get yourself into a lot of trouble.

Suppose I say to my wife, "I just took these pills to help me sleep better."

"We don't have any sleeping pills," she might respond. "What was the name on the bottle?"

"Relax," I'd say.

She would look at me askance and checks the bottle. "That's not *Relax,*" she'd say. "It's *Ex-Lax!*"

We all need to get our spiritual eyes checked. And if we need glasses or contacts, then let's wear them. Why suffer from spiritual double vision if you don't have to?

CHAPTER **44**

Who Was That Masked Man?

> *"Beware of the leaven of the Pharisees, which is hypocrisy. For there is nothing covered that will not be revealed, nor hidden that will not be known."* Luke 12:1-2

Do you remember the old TV show *The Lone Ranger*? Whenever the hero, who wore a black mask across his eyes, did a good deed, someone always asked, "Who *was* that masked man?"

I think many observers today are asking the same question of a lot of Christians. The Bible tells us that men and women in the last days will display a form of godliness, even while denying its power (2 Timothy 3:5). They'll perform a convincing show on the outside while faking it on the inside.

In other words, many will be hypocrites.

The word *hypocrisy* comes from a Greek term that means "to wear a mask." In the Greek theater, actors held masks over their faces to portray different characters. Jesus tells us, in essence, "Beware of hiding behind a mask of hypocrisy. Don't try to appear to be something that you really aren't."

What a curse hypocrisy has been to the church! So many pretend to be something they are not. Yet no mask will stand up to God's scrutiny. Jesus warns us that "there is nothing covered that will not be revealed."

I don't have a lot of experience in wearing masks, except on Halloween when I was a kid. My friends and I would wear cheap, dime-store rubber masks and run around for the night, pretending we were someone other than who we really were. But we always ran into two problems. First, we had trouble seeing through those little eye holes; inevitably we tripped and fell. Second, we had to smell sweaty rubber all night. What a relief to finally tear the thing off and eat the bounty of candy we had scored!

Sadly, many of us hide behind a mask for more than a single evening. We wear one day and night, month after month, year after year. We may put on the mask of respectability, of piety, or even of deep spirituality. But in reality, underneath the latex lives someone else altogether.

There are no secrets with God. In the end, Jesus will pull off every mask and reveal who's really underneath. Paul speaks of the day "when God will judge the secrets of men by Jesus Christ, according to my gospel" (Romans 2:16). And the apostle warns us, "When the Lord comes, he will bring our deepest secrets to light and will reveal our private motives. And then God will give to everyone whatever praise is due" (1 Corinthians 4:5, NLT).

Without question, Jesus saved His most scathing words for the Pharisees (see, for example, Matthew 23:13-33). Why? What did they do that made Him so angry? They were ecclesiastical actors, religious phonies, pastoral pretenders. At the moment they appeared the most righteous, they were the most wicked. Even the old pagan Cicero said, "Of all villainy there is none more base than that of the hypocrite, who, at the moment he is most false, takes care to appear most virtuous."

In speaking of the hypocrisy of the Pharisees (and all who follow their pattern), Jesus said, "These people . . . honor Me with their lips, but their heart is far from Me" (Matthew 15:8). Notice that our Lord warns us of the "*leaven* of the Pharisees, which is hypocrisy." Leaven is yeast, a rising agent. In the Bible, it usually symbolizes evil. It refers to something secret with penetrating power.

Hypocrisy is like yeast. It starts small but gradually works its way through a life. That's why we must carefully guard against it. Small sins inevitably lead to bigger ones—and eventually everything will come out.

While we find it easy to condemn the Pharisees and their hypocrisy, we ought to stop and examine our own lives. Do we back up our profession by our practice? Do we sincerely mean everything we pray in public? Are we honest when we sing "Though none go with me, still I will follow" or "Mold me, melt me, fill me, use me"? Or do we speak mere words through a mask of Sunday devotion?

Whatever the case, it's all going to come out.

The expression "face the music" originated in Japan. One man in the imperial orchestra couldn't play a note, but as a person of great influence and wealth, he demanded to be given a seat; he wanted the emperor to see him "perform." The conductor agreed to let the man sit in the second row. He was handed a flute, and when a concert began, he'd raise his instrument, pucker his lips, and move his fingers. He went through all the motions of playing but never made a sound. His deception continued for two years.

Then a new conductor took over. He told the orchestra that he would audition each player personally. One by one the musicians performed in his presence. At last came this flutist's turn. Frantic with worry, he pretended to be sick—but his lies caught up with him. The doctor who examined him declared him to be perfectly fine. Finally the pretender had to admit he was a fake. He couldn't face the music.

Ready or not, all of us will one day face the music. We will all appear before the Lord, without masks and without deception. Better that we show our true faces to the world now than have someone ask on that day, "Who *was* that unmasked man?"

CHAPTER 45

With You All the Way

> *"Are not five sparrows sold for two copper coins?*
> *And not one of them is forgotten before God. But the*
> *very hairs of your head are all numbered. Do not fear*
> *therefore; you are of more value than many sparrows."*
> Luke 12:6-7

Let's face it: It's not terribly popular to be a Christian in the twenty-first century—especially one who has clear opinions and is unafraid to state them. Fear of how others may react to our faith can tempt us to back down on what we believe, especially in the presence of those who hold opposing views.

Jesus well understood this weakness, and so He addressed the issue head-on. "I say to you, My friends," He told His disciples, "do not be afraid of those who kill the body, and after that have no more that they can do. But I will show you whom you should fear: Fear Him who, after He has killed, has power to cast into hell; yes, I say to you, fear Him!" (Luke 12:4-5).

Jesus does not mean to make us afraid of His Father, yet He does want to remind us that fear of people makes no sense for those who fear God. As God said to the prophet Isaiah, "Do not fear what they fear, and do not dread it. The Lord Almighty is the one you are to regard as holy, he is the one you are to fear, he is the one you are to dread, and he will be a sanctuary" (Isaiah 8:12-14, NIV). The Lord later asked His people through the prophet,

Who are you that you fear mortal men, the sons of men, who are but grass, that you forget the Lord your Maker, who stretched out the heavens and laid the foundations of the earth, that you live in constant terror every day because of the wrath of the oppressor, who is bent on destruction? For where is the wrath of the oppressor? The cowering prisoners will soon be set free; they will not die in their dungeon, nor will they lack bread. For I am the Lord your God, who churns up the sea so that its waves roar—the Lord Almighty is his name.

Isaiah 51:12-15, NIV

One of the best definitions of fearing God that I have heard is this: "a healthy dread of displeasing Him." That's a dread many of us could use a lot more of. Jesus repeated and amplified this message when He declared, "I say to you, *My friends.*" This phrase should be taken in a passive sense (those whom Jesus made His friends) not in an active sense (those who are making Jesus their friend). Jesus thus asserts that He initiates the friendship; that is why we don't have to be afraid of what others might do.

Imagine if the boxer Lennox Lewis said to you, "Look, I know you've been picked on at school. But I'm going to start hanging out with you, so don't worry about it anymore!"

You might reply, "But Lennox, what if you're not there when the bullies come?"

"I'll be all over you like a cheap suit," Lennox might say. "So chill already."

So off you go to school, you and your buddy, the heavyweight champion of the world. I have no doubt the bullies would be kept at bay!

That's what Jesus is promising to do for His friends.

Or let's say you had a bit of trouble with some unpaid bills. So Bill Gates says to you, "I'm going to be around to take care of your expenses from now on, so don't worry about that. And as far as a place to crash and hang your hat, *Mi casa es su casa.*"

Jesus declares to us, "I am extending My friendship to you, so don't worry about any harm to your life. I will be with you all the way."

A story from church history tells about a Christian who was arrested, brought before the Roman emperor, and commanded to renounce his faith. The emperor demanded, "Give up Christ. If you don't, I'll banish you."

"You cannot banish me from Christ," the Christian replied, "for God says, 'I will never leave you or forsake you.'"

"Then I'll confiscate your property," the ruler retorted.

The Christian answered, "My treasures are laid up in heaven. You can't touch them."

"Then I'll kill you," replied the emperor.

The Christian answered, "I've been dead to the world in Christ for forty years. My life is hid with Christ in God. You can't touch it."

At that point the emperor turned to the members of his court and said in disgust, "What can you *do* with such a fanatic?"

May God give us more "fanatics" like that!

Jesus wants us to know that we have nothing to fear, not only from enemies but from the hardships and difficulties of this life. He reminds His friends that He remains vitally concerned about the smallest details of their lives.

"Are not five sparrows sold for two copper coins?" Jesus asks. "And not one of them is forgotten before God. But the very hairs of your head are all numbered. Do not fear therefore; you are of more value than many sparrows."

What can this mean but that God pays great attention to detail? Our Lord's knowledge of us is so detailed and His interest in us so strong that He numbers the very hairs of our heads! The average hair count on the human head is said to be about 140,000 (140 in my case).

In Matthew's version of this passage, Jesus says that God

knows about each sparrow that falls to the ground (see Matthew 10:29). His point? If God knows about something as seemingly insignificant as the fall of a little bird, how much more concerned is He about spiritual matters of far greater consequence?

The answer is, He is *a lot* more concerned. God cares about what you care about. And that's why you do not have to fear.

CHAPTER 46

The Unforgivable Sin

"And anyone who speaks a word against the Son of Man, it will be forgiven him; but to him who blasphemes against the Holy Spirit, it will not be forgiven."

Luke 12:10

Over the years, I've probably been asked one question more than any other: What is the unpardonable sin?

People read the words of Jesus in Luke 12:10 and have all kinds of questions. "What is blasphemy against the Holy Spirit? Is this a sin that I might have committed? After all, before I was a Christian, I cursed just about everyone—and that may have included the Holy Spirit!"

Years ago I talked to a young man who thought he had committed this sin. It seemed as if a dark cloud hung over his head. I was able to explain just what this verse means and assure him that because he was a Christian, he had *not* committed this sin. Immediately the cloud lifted and his countenance changed.

We need to remind ourselves that God forgives *all* confessed sin—lying, cheating, stealing, drunkenness, adultery, immorality, even murder. Even an unbeliever who blasphemes God can be forgiven. Two of God's choicest servants committed this sin and were forgiven.

Paul confessed that even though he "was formerly a blasphemer, a persecutor, and an insolent man," he was nevertheless shown mercy because he acted "ignorantly in unbelief"

(1 Timothy 1:13). And for all practical purposes, Simon Peter blasphemed Jesus Christ with curses (Mark 14:71). The word translated *curse* involved pronouncing death on oneself at the hand of God if the speaker were lying. Peter essentially said, "May God damn me if I am not speaking the truth." But he too was forgiven after he repented.

How then can Jesus say that the blasphemy against the Holy Spirit "will not be forgiven"? It's important to remember that Jesus made this statement after the Pharisees accused Him of casting out a demon by the power of Satan (Matthew 12:24). This was the greatest insult conceivable—to suggest that Jesus was working in harmony with Satan, the very one He had come to destroy. Essentially Jesus was saying to them, "You who know the Word of God should know the hand of God when you see it—yet you are so hardened in your sin, so blinded spiritually, that you actually attribute God's work to the devil."

To blaspheme is to consciously denounce and reject God. It is defiant irreverence, the uniquely terrible sin of intentionally speaking evil against God. The blaspheming of the Holy Spirit does not merely represent unbelief but a *determined* unbelief. These Pharisees had intentionally hardened their hearts. They knew what was right yet deliberately refused to follow it. The blasphemy of the Spirit is the refusal—after having seen all the necessary evidence—even to consider faith in Christ.

When a man becomes so hardened that he makes up his mind not to pay any attention to the nudging of the Holy Spirit, he places himself on the road that leads to certain judgment. For all those who reject the Spirit's mission of bringing lost people to Jesus Christ, there comes a point of no return.

The Bible asks, "How shall we escape if we neglect so great a salvation?" (Hebrews 2:3). Answer: We can't, for the Bible clearly teaches that God's forgiveness and the hope of salvation come from Christ, and Christ alone (John 14:6).

How does one reach the point of no return? It's a process. A man or woman enjoys continued exposure to the truth of God yet refuses to obey. She accepts the message intellectually yet doesn't respond. Eventually he goes too far and loses all perspective, like the Pharisees. She not only disbelieves, she strikes out at God and goes out of her way to insult and even blaspheme Him. Then God slams the door shut and says, "That's it!" There comes a time, known only to God, when an individual's fate is sealed.

During World War II, a small U.S. battle group was patrolling the waters of the northern Atlantic in search of German U-boats. One evening, four pilots took off from the group's aircraft carrier. The squadron leader received instructions to be back by a certain hour, but he purposely stayed out longer, believing that with just a little more time, he and his fellow pilots could find the enemy and score an impressive hit.

As the sun set, a large German armada entered the area. The American fleet knew it was in trouble, for now it was outgunned, outmanned, and outnumbered. The American commander ordered immediate radio silence. As the planes' fuel dipped dangerously low, the pilots radioed the carrier but got no reply. Again and again the pilots radioed in: "Turn on the lights. Turn on the landing lights!" But the lights stayed off, for to turn them on would have jeopardized the lives of thousands of sailors. The men on the darkened carrier stood by in horror as they watched four American planes crash into the icy waters of the Atlantic.

The Scriptures say, "Now is the day of salvation" (2 Corinthians 6:2). The light is shining in your heart. You have heard the Word of the Lord. But there will come a time when the Lord, the Commander-in-Chief, will order radio silence. The lights will be dimmed, and all those who have refused to follow His orders will be unable to find their way home. They will have blasphemed the Spirit and will be without hope.

That is why the Bible says, "Today, if you will hear His voice, do not harden your hearts" (Hebrews 4:7). You can't play games when the Holy Spirit draws you. The stakes are just too high.

CHAPTER 47

Friends of God

"I have called you friends, for all things that I heard from My Father I have made known to you." John 15:15

How do you tell the difference between your acquaintances and your friends? Friends are the ones you call when you have something you just have to get off your chest. Friends are the ones who want to hear what you are going through, good or bad. Friends are the ones you invite to your house to share some joy.

You let friends into your life.

As the time drew near for Him to go to the cross, Jesus gathered His disciples around Him to declare His friendship. He was about to invite them into His life in a way they had never known.

"No longer do I call you servants," He told them gently, "for a servant does not know what his master is doing; but I have called you friends" (John 15:15).

What is a friend? What does a friend do? Jesus had often modeled for His followers the meaning of the beautiful word *friend*.

A FRIEND TELLS THE TRUTH.
If you're wearing the worst clothes ever unearthed and you ask a friend, "How does this look?" she will tell you the truth. An enemy won't; she'd just as soon let you make a fool of yourself.

A true friend also tells you when you're doing the wrong thing. "Faithful are the wounds of a friend," says Proverbs

27:6, "but the kisses of an enemy are deceitful." No doubt it hurt Peter to hear Jesus say to him, "Get behind Me, Satan!" (Matthew 16:23), but the big fisherman needed to know that he was moving dangerously close to running afoul of God's eternal purposes. Jesus, as a true Friend, made sure that didn't happen. Only a true friend would do that. "A true friend always stabs you in the front," said Oscar Wilde.

A FRIEND TELLS HIS OR HER SECRETS.

Friends share their secrets. "A servant does not know what his master is doing," Jesus said, "but I have called you friends." Jesus is basically saying to them, "Initially when I called you, you were simply My servants. While that has not changed, you have become much more than that. Something deeper has developed between us. That's why I'm now bearing My full heart to you. You who have heard such secrets can no longer be regarded as mere servants; you are My friends. Therefore I'm sharing My complete heart with you."

To fulfill prophecy, according to Matthew, Jesus would "utter things kept secret from the foundation of the world" (Matthew 13:35). Our Lord told His followers too much to call them mere servants. The secrets that His Father entrusted to Him, He revealed to His friends.

A FRIEND "GETS REAL."

For three years Jesus had shared His struggles, His pains, and His heartaches with His disciples. In time He would say to His closest friends—Peter, James, and John—"My soul is exceedingly sorrowful, even to death. Stay here and watch with Me" (Matthew 26:38). He would ask them to pray with Him, to share His struggle and His hurt.

Only friends get real enough to display true love. Love demands an open sharing of who you are and what you feel. Love takes down the façades and gets real. And real friends get real together.

A FRIEND CAN BE TRUSTED.

You know true friendship has arrived when you feel free to drop your guard with someone, when you purposefully take chances, when you risk trust.

Throughout His ministry, Jesus showed He could be trusted. The disciples knew they could count on Him to be there for them when they needed Him most. They had seen Him heal their relatives (Matthew 8:14-15) and satisfy their hunger (John 6:10-13). Therefore, as the Cross drew near, Jesus could say to them, "Trust in God; trust also in me" (John 14:1, NIV).

If God is your friend, you can be sure that He will always keep your confidence. The psalmist said to God, "You ... put my tears into Your bottle; are they not in Your book?" (Psalm 56:8). You can trust Him!

In ancient Hebrew, the word *know* speaks of intimacy; the Old Testament frequently uses the term to describe marital intimacy. Jesus makes it clear He wants to be our intimate friend (John 10:1-15) who knows us thoroughly.

You can read all about movie stars in the latest issue of *People* or *Us,* but you don't know these celebrities. You may know about them, but you don't know them—and if you walked up to them and tried to engage them in conversation, much less hang out with them, they would probably have their bodyguards "put the hurt on you."

Knowing someone means establishing a relationship. You exchange home phone numbers, cell phone numbers, e-mail addresses. You can bare your heart to each other and share secrets. You may even let your friend eat off your plate (now *that's* friendship!).

Jesus offers this friendship to you right now. You have His unlisted phone number, His personal e-mail address. He will tell you the truth, hear your secrets, and tell you His. He wants you to bare your soul to Him and let Him earn your trust. Yes, He will always remain the Master. But more than that—He wants to be your friend.

CHAPTER **48**

What Does It Take?

"You are My friends if you do whatever I command you."
John 15:14

Because I moved a lot when I was young, more kids knew me by the moniker "new kid" than by my actual name. I did not always have a lot of steady friends.

That's why it always intrigues me when, every once in a while, someone tells me that he just met my closest friend from high school.

"What is his name?" I ask.

"Joe Smith," he says. "You were best buddies in high school."

And I never even heard of the guy!

I think the Lord has a lot of "friends" like that. Many claim to be His friends who are really just casual acquaintances, lacking any real friendship at all. Or they're fair-weather friends who bail at the first mention of sacrifice or real commitment.

Most of us would like to think of ourselves as friends of God—but what does that mean? What does Jesus require of those who can legitimately be called His friends?

Jesus certainly demonstrated his willingness to have friendship with us. "Greater love has no one than this," He said, "than to lay down one's life for his friends" (John 15:13). And then He backed up His words by dying for us on the cross.

So then, how do we show our love for Him? Jesus tells us five things about true friendship with God.

TRUE FRIENDS OF JESUS OBEY HIM.

How do we demonstrate our friendship with Jesus? Quite simply, we do what He says. If we refuse, we have no right to call ourselves His friends.

In 1 Samuel 15 the Bible tells how King Saul disobeyed the Lord's command to completely destroy the enemies and all their livestock. When Samuel asked the king why he heard the bleating of sheep and the lowing of cattle, Saul basically replied, "Oh right, thanks for reminding me. We're saving those to offer to the Lord later!"

Samuel recognized a lie when he heard one and replied, "Does the Lord delight in burnt offerings and sacrifices as much as in obeying the voice of the Lord? To obey is better than sacrifice, and to heed is better than the fat of rams" (1 Samuel 15:22, NIV). God wants the same from us, not some great annual recommitment that we soon break. He wants consistency. Regularity. Faithfulness. He wants our obedience.

TRUE FRIENDS OF JESUS OBEY HIM ACTIVELY.

Some think it's enough if they avoid what God forbids. "I am not a thief or an adulterer or a liar," they say. But that's like saying, "I am your friend because I do not rob you, cheat you, insult you, or beat you up." Although I appreciate you not pulverizing my face, I have to say that true friendship is much more than that.

Friendship with Jesus is not merely avoiding the wrong but doing the right. So Paul tells us not only to "flee also youthful lusts" but to "pursue righteousness, faith, love, peace with those who call on the Lord out of a pure heart" (2 Timothy 2:22).

TRUE FRIENDS OF JESUS OBEY HIM CONTINUALLY.

I am not perfect, but I keep trying. If I fail, I repent, get up, and try again. Intermittent obedience is like saying "I do" on your wedding day and then breaking your vows two hours later. I made a commitment to my wife on our wedding day many years ago, but I reaffirm my commitment to be faithful to her "for better or worse, for richer or poorer, in sickness and in health" every day. So far I have done this for twenty-eight years, and by God's grace, I intend to continue for twenty-eight more.

Some might say, "Obedience like this is impossible!" And they'd be right; for that very reason the Bible says, "Be filled with the Spirit" (Ephesians 5:18). We can't do it in our own strength. But we can do "all things through Christ who strengthens" us (Philippians 4:13). God gives daily power for daily obedience.

TRUE FRIENDS OF JESUS OBEY HIM
IN EVEN THE SMALLEST MATTERS.

Jesus said, "You are my friends if you do whatever I command you," not "whatever you're personally comfortable with" or "whatever you personally agree with" or "whatever you find easy." No. *Whatever.* It's compromise in the little things that usually snowballs into big things later.

TRUE FRIENDS OF JESUS OBEY HIM
BECAUSE THEY WANT TO.

When you love someone, you naturally want to please your beloved. You buy her a gift because you want to. You do things for him because of your deep love for him, not for fear of what he will do if you don't. Paul said, "the love of Christ compels us" (2 Corinthians 5:14). If you want to rebel more than you want to obey, you can't be a true friend of Jesus. Actions speak louder than words.

A friendship is made up of two people who commit themselves to each other. Friendship can exist only where there is a response.

Will you take Jesus' hand of friendship and forgiveness? He offers it to all humankind. The question is, do we truly want to be His friends?

CHAPTER 49

If Your Knees Are Shaking

Then He spoke a parable to them, that men always ought to pray and not lose heart. Luke 18:1

We all know what it's like to feel overwhelmed. Everything seems to be sailing along smoothly when without warning, your boat starts taking on water. And just when you think it can't get any worse, it does. Sometimes you feel so overwhelmed that you just want to give up and abandon ship.

But Jesus has a better idea. Don't bail out, He says, but *pray!* In other words, if your knees are shaking, then kneel on them.

To highlight that lesson, Jesus once told a story about a judge who had little regard for God or people. A widow repeatedly asked the judge to rule in her favor against a powerful enemy, but he continually snubbed her. The widow refused to take silence for an answer, however, and continued to petition the judge. Finally the exasperated man said, "Though I do not fear God nor regard man, yet because this widow troubles me I will avenge her, lest by her continual coming she weary me" (Luke 18:4-5).

Jesus contrasted the judge's unwillingness to hear the widow's petition with God's eagerness to hear ours. "And shall God not avenge His own elect who cry out day and night to Him, though He bears long with them?" He asked. "I tell you that He will avenge them speedily" (verses 7-8).

Jesus spoke this parable to teach His disciples explicitly "that they should always pray and not give up" (Luke 18:1, NIV).

He knew how frustrated we can become when our prayers don't get answered as fast as we'd like. He knew that we grow tired in prayer and that we sometimes wonder whether we would feel less exasperated if we just gave up.

"Don't quit now," Jesus says. "It may seem as if God is as unsympathetic as the judge, but He's not. He's really eager to hear from you and to give you His best. Just hang in there!"

To those discouraged souls who wonder, *Why pray at all?* the Bible gives at least three strong reasons to keep on praying.

JESUS COMMANDS US TO PRAY.

Why should we pray? Because Jesus told us to! Is there any better reason?

Jesus commanded us to pray for those who mistreat us (Luke 6:28). He instructed us to pray for our daily sustenance (Matthew 6:11). He not only commanded us to pray, He took it as a given that we would do so (Matthew 6:5). The epistles overflow with God's directives to pray (for example, see Ephesians 6:18; Colossians 4:2-3; 1 Thessalonians 5:17).

Even if prayer were an extremely difficult thing to do (which it is not) or very unpleasant (again, which it is not), we should still pray because God commands us to do so.

And let's not forget the fabulous blessings that come from seeing our prayers answered—such as the salvation of a loved one, a divine healing, or a wonderful and unexpected provision!

PRAYER IS GOD'S WAY FOR US TO OBTAIN WHAT WE NEED.

God has so wired this universe that His children get certain delightful things only by asking for them. James tells us, "You do not have because you do not ask" (James 4:2).

You might ask, "Why is it that I never seem to know the will of God for my life?"

James answers, "You have not because you ask not."

"Why don't I ever have the opportunity to lead people to the Lord?"

You have not because you ask not.

"Why am I always just scraping by, never having enough?"

You have not because you ask not.

So ask, already!

PRAYER IS GOD'S WAY FOR US TO OVERCOME ANXIETY.
Nothing is too big or too small to bring to God in prayer. He's interested in even the smallest details. So Paul writes, "Don't worry about anything; instead, pray about everything. Tell God what you need, and thank him for all he has done. If you do this, you will experience God's peace, which is far more wonderful than the human mind can understand. His peace will guard your hearts and minds as you live in Christ Jesus" (Philippians 4:6-7, NLT).

We tend to pray only about the "big" things and not the "little" ones, until the little things become big things. But your heavenly Father is interested in every detail of your life; therefore you can come boldly to His throne of grace and open your heart to Him (Hebrews 4:16). Do not reduce the infinite to the finite by placing a limit on God! Remember, the Lord Himself asked, "Is anything too hard for the Lord?" (Genesis 18:14). Jeremiah was wise enough to answer God's question with a resounding, "There is nothing too hard for You" (Jeremiah 32:17).

The next time it looks as if your ship is taking on water and listing dangerously to port, remember Jesus' parable about the unresponsive judge—and remind yourself that He told it so that *you* would always "pray and not lose heart."

We all have a choice about what to do when a crisis hits. We can lose heart or we can pray. Jesus advises us that the latter is a far better choice than the former.

So is anything in your life causing you to lose heart? Then pray!

CHAPTER 50

Faithfully Persistent

"And shall God not avenge His own elect who cry out day and night to Him, though He bears long with them?"
Luke 18:7

Jesus commands us to pray, and we know we should do so. But what about those times when we pray and nothing seems to happen? What then?

The Savior's answer? We should pray with persistence.

In Jesus' day, Israel had two kinds of judges. The first was the Orthodox judge who upheld the principles of the law of Moses; most of the people put their trust in him. The second type was appointed either by the Romans or by King Herod. These men tended to be dishonest. As one ancient historian said, they would pervert justice for a dish of meat.

The judge in Jesus' parable was corrupt, by his own admission. He bragged that he did "not fear God nor regard man" (Luke 18:4). To make matters worse, the victim was a widow, and any widow had to overcome two huge obstacles in the culture of ancient Israel. First, females had little standing before the law; women did not even go to court. Second, widows usually had no money to pay a bribe.

So what did this woman do? She persisted (with a capital *P*).

It almost sounds as if this woman stalked the judge. He would get up in the morning to get his paper, and there she would be. He'd go out for dinner at night, and she would show up to harass him. The judge said this behavior troubled him (verse 5), but the original Greek word means more literally "to beat black and blue or give one a black eye." Perhaps the widow tended toward the brawny side, because the judge feared her. *By the time she's finished,* the judge probably thought, *she may end up in prison—but I'll be six feet under!*

So at last the judge declared, "This woman is driving me crazy. I'm going to see that she gets justice, because she is wearing me out with her constant requests!" (verse 5, NLT).

Why did Jesus tell us this story? To teach us that we need to threaten God to get answers to prayer? "Lord, you better come through on this, or you'll have *me* to deal with!" Hardly. The only guy I know of who ever wrestled with God lost miserably (see Genesis 32:24-32).

Some believers think they can convince God of their cause. They assume that the louder or longer they pray, the more effective they will be. But such an idea is pagan; the prophets of Baal did exactly this in their contest with Elijah (1 Kings 18:26-29).

Believers need not approach God like this, for our God is the exact opposite of the judge in Jesus' story. "And shall God not avenge His own elect who cry out day and night to Him, though He bears long with them?" Jesus asks. In other words, "If a poor woman got what she deserved from a selfish judge, how much more will God's children receive what is right from a loving heavenly Father!" The unjust judge and our heavenly Father differ from one another in at least three ways:

1. The widow was a stranger, but we are God's children.
2. The widow had no access to the judge, but God's children have open access to Him every minute of every day (Hebrews 10:19).
3. The widow had no friend at court to help her plead her case, no husband to stand up for her, no attorney, no inside connection. All she could do was walk around

outside the tent and shout at the judge. But believers have an Advocate with the Father (1 John 2:1).

We don't have to threaten God or wear Him out. We come to a loving Father through His Son with prayers energized by His Spirit. True prayer is not bending God my way but bending myself His way. It's not getting my will in heaven but His will on earth. Still, Jesus told this parable to encourage us to persist in our prayers even when they don't seem to be answered.

We must realize that a spiritual battle rages behind the scenes. The answer to at least one prayer of the prophet Daniel was hindered for twenty-one days by behind-the-scenes spiritual warfare. It took the intervention of the archangel Michael to get things rolling (Daniel 10:13).

Sometimes when it seems as if God is putting us off, He is really drawing us in. A pagan woman once approached Jesus on behalf of her demon-possessed daughter. "Lord, help me," she begged. For a long time Jesus made no reply. Finally, after she persisted He answered, "It is not right to take the children's bread and toss it to their dogs."

"Yes, Lord," she said, "but even the dogs eat the crumbs that fall from their masters' table."

"Jesus answered, 'Woman, you have great faith! Your request is granted.' And her daughter was healed from that very hour" (Matthew 15:21-28, NIV).

Why did Jesus treat the woman in such a rough way? He erected obstacles that only genuine, persistent faith could hurdle—and through her persistence and faith, the woman's daughter got her life back.

Jesus does not ask us to understand His ways and timing. He asks only for our trust, demonstrated by our persistence.

CHAPTER **51**
A Good Way to Unmake a Prayer

"For everyone who exalts himself will be humbled, and he who humbles himself will be exalted." Luke 18:14

Never forget, attitude can make or unmake a prayer.

You can pray with all the persistence in the world, but if your heart is not right before God, it will not matter. Jesus shows us that while some prayers lead to heaven, others grease the way to hell.

Our Lord made a strong statement about the attitude God accepts by comparing two prayers, one by a Pharisee and the other by a tax collector. Listen to the Pharisee's prayer: "God, I thank You that I am not like other men; extortioners, unjust, adulterers, or even as this tax collector. I fast twice a week; I give tithes of all that I possess" (Luke 18:11-12). In direct contrast, consider the tax collector: "And the tax collector, standing afar off, would not so much as raise his eyes to heaven, but beat his breast, saying, 'God, be merciful to me a sinner!'" (verse 13).

Whose prayer did God hear? Jesus tells us that the tax collector "went down to his house justified" (verse 14). The Pharisee didn't.

Jesus' story must have shocked His listeners, for in that culture, the Pharisees enjoyed a stellar reputation. People considered them to be devoutly religious men who were rightly related to God. On the other hand, everyone despised tax collectors because they were Jews who had sold out their own people to collect taxes for Rome. Yet Jesus made a hero of the tax collector and a villain of the Pharisee.

This would be like saying, "Mother Teresa and Adolf Hitler went to church to pray." Most listeners would immediately assume that God will hear the prayer of Mother Teresa and dismiss Hitler. But in His story, our Lord turns the tables. Why?

Jesus explicitly told this parable "to some who trusted in themselves" (verse 9). The Pharisee trusted in himself rather than in God. He placed his confidence in what *he* did for God instead of what *God* had done for him.

God does not hear our prayers because we go to church (though that is great) or because we spend time in the Word and prayer (though that is essential for the Christian). Nor does He hear us because we volunteer to help in Sunday school or elsewhere at church. God hears our prayers because of the sacrifice of Jesus on the cross (Ephesians 2:18).

It is good that the Pharisee did not extort, commit adultery, or behave unjustly. We need more people like that! But he erred, not only in trusting in his own works but also in praying loudly enough so that everyone could hear. That is not prayer; that is bragging.

Billy Graham and his late associate T. W. Wilson once visited the Oval Office to see President Lyndon B. Johnson. The president asked Dr. Wilson to pray but soon told him to speak up so he could hear.

"I'm not talking to you, Mr. President!" T. W. replied.

Some use prayer as an opportunity to brag about their accomplishments: "Lord, I fasted this week and shared the gospel with hundreds." Others use it as an opportunity to gossip: "Lord, you know that Jim has been unfaithful to his wife, although she doesn't know it yet. So we do pray . . ." Others use it as an opportunity to impress, praying in their most eloquent King James English.

Of course, there is nothing wrong with praying eloquently; in fact, it can be quite beautiful—so long as it's from the heart!

That is what God cares about. Yet we can pray the most elo-quent and lengthy prayers known to humanity and never get heard by our Father in heaven if our heart is not in the right place. God says, "These people come near to me with their mouth and honor me with their lips, but their hearts are far from me. Their worship of me is made up only of rules taught by men" (Isaiah 29:13, NIV).

When we pray like that, it really has nothing to do with God but everything to do with us. And prayers like this go no higher than the ceiling (if that far). Know this: many people who "say their prayers" don't really know how to pray. Why? Because their hearts are not right with the Lord.

Beyond that, this Pharisee did not merely lack compassion for the tax collector; he actively disdained him. Yet every man and woman is made in God's image and needs God's salvation. Remember this when you come into contact with nonbeliev-ers: they're blind, like "sheep without a shepherd" (Mark 6:34, NIV). We believers are not better then they are, though we are better off. So have compassion on them.

And what of the tax collector? First of all, he stands "afar off," or at a distance. Instead of loudly announcing his virtues, he quietly confesses his sins. He has no desire to compare himself with this Pharisee or with anyone else. He knows he falls far short of God's standards. He makes no excuses but takes total responsibility for his sins. He prays the only real "sinner's prayer" we know of in the Bible: "God, be merciful to me a sinner."

Through this story, Jesus teaches us that the closer we get to God and the more we become like Christ, the more we recog-nize our sinful nature. The most godly people I know are deeply humble. They see themselves as they really are—and as God sees them.

Whenever we bow in prayer, we must always check our atti-tude because God looks on the heart: "People judge by out-ward appearance, but the Lord looks at a person's thoughts and intentions" (1 Samuel 16:7, NLT). When we come to God in prayer, we must come in complete humility: "Humble yourselves in the sight of the Lord, and He will lift you up" (James 4:10).

If we fail to come to the Lord with the right attitude, our prayers will rise no higher than the ceiling—and we won't get answers from there!

CHAPTER 52
How to Come to Jesus

*"Assuredly, I say to you, whoever does not receive
the kingdom of God as a little child will by no means
enter it."* Luke 18:17

You've got to love children. Jesus sure did! As the children's
song says, "Jesus loves the little children." He always has, and
He always will.

A Sunday school teacher once asked her students to write
letters to God, saying anything that occurred to them. Consider some of their comments addressed to God:

> In Sunday school they told us what You do. Who does
> it when You are on vacation?
> I read the Bible. What does "begat" mean? Nobody will
> tell me. Love, Allison
> Are You really invisible or is that just a trick?
> Is it true my father won't get into heaven if he uses his
> bowling words in the house?
> Did You mean for giraffes to look like that, or was it
> an accident?
> Who draws the lines around the countries?
> I went to this wedding and they *kissed* right in the
> church. Is that okay?
> I like the Lord's Prayer the best of all. Did You have to
> write it a lot, or did You get it right the first time?
> I have to write everything I ever write over again.

I would like to know why all the things You said are in *red.*

My grandpa says You were around when he was a little boy. How far back *do* You go?

Thank You for the baby brother, but what I prayed for was a *puppy!*

Please put another holiday between Christmas and Easter. There is nothing good in there now.

I wish You would not make it so easy for people to come apart. I had three stitches and a shot.

We read that Thomas Edison made light. But in Sunday school they said You did it. So, I bet he stole Your idea.

I bet it is very hard for You to love all of everybody in the whole world. There are only four people in our family, and I can never do it.

I want to be just like my daddy when I get big, but with not so much *hair* all over!

If You watch in church on Sunday, I will show You my new shoes.

Many of Jesus' teachings and miracles involved children. Luke tells us that one day many parents "brought infants to Him that He might touch them; but when the disciples saw it, they rebuked them. But Jesus called them to Him and said, 'Let the little children come to Me, and do not forbid them; for of such is the kingdom of God'" (Luke 18:15-16).

Mark's Gospel adds that Jesus took the children into His arms and began to fervently bless them. So, clearly He was passionate about this.

What a refreshing change these children must have been from the adults Jesus encountered most of the time. The children were trusting, loving, laughing; the adults were full of verbal jousting and theological traps. When the children scampered up onto His lap, I imagine Jesus enjoyed Himself immensely!

Jesus used this incident as an opportunity to show us how we should approach God. "Assuredly, I say to you," He declared, "whoever does not receive the kingdom of God as a little child will by no means enter it" (verse 17). Conventional thinking insists that to know God, a child should become like an adult. Jesus says the very opposite: an adult should become like a child. The child is the model for faith, not the adult. Of course, Jesus wants us to be childlike, not childish. There is a difference.

CHILDREN COME TO GOD WITH COMPLETE HONESTY.
At the beginning, children are very honest. When they feel happy, they laugh. When they feel sad, they cry. When they fall, they come running to mom for comfort. So many of us have lost this childlike honesty. We try to be what we think others expect us to be.

CHILDREN COME WITH COMPLETE HELPLESSNESS.
Very small children cannot care for themselves. They can't feed themselves. They depend completely on their parents. In the same way, we must realize that we are spiritually helpless. We must depend completely on God to be saved and forgiven.

CHILDREN KNOW HOW TO RECEIVE GIFTS.
Give an adult a birthday gift, and he or she will thank you, set it on a table, and plan to open it later. When I give someone a gift, I want him to open it then and there. So do kids! Kids just take the gifts offered to them. Children would never say, "I'm not worthy of such a present" or "What can I do to repay you?" They just gladly receive the gift and immediately start enjoying it.

Jesus not only took time for children, He used them as an example of how we must behave if we want to enter the kingdom of God. Like little children, we must forget ourselves and come to God humbly and expectantly. Like little children who depend completely on their parents, we are simply to receive and use the gifts that God lavishes upon us.

CHAPTER **53**

Be Ready

"You also be ready, for the Son of Man is coming at an hour you do not expect." Luke 12:40

Do you ever wonder if the Lord will really come again? Many throughout the centuries have felt certain that Jesus would return in their lifetime. He didn't.

As recently as the early 1970s, with the Jesus Movement in full swing, many of us felt sure that Jesus was coming any day. He didn't.

Some of us have lived through at least a dozen versions of the "Jesus is coming" bumper sticker—and still He's not here!

So what gives? Is Jesus late? No, He is not late; we are just a bit early. "The Lord is not slow in keeping his promise, as some understand slowness," writes Peter. "He is patient with you, not wanting anyone to perish, but everyone to come to repentance" (2 Peter 3:9, NIV). Jesus is right on schedule, and He will come at the time set by His Father (Matthew 24:36). But He *will* come!

In the 260 chapters of the New Testament, Christ's return is mentioned no less than 318 times. Jesus Himself often spoke of His second coming. After challenging His disciples to take up the cross and follow Him, He warned, "For whoever is ashamed of Me and My words in this adulterous and sinful generation, of him the Son of Man also will be ashamed when He comes in the glory of His Father with the holy angels" (Mark 8:38). Christ later told His disciples, "I go to prepare a place for you. And if I go and prepare a place for you, I will come again and receive you to Myself; that where I am, there you may be also" (John 14:2-3).

The last book of the Bible declares, "Behold, He is coming

with clouds, and every eye will see Him, even they who pierced Him. And all the tribes of the earth will mourn because of Him. Even so, Amen. 'I am the Alpha and the Omega, the Beginning and the End,' says the Lord, 'who is and who was and who is to come, the Almighty'" (Revelation 1:7-8).

Make no mistake, Jesus Christ is coming again to our planet. But how are we to respond to the Second Coming? How can we best prepare for His imminent return? Jesus Himself gave us a key in Luke 12:35-48.

Jesus compared His return to a first-century Jewish wedding. Unlike modern nuptials, a first-century Hebrew marriage celebration lasted days, not hours. Families used the event for an extended time of merriment and fun. No one knew exactly when the groom would arrive, so all the guests and servants waited with great anticipation.

Such servants were to wait with their waists "girded" and their "lamps burning." In those days, everybody wore long, flowing robes as well as belts to which they attached things, such as oil flasks. To "gird your waist" meant to "tighten your belt." This gave the servant freedom of movement so he could answer the door quickly. To have "lamps burning" meant to have sufficient oil to keep the house illuminated, regardless of when the master arrived.

"And if he should come in the second watch, or come in the third watch, and find them so," Jesus said, "blessed are those servants" (verse 38). People in New Testament times divided the night into four watches, or shifts. The first watch lasted from 6 to 9 P.M.; the second, from 9 P.M. to 12 A.M.; the third, from 12 to 3 A.M.; and the fourth, from 3 A.M. until the time just before dawn. Note that even if the master did not come as quickly as the servants would have liked, they were to remain decisively ready.

In the same way, even if Jesus comes in the third or fourth watch—that is, later than we expect—we need to stay ready. We don't want to be like the foolish servant who said, "My master is delaying his coming" (verse 45). Jesus may come in the third watch, even the fourth, but know this—*He is coming!*

And what a reward awaits those who stay ready! "Blessed are those servants whom the master, when he comes, will find watching," Jesus said. "Assuredly, I say to you that he will gird himself and have them sit down to eat, and will come and serve them" (verse 37).

The master in Jesus' story feels so moved by the faithfulness of his servants that instead of sitting down at the table, he changes his clothes and serves *them!* The disciples did not miss the Lord's meaning here; they knew that they were the servants and Jesus was the Master.

These teachings have never been more relevant than they are today, for we have never been closer to the Lord's return. One looks around and wonders if we are not already in the third or the fourth watch.

So when will Jesus come? Listen to Peter again: "The day of the Lord will come like a thief. The heavens will disappear with a roar; the elements will be destroyed by fire, and the earth and everything in it will be laid bare. Since everything will be destroyed in this way, what kind of people ought you to be? You ought to live holy and godly lives" (2 Peter 3:10-11, NIV).

As we await the return of Jesus, let's make sure that we live in a productive way, a way that honors Him. For only that kind of being ready results in the Lord's blessing.

CHAPTER **54**
So What Now?

"And what I say to you, I say to all: Watch!"

Mark 13:37

As I write, Palestinian suicide bombers have killed scores of Israeli citizens, while Israeli soldiers are desperately trying to defend themselves. We watch with trepidation any talk of Arab nations attacking Israel, for we recognize this as a key sign of our Lord's imminent return. "Now when these things begin to happen, look up and lift up your heads," Jesus said, "because your redemption draws near" (Luke 21:28).

While I certainly do not mean that the events currently taking place in the Middle East will lead directly to the return of Christ, I think they could. Whatever happens, the turmoil in Israel reminds us that Christians are to prepare themselves for the Lord's return. And how are we to do this?

WE ARE TO BE WATCHING FOR HIM.
"Blessed are those servants whom the master, when he comes, will find watching," Jesus said (Luke 12:37). Christians should not worry about the things that dominate the minds and hearts of nonbelievers: what we shall eat, drink, and wear (see Matthew 6:31-32). But we must seek first Christ's rule and reign in our lives. No day should pass without our asking, "Could this be the day?"

WE ARE TO BE READY TO GO WITH HIM.
I always pack my bags the night before I leave on a trip; I want to be ready to go when the moment arrives. That's the modern

counterpart to having "your waist girded and your lamps burning" (Luke 12:35). We who wait for the Lord's return should have our bags packed and comfortable shoes on. We need to be ready to go at a moment's notice.

To be ready for Christ's return is to be engaged in activities that would bring us no shame were Jesus to return at that moment. Ask yourself, "This place that I'm about to go to, this thing that I am ready to do—would I be ashamed or embarrassed to be doing it when Jesus came back?" If the answer is yes, *then don't do it!* "And now, dear children, continue in him, so that when he appears we may be confident and unashamed before him at his coming" (1 John 2:28, NIV).

Since Christians someday will be like Jesus, right now we ought to be growing in our desire to become more like Him. That was certainly Paul's passion: "I press on, that I may lay hold of that for which Christ Jesus has also laid hold of me. Brethren, I do not count myself to have apprehended; but one thing I do, forgetting those things which are behind and reaching forward to those things which are ahead, I press toward the goal for the prize of the upward call of God in Christ Jesus" (Philippians 3:12-14).

I have the privilege of serving on the board of directors of the Billy Graham Evangelistic Association. During one of our meetings in 2001, my friend Joseph Stowell of Moody Bible Institute asked Mr. Graham to name his greatest passion and joy in life.

We all wondered, was it in personally knowing presidents and world leaders? Was it in standing before thousands in the great stadiums of the world? We all were pleasantly surprised when Billy said his greatest joy came from talking to and hearing from Christ. In the hospital during an operation that year, he thought he was going to die. "I came face-to-face with my own sins and the glory of God!" he said. And I wondered, *If Billy Graham came face-to-face with his sins, what about me?*

WE ARE TO ANXIOUSLY AWAIT HIS RETURN.

My dog likes to sleep against my door at night. He waits for me to wake up. He greets me excitedly. He wags his tail and runs around in circles. He certainly makes me feel *wanted!* I recall a bumper sticker that read, "Lord, make me the person my dog thinks I am!"

Maybe we can learn a lesson from our dogs. Most dogs can't wait to see their master—and that is how we are to await the Lord's return.

Jesus says, "Surely I am coming quickly." The answer of the true Christian will always be, "Even so, come, Lord Jesus!" (Revelation 22:20).

Anything that would prevent us from feeling such excitement for our Lord's return is out of place in our lives. Anything that makes it difficult to say "Come quickly, Lord Jesus" is an element of weakness. We must test all ambitions, all pursuits, all hopes by the truth of the Lord's imminent return.

WE ARE TO WORK IN LIGHT OF HIS RETURN.

If watching is the evidence of our faith, then working is the evidence of our faith in action. Watching for the Lord's return will help us to prepare ourselves, but working will assure that we bring others with us.

"Blessed is that servant whom his master will find *so doing* when he comes," said Jesus (Luke 12:43, emphasis added). The sentence could be more literally translated, "How happy are those servants!" Jesus means that living in this way brings a special blessedness.

To watch for Christ's return does not lead to a miserable, repressive, confining way of life. Much to the contrary, it yields a happy, joyful, purposeful way of living. I agree with Charles Spurgeon, who said, "It is a very blessed thing to be on the watch for Christ, it is a blessing to us now. How it detaches you from the world! You can be poor without murmuring. You can be rich without worldliness. You can be sick without sorrowing. You can be healthy without presumption. If you are always waiting for Christ's coming, untold blessings are wrapped up in that glorious hope."

Indeed they are.

CHAPTER 55
Beware the Pitfalls

"But if that servant says in his heart, 'My master is delaying his coming,' and begins to beat the male and female servants, and to eat and drink and be drunk, the master of that servant will come on a day when he is not looking for him, and at an hour when he is not aware, and will cut him in two and appoint him his portion with the unbelievers." Luke 12:45-46

Not everyone who claims to serve Christ will be ready on the day He returns. The longer Jesus stays in heaven, the more these individuals act up—and the bigger trouble they'll have when He comes back.

"The master of that servant will come on a day he is not looking for him," Jesus said, "and at an hour when he is not aware, and will cut him in two and appoint him his portion with the unbelievers."

This is not the only time in Scripture that believers are told to avoid the pitfalls of spiritual unreadiness. Paul gives us another set of verses that really bring this home to us:

And do this, knowing the time, that now it is high time to awake out of sleep; for now our salvation is nearer than when we first believed. The night is far spent, the day is at hand. Therefore let us cast off the works of darkness, and let us put on the armor of light. Let us walk properly, as in the day, not in revelry and drunkenness, not in lewdness and lust, not in strife and envy. But put on the Lord Jesus Christ, and make no provision for the flesh, to fulfill its lusts. Romans 13:11-14

J. B. Phillips paraphrases the first part of this passage, "Why all this stress on behavior? Because, as I think you have realised the present time is of the highest importance." And what is this "present time"? It is the time before the Lord's return.

We Christians need to wake up. Paul is calling us to awaken from spiritual sleep—from unconsciousness, unresponsiveness, and inactivity concerning the things of God. Paul tells us that servants waiting and working for their Lord's return must "put off" one thing and "put on" something else. "Let us cast off the works of darkness, and let us put on the armor of light," he says (verse 12). Paul specifically lists some of "the deeds of darkness" we are to discard.

DON'T PARTY AND DRINK.

Don't participate "in revelry and drunkenness," he says (verse 13). These words picture drunken individuals stumbling through the streets—your basic party animals, drunken fools making a lot of noise.

It seems almost ridiculous to bring up such an issue among Christians, but I see more and more believers becoming lax in this very area. You might say, "We can handle it; we have the liberty!" True, you do have the liberty; but can you *really* handle it? I know of a Christian couple who flaunted their "freedom to drink," and the next thing they knew, their son had developed a drinking problem. When they tried to get him under control, he said, "But you guys drink—why can't I?"

Christians are not to be under the influence of "spirits," but under the control of the Holy Spirit. "Do not be drunk with wine . . . but be filled with the Spirit" (Ephesians 5:18).

AVOID IMMORALITY.

Paul further tells us to reject "lewdness and lust" (verse 13). The Greek term translated *lewdness* can more simply be rendered *bed*. The word had the same connotation in ancient days as it does today, as in "going to bed" with someone. The word *lust* is one of the ugliest terms in the Greek language. It describes someone not only given to immorality but someone incapable of feeling shame. It speaks of brazen excess and the absence of restraint.

AVOID ENVY AND STRIFE.

The third pitfall Paul names is more subtle and definitely more widespread among Christians. At the same time, it is severe enough to be highlighted as a serious problem for believers. He tells us not to engage "in strife and envy" (verse 13).

Strife refers to persistent contention, bickering, petty disagreements, and enmity. It reflects a spirit of antagonistic competitiveness that fights to get its own way, regardless of the cost to itself or the harm to others. It comes from a deep desire to prevail, to gain the highest possible prestige, prominence, and recognition. *Envy* describes someone who cannot stand being surpassed and who grudges others' successes and positions.

So much for what we are *not* supposed to do; what *should* we be doing as we await the Lord's return? "But put on the Lord Jesus Christ, and make no provision for the flesh, to fulfill its lusts," answers Paul (verse 14). We must practically, repeatedly, and day after day, put on Christ. We are to embrace Jesus again and again.

When you get up in the morning and put on your clothes, you intend for them to cover you, to bend when you bend, and to make you presentable to others. In the same way, when you "put on" Christ, you get up in the morning and make Him an integral part of your life that day. You intend that He go with you everywhere and that He act through you in everything you do.

J. B. Phillips had the right idea, and I can say it no better: "Let us be Christ's men from head to foot and give no chances to the flesh to have its fling" (Romans 13:14, Phillips).

CHAPTER 56

The Parable of Equal Opportunity

[He] said to them, "Do business till I come." Luke 19:13

Suppose you had ten cars to sell. You select ten individuals to sell one car apiece and tell each seller, "Get the most money for my car."

You return in a month and discover that one man has not only failed to sell your car, but he's put more miles on it and neglected it so badly that it is worth less now than it was before you left. A second guy sold your car and made a tidy profit, which he hands over to you. A third fellow sold your car at a profit the first day, bought another two cars with what he made, sold them at a profit, then bought several more and sold them. By the time you return, he's set you up with a Ferrari dealership. Lines of people snake around the block, salivating to buy one of your cars.

Now, that's a good return! And that's the idea behind the parable of Luke 19–doing the most with what God gives you.

"A certain nobleman went into a far country to receive for himself a kingdom and to return," Jesus said. "So he called ten of his servants, delivered to them ten minas, and said to them, 'Do business till I come'" (Luke 19:12-13).

A mina amounted to about one hundred days' wages, nearly four months' salary. Through shrewd investments, one man multiplied his mina by a factor of ten; a second man earned five additional minas; and a third servant did nothing with the money but hide it. When his master returned, he returned his funds to him. Jesus called that man a "wicked servant" (verse 22).

Note that every servant was given the same amount to invest. This is the parable of equal opportunity. Our Lord speaks here of something that every Christian has and should use. And what one thing do all Christians have?

Answer: the message of the gospel.

The great commission was given to *all* (Matthew 28:19-20). Every Christian is to go and preach the gospel; no believer is excused. While not everyone is called as an evangelist, all are called to evangelize.

Jesus is saying to us, "Look, I am coming soon! Take this message that I have entrusted to you and get it out to others. Do God's business until I return!"

It's perfectly fine to find that right person, marry, have children, pursue a career, buy a home, etc. But we must each ask ourselves, "How am I personally fulfilling my responsibility to get out the gospel?"

Every Christian will one day stand before the judgment seat of Jesus Christ (2 Corinthians 5:10; 1 Corinthians 3:10-15). When we get to heaven, God will lavishly reward those who have been faithful to Him. The Lord will not overlook even the smallest and most insignificant gesture on behalf of His kingdom.

While the promises of God guarantee our *presence* in the kingdom, we earn or lose our *position* in the kingdom by the quality of service we render here and now. *Salvation* is a gift through faith in Jesus Christ; *honor* is a reward for service to Jesus Christ.

God will want to know what you did with your gifts, talents, abilities, and time. He will want to know what you did with the sacred charge of the gospel (1 Timothy 1:11). The Master has given you this charge and has said, "Do business till I come."

Peter declared that we can enjoy "a rich welcome into the eternal kingdom" (2 Peter 1:11, NIV). How important this is!

When I am asked to speak at a memorial service, I always try to find out about the deceased. I ask family members and friends to describe the individual. I never mention how successful in business the person may have been, nor do I describe how large a house they lived in or what kind of car they drove. The reason? People don't really care about such things at a time like this. Instead, I try to highlight the good qualities of the individual's life, his unknown acts of kindness, her sacrificial acts, a story that sums up what really mattered to the person.

How deeply it grieves me when I find nothing of this kind and realize I am speaking of a life largely wasted! That is just pathetic. But it happens far too often.

What if we did not try to sugarcoat the life of the deceased but told the bare-bones truth? What if we said, "This man wasted his life pursuing a bunch of stuff his family will now fight over. He was selfish, never spent time with his kids, and was dishonest. And I suppose this would be as good a time as any to mention that he was having an affair!"

Of course, we would never do that. But let me ask you this: If someone were to honestly sum up *your* life at your funeral service, how would you be remembered?

When crime boss John Gotti died of cancer at age sixty-one, he was in prison. He had been convicted of murder, among other things. A who's who of gangland figures attended his wake. The florists delivered floral displays that, to some degree, symbolized Gotti's life: a six-foot replica of a martini glass, a racehorse, a royal flush, and a Cuban cigar.

What floral displays could symbolize your life at your funeral?

A believing friend once spoke to celebrated Christian author Alan Redpath of a "saved soul but a wasted life." The comment haunted Redpath and caused him to rededicate his life to Christ.

Jesus has told each of us to "do business" till He comes. We have a sacred trust to do what we can to get the gospel out. Each of us has 1,440 precious minutes a day to invest in that endeavor. Let's not settle for a saved soul but a wasted life.

PART THREE

the promises
of jesus

CHAPTER **57**

The Happy Ones

"Blessed are you poor, for yours is the kingdom of God."
Luke 6:20

Have you ever met someone who said, "I really do *not* want to be happy. Happiness might be okay for some people, but it's really not for me"? Neither have I. That's because deep down inside, we all want to be happy.

And by the way, there's nothing wrong with that. As a matter of fact, Jesus understood this basic human desire and so made happiness the subject of some of the first promises He ever made.

In what we know as the Beatitudes, Jesus described how we can be "blessed," which means "happy." If we live according to His directions, we will be happy men and women.

The sermon in Luke 6 may be the same message recorded in Matthew 5-7 (commonly called the Sermon on the Mount), but I believe that these were two separate events. A number of differences exist between the two talks. Matthew devotes three long chapters to Jesus' message; Luke, only one. Matthew records nine Beatitudes; Luke, just four. In Luke, Jesus "came down" and delivered His message on "a level place" rather than going "up on a mountain" (Luke 6:17; Matthew 5:1). One commentator described it as "the sermon on the level."

In any event, this sermon contains some of the hardest teachings found anywhere in the Bible. Jesus tells us plainly what it means to be His true followers. His sermon applies to life today and describes the kind of godly character God wants believers to develop.

Jesus spoke His message not to the crowds but to His disciples. The Savior momentarily left the multitude in order to give some in-depth teaching to the Twelve.

"Do you want to be happy?" Jesus was asking them (and us). "Then listen up: Happy are the poor, for theirs is the kingdom of God."

What did He mean? Does poverty make us more spiritual and wealth make us less so? Are we to believe that the fewer possessions we have, the more godly we become?

No, He doesn't mean that at all. The first beatitude simply promises the person who has nothing that possessions are *not* what matter most in life. What really matters is what lasts for eternity—and possessions don't.

The problem with those who own a bunch of stuff is that they tend to become preoccupied with it. So Psalm 62:10 warns us, "If riches increase, do not set your heart on them." Yet that's precisely what we often do.

The apostle Paul wrote to Timothy:

> *Tell those who are rich in this world not to be proud and not to trust in their money, which will soon be gone. But their trust should be in the living God, who richly gives us all we need for our enjoyment. Tell them to use their money to do good. They should be rich in good works and should give generously to those in need, always being ready to share with others whatever God has given them. By doing this they will be storing up their treasure as a good foundation for the future so that they may take hold of real life.* 1 Timothy 6:17-19, NLT

Think of the compromises many individuals make for money. No matter how hard one may try, who can forget the TV program *Who Wants to Marry a Multimillionaire?* Network executives chose fifty women from a pool of some three thousand applicants to have the "privilege" of marrying—sight unseen—a genuine, living, breathing millionaire. The girls had to don bathing suits so the millionaire could check them out. They took a personality test in which they answered several questions, such as what they would do with his money. And, by the way—would they mind if he went to strip clubs?

As the girls completed their interviews, the millionaire, Rick Rockwell, watched from a high-tech perch. The eventual winner, Darva Conger, took the honeymoon and $100,000 prize—but only days later announced that she had made a big mistake and sought an annulment.

What next? *Who Wants to Sell Their Soul?*

Some individuals will compromise their values or abandon them altogether for a few bucks or a little notoriety.

In the Sermon on the Mount recorded in Matthew's Gospel, Jesus said, "Blessed are the poor in spirit, for theirs is the kingdom of heaven" (Matthew 5:3). To be "poor in spirit" is to see yourself as you really are—spiritually impoverished. The poor in spirit have confronted God and realized how utterly bankrupt they are spiritually. The poor in spirit recognize their dilemma. They don't look to themselves for answers but to Jesus. To be poor in spirit means to know that you are a helpless sinner in need of God's help.

Our Lord emphasized four essentials for true happiness: faith in God, love toward others, honesty with ourselves, and obedience toward God. Jesus is telling us, "Don't envy those who make spiritual compromises. Though you may not be rich in this world's eyes, you have true riches. And I promise you this: You'll be the happy one."

CHAPTER **58**

Happy People Are Hungry People

> *"Blessed are you who hunger now, for you shall be filled."* Luke 6:21

Do you appreciate a meal much more when you feel really hungry? I do.

Thanksgiving embodies this principle. Every year, it seems as if the meal or the people who are joining me for the meal are always late, so I have to wait. And wait. And wait some more. Meanwhile, the heavenly aroma of cooked turkey, fresh stuffing, sweet potatoes, and pumpkin pie wafts from the kitchen to entice my olfactory nerves and taunt my taste buds. Oh, how I want to say the blessing and chow down!

Jesus said that spiritual hunger works in much the same way. You can tell if someone is spiritually alive by the way he or she salivates at the thought of dining on God's heavenly banquet. If you get ravenously hungry when you get a whiff of the Bread of Life, if you can't wait to dig into heavenly meat and you long to slake your thirst with Living Water, then you're on your way to true blessedness. "Blessed are you who hunger . . . ," Jesus said, "for you shall be filled."

Jesus Christ, the Bread of Life and the Living Water, has what you hunger and thirst for. If your stomach growls for more of Him, be glad, for He plans to host you at the wedding supper of the Lamb (Revelation 19:9). There you will feast to your heart's content, and there you shall be filled.

In our diet-obsessed culture, we want to find ways to dramatically curb our hunger because hunger leads to eating and eating leads to weight gain. But Jesus insists that spiritual hunger is an incredibly good thing. In fact, without it, you can never be truly happy.

If you want authentic, world-changing, New Testament Christianity as Jesus taught it and as the first-century apostles lived it, then you will find it wherever you see true spiritual hunger. Surprised? Many are. They imagine the Christian life as a playground, not a battleground. But anyone who wants to live on easy street without any troubles doesn't want real Christianity. Those who really want to know God find that it costs them something, not the least of which is spiritual hunger. It's important to remind ourselves of this fact, for occasionally we'll hear someone say, "Oh, I tried Christianity and it just didn't work for me."

Nonsense!

Christianity "works" for every person because true Christianity *is* Jesus Christ—and He did not say, "And only certain people who are predisposed to this will have eternal life." Rather, He said, "*Whoever* believes in Him should not perish but have everlasting life" (John 3:16, emphasis added). That means everyone, including you.

Spiritual hunger is one of the great earmarks of true Christianity. The apostle John gives us at least five more.

DO YOU CONFESS JESUS AS LORD?

"If anyone acknowledges that Jesus is the Son of God," writes John, "God lives in him and he in God" (1 John 4:15, NIV).

ARE YOU MISERABLE WHEN YOU SIN?

"No one who is born of God will continue to sin," insists John, "because God's seed remains in him; he cannot go on sinning, because he has been born of God" (1 John 3:9, NIV). The original Greek says more literally, "Every one who has been born of God does not habitually sin because His seed remains in him.

And he is not able to habitually to sin, because out of God he has been born."

If a person can continue in sin without any sense of remorse or conviction, it probably indicates that he or she does not really know God. So when you sense guilt and conviction when you do the wrong thing, rejoice! It's a reminder that you are a child of God.

DO YOU ENJOY FELLOWSHIP WITH OTHER BELIEVERS?

"Everyone who believes that Jesus is the Christ is born of God, and everyone who loves the father loves his child as well" (1 John 5:1, NIV). A true Christian will want to hang around other Christians who also hunger for God. Those who isolate themselves from other Christians do so at their own peril (Hebrews 10:24-25).

DO YOU OBEY CHRIST'S COMMANDS?

"This is love for God: to obey his commands. And his commands are not burdensome" (1 John 5:3, NIV). Plain and simple, the person who blatantly and continually breaks the commands of God does not know Him.

DO YOU LOVE GOD'S WORD?

"If anyone obeys his word, God's love is truly made complete in him. This is how we know we are in him" (1 John 2:5, NIV). You cannot effectively live the Christian life without a love for the Word of God.

All true disciples of Jesus long to be students of Scripture and to walk according to its teaching, for they hunger for the God of whom the Scripture testifies. Success or failure in the Christian life largely depends on how much of the Bible we get into our heart and mind on a daily basis and how obedient we are to it.

Do you hunger for the Bread of Life? "I am the living bread which came down from heaven," Jesus said. "If anyone eats of this bread, he will live forever; and the bread that I shall give is My flesh, which I shall give for the life of the world" (John 6:51). Hunger can be a very good thing—so long as Jesus is the meal that satisfies.

So lose the guilt, sit down for a spiritual feast, and dig in. Don't be late!

CHAPTER 59

The Joy of Thrown Bricks

"Blessed are you who weep now, for you shall laugh."
Luke 6:21

Tobey Maguire has become one of Hollywood's hottest young actors (*Spider-Man, Cider House Rules, The Wonder Boys*). According to one article, Maguire grew up poor and never expected to have anything handed to him. He feels overwhelmed by his sudden stardom.

"Sometimes I get panicky," Maguire said. "I ask myself what life is, you know? Is it the pursuit of material success? Is it a spiritual journey? I'm really learning about responsibility and mortality—these are two big things. The concept that this is not a dress rehearsal."[3]

He's right; life is not a dress rehearsal. *This* is the real deal. And no, life is not about material success. Life is about knowing the God who made you and discovering His plan for you.

The same questions that trouble Maguire also perplex others. But in the meantime, they're living it up and laughing it up—just like one of Israel's ancient kings. Solomon went on a sin binge, trying everything this world has to offer: "I said to myself, 'Come now, let's give pleasure a try. Let's look for the "good things" in life.'" But what happened? "I found that this, too, was meaningless," he wrote. "'It is silly to be laughing all the time,' I said. 'What good does it do to seek only pleasure?'" (Ecclesiastes 2:1-2, NLT).

Perhaps Jesus had Solomon in mind when He declared,

"Blessed are you who weep now, for you shall laugh"—essentially, "Happy are the unhappy!" What did He mean?

As we grow "poor in spirit" and see ourselves as we really are, we may realize we have wasted our lives trying to fill spiritual hunger with the wrong things. As a result, we feel sorry, remorseful. We weep over our behavior. But it's better to mourn now and laugh later than to laugh now and mourn later! "His anger lasts only a moment," the psalmist says of God, "but his favor lasts a lifetime; weeping may remain for a night, but rejoicing comes in the morning" (Psalm 30:5, NIV).

It is good that we repent of foolish behavior—but there may be more to this idea of "happy weeping" than sorrow over sin. We know this because Jesus follows up His unusual comment with a related one: "Blessed are you when men hate you, and when they exclude you, and revile you, and cast out your name as evil, for the Son of Man's sake. Rejoice in that day and leap for joy! For indeed your reward is great in heaven, for in like manner their fathers did to the prophets" (Luke 6:22-23).

Many of us would like to avoid this area of the Christian life; who wants to face persecution? Yet God made us another promise: "All who desire to live godly in Christ Jesus will suffer persecution" (2 Timothy 3:12). We believers are quick to claim God's promises of provision, protection, and guidance, but when is the last time you said to the Lord, "Father, you promised that if I lived a godly life, I would be persecuted. So please, Lord, bring it on!"

Right. (I haven't prayed that prayer either.) None of us enjoys being mocked and laughed at.

This was a real shocker to me as a young Christian. After all, I had always been the one mocking—and suddenly others were mocking *me!* That hurt. Yet Jesus says, "Rejoice!" And Peter explains, "Be happy if you are insulted for being a Christian, for then the glorious Spirit of God will come upon you. If you suffer, however, it must not be for murder, stealing, making trouble, or prying into other people's affairs. But it is no shame to suffer for being a Christian. Praise God for the privilege of being called by his wonderful name!" (1 Peter 4:14, NLT).

Persecution can appear in many forms. It may be violent; many believers throughout church history have lost their lives for Jesus' sake. The Romans made early Christians into human torches or wrapped them in animal skins and threw them to wild dogs. Persecution can also take a more subtle form, such as losing a job, being the brunt of jokes, or enduring the betrayal of friends. Bottom line: If you are living a godly life, you *will* suffer some kind of persecution.

And how should we react? "Rejoice in that day and leap for joy," says Jesus, "for indeed your reward is great in heaven." The sentence might be more literally translated, "Jump and skip with happy excitement." In Greek, the words appear in the imperative mood. Jesus *commands* us to be glad, not sad.

The great preacher John Wesley was riding along a road one day when it dawned on him that he had suffered no persecution for three whole days. No one had thrown so much as a brick or an egg at him. Alarmed, he stopped his horse and exclaimed, "Can it be that I have sinned and am backslidden?" Wesley fell to his knees and asked God to show him if he had committed some transgression.

As Wesley prayed, a rough fellow on the other side of the hedge heard him. Irritated, the man picked up a brick and threw it at the preacher, barely missing him. When Wesley saw the brick, he leaped to his feet and joyfully exclaimed, "Thank God, it's all right. I still have His presence."

No one likes to be persecuted; brick throwers can make us weep. Yet persecution can also draw us closer to Jesus and farther away from a world system hostile to Him. And it guarantees us a reward. Shouldn't that make us smile at least?

CHAPTER 60

Life Is More Than Food

"Do not labor for the food which perishes, but for the food which endures to everlasting life, which the Son of Man will give you." John 6:27

In the days leading up to the miracle of the feeding of the five thousand (a bit of a misnomer, because probably more than ten thousand persons ate the multiplied loaves and fish that day, counting women and children), Jesus had become exceedingly popular. John tells us, "Then a great multitude followed Him, because they saw His signs which He performed" (John 6:2).

The Lord's popularity soon reached a fever pitch, so much so that the people wanted to "take Him by force to make Him king" (verse 15). To prevent that from happening, Jesus told His disciples to leave the area immediately; He would join them later.

As the sun arose the next morning, the stomachs of the well-fed multitudes began to growl. They had no restaurants to patronize, no vendors selling bread from carts, no fishermen bringing in the catch of the day. So they thought, *Where's that bread guy? The one who multiplies food?*

When they realized He had gone, they went searching for Him, finally finding Him on the other side of the lake. "Rabbi, when did You come here?" they asked (verse 25). Although they asked *when He* had come, He told them *why they* had come: "You're here because you're hungry!"

Jesus had compassion on the hungry crowds the day before, but now He sees that they care only about filling their stomachs. So He uses the opportunity to remind them of what life's priorities ought to be. "Do not labor for the food which perishes," He says. In other words, "Life is more than filling your stomachs. Think about the spiritual!"

At another time He said,

> *Don't worry about having enough food or drink or clothing. Why be like the pagans who are so deeply concerned about these things? Your heavenly Father already knows all your needs, and he will give you all you need from day to day if you live for him and make the Kingdom of God your primary concern. So don't worry about tomorrow, for tomorrow will bring its own worries. Today's trouble is enough for today.* Matthew 6:31-34, NLT

Jesus says our priority should be the kingdom of God. Well, then, what is the kingdom of God? Jesus said to Nicodemus, "Most assuredly, I say to you, unless one is born again, he cannot see the kingdom of God" (John 3:3). So the entry point is to be "born again." To enter into the kingdom is simply to trust in Jesus, follow Him, and surrender to His reign in your life.

On one occasion Jesus told the Pharisees, "The kingdom of God is within you" (Luke 17:21). Wherever Jesus is, so is the kingdom of God. To "seek first the kingdom," as Matthew 6:33 says in the New King James Version, is to desire the rule and reign of Jesus Christ in your life. To seek God's kingdom is to try to win people into that kingdom so that they might be saved and God might be glorified. We also seek God's kingdom when we yearn for the return of the Lord to this earth to physically take up His rule.

Some see this as a miserable, restrictive lifestyle. Nothing could be further from the truth. The book of Romans tells us, "The kingdom of God is not eating and drinking [rules and regulations], but righteousness and peace and joy in the Holy Spirit" (Romans 14:17). Instead of longing after the things of this world, we are to hunger and thirst for the things of the world to come, which are characterized, above all else, by God's perfect righteousness and holiness. "Since, then, you have been raised with Christ, set your hearts on things above, where Christ is seated at the right hand of God. Set your minds on things above, not on earthly things" (Colossians 3:1-2, NIV).

And what is the result of living like this? "He will give you all you need" (Matthew 6:33, NLT). What an aftereffect of a life in proper balance! And what things will God give us? Whatever we need—what we shall eat or drink or wear, where we will work, whom we will marry, how we will minister.

When was the last time you sought the Lord? When was the last time that, instead of muttering a mechanical prayer, you took time to wait upon Him and seek His purpose and direction for your life? The psalmist could testify, "I sought the Lord, and He heard me, and delivered me from all my fears" (Psalm 34:4). Can you say the same?

Jesus is saying to us, "Don't make the things that pass away the driving force of your life. There is more to life than this."

Professor David Meyers spent six years examining hundreds of studies on happiness. He concluded that once people get past poverty, money doesn't add to their happiness, and it doesn't matter how much stuff they buy. "The stockpiles of CDs, the closets full of clothes, the big screen stereo TV systems. But clearly that doesn't do it. Once people achieve that level of wealth, they adapt to it, and it takes new increments, a faster computer, a bigger TV screen or whatever to re-juice the joy that the initial purchase gained for them."[4]

So don't seek mere success or power or possessions or happiness, Jesus tells us. Seek God first and foremost in your life, and everything you need will be provided for you. As Paul could testify, "My God shall supply all your need according to His riches in glory by Christ Jesus" (Philippians 4:19).

CHAPTER 61

The Division That Brings Unity

> *"Do you suppose that I came to give peace on earth? I tell you, not at all, but rather division. From now on five in one house will be divided: three against two, and two against three."* Luke 12:51-52

Not all the promises from Jesus' mouth sound positive. Many do not burst with sunshine and roses. Yet He gave them all for our benefit—even the ones that seem ominous.

When our Lord promised that members of many households would find themselves pitted against one another, He simply wanted to prepare His followers for the future. His words in Luke 12 do not contradict the idea that He is the Prince of Peace (Isaiah 9:6). Nor do they mock the angelic message to the shepherds on the first Christmas: "On earth peace, goodwill toward men!" (Luke 2:14). Rather, Jesus spoke of the division that brings unity.

I would never suggest that Christians should be unnecessarily divisive, seek to misunderstand others, or refuse to accept them and instead act with complete intolerance. But neither can we have unity at any cost; down that road lies communism or fascism.

While unity is important, truth is even more important. Unity based on a lie cannot do anything in the long run but bring disaster. For the most part, the German nation under Nazism remained unified—but it was a unity based on lies that ended in worldwide catastrophe. Unity has its crucial place, but only within the proper framework of what is true and right.

Today we often hear that right and wrong is up to the individual. We are told what is right for one may be wrong for another, for there is no such thing as universal or absolute truth. My truth may not necessarily be your truth. Therefore, if I warn someone about pursuing a lifestyle that harms not only him or her but others as well, I am branded as intolerant and mean-spirited and, of course, judgmental.

Jesus reminds us that before we can have real unity, sometimes we first must have division. Before we can have real healing, we must get some surgery. Suppose you visit a dermatologist who diagnoses you with a life-threatening skin cancer, like malignant melanoma. While he knows it threatens your life, he also knows that if he cuts it out, you have a good chance of survival. But he says to you, "I wouldn't worry about this strange growth. Go ahead on that vacation. No worries!" So you leave—at peace with his answer—and die two months later.

The problem? You felt good and suffered no immediate pain, but you desperately needed surgery. A doctor who gives such advice should be punished and have his credentials pulled. He is largely responsible for your premature death.

Now let's change the story. Let's imagine that the doctor tells you, "You have a malignant melanoma. It's a serious form of skin cancer and if left untreated, it will kill you."

How do you feel at that moment? You feel no peace; in fact, your stomach drops and your world spins. But then he says, "If I can get you into surgery today, I think we can get all of it and you will live a long life."

I admit, it would be no fun to hear that you have cancer. The operation will cause you a certain measure of pain—but the result is well worth it. By cutting into your body, the doctor is giving you hope. By bringing pain, he will bring healing. By removing the cancer, he will add years to your life.

In the same way, Jesus explained that He had a baptism of

fire to undergo, but that very fire would bring life to others. Jesus' death on the cross set ablaze a worldwide firestorm of division and strife. Yet it is that very strife, that very conflict, that ultimately will bring the greatest unity—not unity at any cost, but unity built firmly on truth and righteousness.

Jesus did not come to bring peace to those who willfully live in opposition to Him. Rather, He wants to wake them up to the reality of their situation. If they do not truly repent, they will not only suffer on this earth the results of their rebellion but will face an eternal judgment.

The Christian message, according to Scripture, is "the gospel of peace" (Ephesians 6:15) because it offers the only way to bring peace between a holy God and sinful man. It also shows the only way for securing truly peaceful relationships between people.

But because both the world system and human nature are sinful, God's offer of peace continues to be rejected and considered offensive. This brings conflict into the most intimate of human relationships so that sometimes people's enemies are the members of their own household.

Remember, though, only this division can ultimately bring unity. Suppose one person in a family comes to Christ. Immediately that decision causes a certain amount of friction because that person adopts an entirely different outlook on life and a new set of values and interests. The individual wants to read the Bible, go to church, talk about the Lord, maybe even wants to pray before meals.

Yet that kind of division can be good. Why? Because that new believer is merely being light in a dark place—and that's our job as Christians. The friction caused by this person's newfound faith also brings a positive influence that can ultimately result in the conversion of those who don't know the Lord.

It is the division that brings unity.

And that's a promise that brings peace!

CHAPTER 62

How to Quench Your Thirst

Jesus answered and said to her, "Whoever drinks of this water will thirst again, but whoever drinks of the water that I shall give him will never thirst. But the water that I shall give him will become in him a fountain of water springing up into everlasting life." John 4:13-14

Have you ever grown so thirsty that nothing seemed to quench your thirst? Not Coke or water, not even Gatorade! No matter how much you drank, your thirst raged on.

In the same way, deep inside each one of us boils a deep, spiritual thirst—a thirst for God Himself. All attempts to quench and satisfy this thirst by other means inevitably meet with failure.

One hot afternoon Jesus met a thirsty woman who had come five times to the well of personal fulfillment in marriage, hoping to meet the perfect man capable of granting all her desires. But time and again she had gone away disappointed.

Jesus encountered this Samaritan woman at the well of Jacob, where she came during the hottest part of the day. Others visited the well to draw water during the evening, but as a social outcast, she had to brave the simmering heat. She had been married and divorced five times and at that moment was living with a man outside of wedlock. The villagers considered her immoral, and she had no desire to mingle with the women of the town as they trudged to the well in the coolness of the evening.

But Jesus was different. He asked her for a cup of water—an outrageous request, since Jews and Samaritans hated one another. An ordinary, orthodox Jew would have thrown the cup to the ground, but Jesus immediately appealed to the woman's curiosity and her inner spiritual thirst.

She responded to His request with flippant, cynical words. No doubt she had grown distrustful of all men since so many had mistreated her. Although she had looked, she had never found the fulfillment she longed for in a relationship with a man. She probably thought, *What is this guy doing? What game is he playing with me? What does he really want?*

Many today are searching for the perfect relationship. Disgruntled husbands or wives sometimes say, "My marriage isn't working out. We've lost the romance." So they start looking around for someone else. They think, *He's so much kinder than my inconsiderate husband,* or, *She's so much more attractive than my ungrateful wife.* So they engage in extramarital affairs and adulterous relationships. Finally, when they terminate their marriages and marry another, they feel great shock to discover that their problems follow them—and actually get worse!

Possibly this woman thought that if she didn't marry her sixth lover, the excitement might remain—but that didn't work, either. Still, she sensed something missing in her life. What she and so many like her don't understand is that they are trying to fill a void in their lives created by the Lord Himself. When you get down to it, it's really a loneliness for God. So Jesus told her, pointing to the well, "Whoever drinks of this water will thirst again" (John 4:13).

One could write those words, "Whoever drinks of this water will thirst again," over many pursuits in life.

If you drink from the well of materialism and possessions, you will thirst again. Once you get what you want, you'll soon tire of it and want more. "Hell and Destruction are never full; so the eyes of man are never satisfied" (Proverbs 27:20). There will always be a newer model, a better version just a little faster than yours.

If you drink of the well of pleasure, you will thirst again. Pleasure is so short-lived and if the activity is sinful in nature, the consequences so severe.

So Jesus offered the woman "living water"–flowing water, as from a stream or river. Jesus promised her inner satisfaction, a spring in her heart that would satisfy her deepest longings and spiritual needs. Yet before she could drink of this living water, something in the woman's life had to be set straight. Jesus forced her to admit her sin because there can be no conversion without conviction, no forgiveness without repentance.

The woman had come to Jacob's well to get water, but there she found a greater purpose. She believed Jesus' testimony about Himself, and her heart instantly filled up with living water. Just as Peter, James, John, and Andrew had earlier forsaken their nets and boats, so she forsook her waterpot and followed Jesus (John 4:28).

What a change came over her! She immediately became the first female evangelist of the New Testament. "Come, see," she told her neighbors. She just had to tell others what she had found. A changed life wields tremendous power. It's hard to dismiss a witness like the man Jesus healed from blindness, who testified, "One thing I know: that though I was blind, now I see" (John 9:25).

From what well are you seeking to be satisfied? The well of pleasure? Sin *is* pleasurable for a season (Hebrews 11:25)–but the wages of sin is death (Romans 6:23). The well of possessions? "For what profit is it to a man if he gains the whole world, and loses his own soul?" (Matthew 16:26). The well of some "perfect" relationship? Look at this woman!

There is a void in your life that only God can fill, a thirst only Jesus can quench. So Peter says, "Repent therefore and be converted, that your sins may be blotted out, so that times of refreshing may come from the presence of the Lord" (Acts 3:19).

Stop drinking from the stagnant mud puddles of this world and take a long, refreshing, cool drink of living water!

CHAPTER 63

A Real Choice

"All that the Father gives Me will come to Me, and the one who comes to Me I will by no means cast out."

John 6:37

Missionary George Smith may have considered his ministry a failure. He had been in Africa only a short time when fierce opponents drove him from the continent. He left behind only one convert, a poor woman. He died soon after, while on his knees praying for Africa.

Years later, a group of men stumbled onto the place where George Smith had ministered. They found a copy of the Scriptures the missionary had left behind, and they met the sole convert of Smith's ministry. In God's providence, the encounter these men had with Smith's Bible and his solitary convert had far-reaching effects. A century afterward, a mission agency discovered that more than 13,000 converts had emerged from the ministry George Smith began.

God loves to bring men and women to Himself, especially against long odds. And He loves to honor Jesus' promise: "All that the Father gives Me will come to Me, and the one who comes to Me I will by no means cast out." Notice three things about this promise:

ALL WHO ARE CHOSEN WILL COME.

Is it true that God chooses some and not others? In a sense, the answer is yes. Yet that is not to say that God wants any to perish, for He wants all to come to repentance (2 Peter 3:9).

So does God pick and reject people randomly? Is His choice

totally arbitrary? That certainly does not seem to be the case. The Bible insists that both God's choice (Romans 8:29-30; Ephesians 1:5, 11; 2 Thessalonians 2:13) and our choice (2 Corinthians 5:11; Deuteronomy 30:19; Ezekiel 33:11) are real choices.

"But that's too hard for me to grasp!" someone says. "I can't reconcile that in my mind!" Welcome to the club. But don't worry; if God were small enough for us to understand, He wouldn't be big enough to worship.

Think of it this way. Before you were saved, there was a door in front of you with the words inscribed on it, "Whosoever will, let him come." After you walked in that door you saw inscribed on the other side, "Chosen in Christ from the foundation of the world."

ALL WHO COME ARE WELCOMED.

Jesus promises that He will never drive away anyone who comes to Him. No matter what sin you have committed or wrong you have done, God will welcome and forgive you. All you must do is come.

ALL WHO COME ARE SAFE FOREVER.

"This is the will of the Father who sent Me," Jesus said, "that of all He has given Me I should lose nothing" (John 6:39). No believer can be plucked out of His hand (John 10:28-29). We do not have to live in fear of falling away, for no one who has fallen away has ever been taken against his or her will.

When Jesus uttered some of His most difficult teachings (John 6:48-66), many followers "went back and walked with Him no more" (verse 66). When He asked the Twelve if they too would leave, Peter answered, "Lord, to whom shall we go? You have the words of eternal life" (verse 68). This is the mark of a true believer: he or she *will not* quit! It is clear that Jesus would have let His disciples go had they chosen to leave. He does not hold any of us against our will.

Peter replied to the Lord's question, in effect, "Lord, we

have been thinking about it. We have investigated the alternatives. We don't understand You at times. What You say does not always make sense at the time. Others have laughed at us for following You. But we have looked at the alternatives and it comes down to this: Lord, we have never found anyone who can do what You do. To whom else shall we go? What You say to us has met our deepest need, has delivered us from our sins, and freed us from our fears. We have never heard words like Yours. They explain us and they explain life to us. They satisfy us. Nobody speaks like You do; nobody understands life like You do. That holds us."

This passage reveals three groups of "disciples."

1. There are those who won't quit, who can't quit, because the Lord has captured their hearts. May this group grow—and may you be among them.
2. There are those who start out well, who follow Jesus for a while, but who eventually drop out and quit.
3. Finally, there are those who are like Judas. These individuals appear to be Christians but are not. They are connivers, deceivers, and liars. The apostle John calls them "antichrists" (1 John 2:18-19). Quite frankly, they are on their way to hell.

George Smith teaches us that evangelism can be tough work. You may not see the fruit of the seed you planted until much later in life, or perhaps not until after you reach heaven. But Jesus promises, "All that the Father gives Me will come to Me, and the one who comes to Me I will by no means cast out." So keep praying for those who don't know the Lord. Keep sowing those seeds. And never give up!

CHAPTER **64**

The Death of Death

> *"Most assuredly, I say to you, if anyone keeps My word he shall never see death."* John 8:51

On the last night of our Harvest Crusade in San Diego, a ninety-year-old woman named Henny listened intently to a message called, "What Happens beyond the Grave." At the conclusion of the service and at Henny's urging, a few close friends grabbed her wheelchair and helped her get down to the field to make a public commitment to Jesus Christ.

Henny was also blind. After she prayed to receive the Lord into her life, she turned to her counselor and said that she couldn't wait to get to heaven, because there she would enjoy eternal sight.

While Henny had no hope of seeing before she died, she fully expected to have 20/20 vision (at least!) after she entered the Savior's presence. As a blind woman, Henny will never "see death." But as a believer, she will "see life"—forever!

The wonderful thing about Jesus' promise in John 8:51 is that it applies equally to the blind and the sighted, to men and women, to the rich and the poor, to the old and the young. Jesus' promise applies to everyone who will accept His offer: "Most assuredly, I say to you, if anyone keeps My word he shall never see death."

What does it mean to "keep" Jesus' word? And in what sense will those who keep that word "never see death"?

Just a little while after Jesus made this promise, He fleshed out His meaning in an encounter with His friends Mary and Martha (John 11:1-44). The sisters' only brother, Lazarus, had died after a short illness. When Jesus arrived, Martha gently scolded Him:

> "Lord, if You had been here, my brother would not have died. But even now I know that whatever You ask of God, God will give You." Jesus said to her, "Your brother will rise again." Martha said to Him, "I know that he will rise again in the resurrection at the last day." Jesus said to her, "I am the resurrection and the life. He who believes in Me, though he may die, he shall live. And whoever lives and believes in Me shall never die." John 11:21-26

How does this passage flesh out the Lord's meaning? On the one hand, Jesus declares that the one who believes in Him "*may* die." On the other hand, whoever lives and believes in Him "*shall never* die." So which is it?

It's both.

On the one hand, physical death comes to every mortal man and woman. No one escapes death; it comes by divine decree: "It is appointed for men to die once, but after this the judgment" (Hebrews 9:27). Even believers in Christ have to pass through this shadowy doorway. So Jesus says, "He who believes in Me, though he may die . . ."

Yet Jesus came to earth for the very purpose of triumphing over what might be called the "first death." The apostle Paul tells us that the "last enemy that will be destroyed is death" (1 Corinthians 15:26) and that Jesus Christ "has abolished death and brought life and immortality to light through the gospel" (2 Timothy 1:10). The book of Hebrews declares that through His death Jesus will "destroy him who had the power of death, that is, the devil, and release those who through fear of death were all their lifetime subject to bondage" (Hebrews 2:14-15). This means that although the first death continues to operate in our world, it can no longer bite and sting the believer as it once did. Jesus has taken care of that (1 Corinthians 15:55).

The "second death," however, is an altogether different matter. The Bible teaches that those who refuse Jesus' offer of life "shall have their part in the lake which burns with fire and brimstone, which is the second death" (Revelation 21:8). Not so for those who place their faith in Jesus! They have nothing to fear, for they "shall not be hurt by the second death" (Revelation 2:11). In fact, over them "the second death has no power" (Revelation 20:6). While everyone experiences the first death, only unbelievers suffer the second death.

We will all die physically, but we do not need to fear the second death.

This is why Jesus could say that "whoever lives and believes in Me shall never die." No one who puts his or her trust in Christ will ever have to face even a moment, even a nanosecond, in the lake of fire, which is the second death. These believers—those who keep Jesus' word—shall never see death. They go from life to life, passing through the first death yet untouched by the second death.

"The one who believes in Christ has eternal life that transcends physical death," writes Bible scholar Merrill C. Tenney. "If he is living and believing, he will never die but will make an instant transition from the old life to the new life."[5]

Those who keep Jesus' words both *believe* them and *live* them. True belief in Jesus Christ is the quality of faith that takes you unto Him, to commit yourself to Him, to rest completely upon Him, to trust Him fully. And such genuine faith results in a radical change in attitudes and lifestyle.

It also results in something else: a blessed eternity without a single glimpse of death. And that goes whether you're blind or not.

Henny is in heaven now and knows that by personal experience. You can, too.

CHAPTER 65

May the Force Be with You?

"Behold, I send the Promise of My Father upon you."
Luke 24:49

What's the best gift you ever received? Was it something you asked for? Something you saw in an advertisement? Chances are, whatever it was, it could truly be characterized as an "it" rather than a "who."

Not so the greatest gift promised to us by the Savior. For when Jesus said to His disciples, "Behold, I send the Promise of My Father upon you," He spoke of a Person, the very Holy Spirit of God, not some "thing."

Sometimes believers think of the Holy Spirit like the fictional Force of the *Star Wars* films, as in "May the Force be with you." And granted, sometimes Scripture *does* compare the Spirit to inanimate forces, such as wind or fire, or says that He came upon Jesus in the form of a dove.

Yet we must be careful how we handle such descriptions, for Jesus referred to Himself as "the bread of life" (John 6:35) and "the door of the sheep" (John 10:7). The Bible also refers to God the Father as a "refuge" who will protect us under "His wings" (Psalm 91:4) and as a "consuming fire" (Hebrews 12:29). Does this mean that Jesus is a literal loaf of bread or a door, or that God the Father is a pile of rocks, a blast furnace, or some kind of giant bird? Of course not.

In the same way, the Bible never suggests that the Holy Spirit is a mere force or power. Jesus said of the Spirit, "And when *He* has come, *He* will . . ." (John 16:8, emphasis added). The Holy Spirit is not an it or a force, but a definite, divine personality.

While certain soulless things *seem* to have a mind of their own, they really don't. Consider the amazing power of today's computers. While the first-generation computers took up whole buildings, they did far less than what a high-end laptop can do today. Yet as incredible as they are, computers don't have personality.

Every person possesses at least three characteristics: intelligence, will, and emotion. Since human beings possess all three, they can be considered persons. But trees, plants, rocks, cars and yes, even computers, cannot be considered persons because they all lack personality. Not so the Holy Spirit!

THE HOLY SPIRIT HAS INTELLIGENCE.

Paul writes, "The Spirit searches all things, even the deep things of God. For who among men knows the thoughts of a man except the man's spirit within him? In the same way no one knows the thoughts of God except the Spirit of God" (1 Corinthians 2:10-11, NIV). Paul declares that the Spirit knows the thoughts of God. Only a person with intelligence can know things. A fire doesn't know anything, nor does a plant, a tree, or even a computer. But the Holy Spirit *does* know—to a far greater degree than we ever will.

THE HOLY SPIRIT HAS A WILL.

Paul informs us that the Holy Spirit distributes the gifts of the Spirit "to each one individually as He *wills*" (1 Corinthians 12:11, emphasis added). It is the Holy Spirit who decides what kind of spiritual gifts each believer should receive. He decides that this one should get the gift of faith and that one should receive the gift of prophecy. Such decisions require that He possess a will.

The apostles once prefaced their judgment on a question of church doctrine by saying, "It seemed good to the Holy Spirit, and to us" (Acts 15:28)—thus demonstrating the will of the Holy

Spirit. We're told that the Spirit also sets apart individuals for service: "While they were worshiping the Lord and fasting, the Holy Spirit said, 'Set apart for me Barnabas and Saul for the work to which I have called them'" (Acts 13:2, NIV). Only a person with a will can communicate in this way.

THE HOLY SPIRIT HAS EMOTION.

Does it surprise you that the Spirit has emotion? It really shouldn't. Just as someone can say or do something to hurt, sadden, grieve, or anger you, so the Holy Spirit also can be hurt, saddened, grieved, or angered (Ephesians 4:30; Hebrews 3:11). When Ananias and Sapphira lied to the Holy Spirit (Acts 5:3)—something, by the way, that one can do only to a person—the Spirit responded by requiring their very lives. His action caused "great fear [to come] upon all the church and upon all who heard these things" (Acts 5:11). The Holy Spirit of God is not some emotionless automaton or heartless force but a divine Person with powerful emotions.

We must remember this when we speak to our children about the "Promise of the Father" who indwells us. They sometimes hear what we say but understand our words in a way different from what we intend. I heard about a mom and her three-year-old daughter who were riding in their car. The little girl suddenly put her head on her mother's chest and began to listen.

"What are you doing?" the mom asked.

"I'm listening for Jesus in your heart," came the reply.

"Well, what do you hear?" her mom inquired.

The little girl innocently replied, "Sounds to me like He's making coffee!"

Let's make sure our kids know that the Holy Spirit who indwells us is a living Person, not an automatic coffeemaker!

The Holy Spirit is more than a force. He is God, and He is in your life today, ready to empower and enable you to be the person God wants you to be.

May the Holy Spirit be with you!

CHAPTER **66**

The Worst Sin You Can Commit

"And when He has come, He will convict the world of sin, and of righteousness, and of judgment." John 16:8

What would you consider the worst sin you could commit? Adultery? Stealing? Murder? You might be surprised by the answer the Bible gives.

The worst sin—and the one with the most far-reaching consequences—is this: to refuse to believe in Jesus Christ. Murder and rape and other heinous sins merely reveal the sin inside those who do not know God. The worst sin we can commit is not believing in Jesus; it is for that sin that people will be judged.

Jesus taught that the Holy Spirit convicts guilty men and women of sin "because they do not believe in Me" (John 16:9). Notice that this sin is singular, not plural. The Spirit will convict the individual not of sins in general but of sin—of missing the mark of righteousness set by God in Christ. Again, on that final day, it will not so much be the sin question as it will be the Son question. The same issue that faced Pilate faces us: What do you think of Jesus Christ? All sins can be dealt with and forgiven if we believe in Jesus.

Notice, too, that it is the Spirit's work to bring about this conviction. We can try all we want to produce a sense of guilt and wrongdoing. But only the Holy Spirit can effectively convict a person of sin. Our interference can even hinder the process of conversion. Well-meaning but misguided believers sometimes turn to pressure tactics; but if someone can be "pressured into" the kingdom, they can also be "pressured out." We must leave conviction of sin to the Holy Spirit.

At the same time, we must not forget that knowledge brings responsibility. Jesus said, "If I had not come and spoken to them, they would have no sin, but now they have no excuse for their sin" (John 15:22). It is a grave thing to shake off the conviction of the Spirit. "He who believes in the Son of God has the witness in himself," wrote John; "he who does not believe God has made Him a liar, because he has not believed the testimony that God has given of His Son" (1 John 5:10).

Jesus reveals that the Holy Spirit has come not only to convict of sin but also to convict "of righteousness, because I go to My Father and you see Me no more" (John 16:10). And Jesus insisted that our righteousness must exceed that of the scribes and Pharisees.

I remember when I first read that statement as a young believer. I knew the Pharisees were devoutly religious men. And I thought, *How could my righteousness possibly surpass theirs?* But then I realized this is not a righteousness I can produce on my own. In fact, even on my best day, my righteousness is pretty much throwaway because "our righteousnesses are like filthy rags" (Isaiah 64:6). So for the proud, self-confident individual who thinks he or she doesn't need Jesus, the Holy Spirit comes with convicting, convincing power to set the record straight.

Before any of us can appreciate the love of God, we must first see our utter depravity and desperate need for a Savior. We must let go of this flimsy branch of self-righteousness that keeps us from the true righteousness of God. True righteousness remains unavailable to us until we become aware of personal sin.

Last, Jesus said the Spirit came to convict us "of judgment, because the ruler of this world is judged" (John 16:11). We might have expected Him to say, "Of the judgment to come against all sinners," for that day clearly looms large in the life of every nonbeliever. But Jesus threw us a curve. The Savior did not speak of some future judgment but of a judgment that already has taken place.

The ruler or prince of this world, Satan, was judged at Calvary. When Jesus went to the cross and died in our place, Satan lost his death grip on humanity. Jesus blotted out "the handwriting of requirements that was against us, which was contrary to us. And He has taken it out of the way, having nailed it to the cross. Having disarmed principalities and powers, He made a public spectacle of them, triumphing over them in it" (Colossians 2:14-15).

This wonderful promise is true *only* for the child of God. The nonbeliever has no protection against the onslaught of the devil; he or she remains fair game.

Could Satan have you in his grip right now? Do you feel trapped by a lifestyle of lust and immorality, drugs and alcohol, violence and crime? Or perhaps you feel self-righteous, like you don't need God.

Meanwhile, the clock continues to tick. With every movement of the second hand, you move a step closer to eternity. The Holy Spirit has been convicting you of your sin, showing you that your righteousness is not enough, calling you to Jesus. Through the Bible He says to you, "And the Spirit and the bride say, 'Come!' And let him who hears say, 'Come!' And let him who thirsts come. Whoever desires, let him take the water of life freely" (Revelation 22:17).

The Spirit convicts us of sin, righteousness, and judgment, but He wants most of all to give us the assurance of forgiven sin. Why not let Him do what He really desires to do? Why not come to Jesus? Or if you have already done that, help someone else to follow your example.

CHAPTER 67

He Teaches Us

"But the Helper, the Holy Spirit, whom the Father will send in My name, He will teach you all things, and bring to your remembrance all things that I said to you."

John 14:26

One night a new Christian attended a meeting in which the speaker stressed the need to share the gospel with others. The young man, a barber, knew he was lacking in this area, so he determined to speak about the Lord to the first person who entered his barber shop the next day.

The following morning, after the first customer of the day sat down and got a cape tucked around his neck, the barber began to strap his razor vigorously. Testing the edge, he turned to the man in the chair and asked, "Friend, are you ready to die and meet God?"

The man took one look at the razor and fled out the door—cape and all!

While the young barber meant well, he really could have taken better advantage of the wonderful promise Jesus gave us in John 14: "But the Helper, the Holy Spirit, whom the Father will send in My name, He will teach you all things, and bring to your remembrance all things that I said to you."

Paul said it like this: "It is written: 'Eye has not seen, nor ear heard, nor have entered into the heart of man the things which God has prepared for those who love him.' But God has revealed them to us through His Spirit" (1 Corinthians 2:9).

So how does the Spirit teach us, and in what ways does He bring to our remembrance the lessons that Jesus taught?

Consider just three aspects of the teaching ministry of the Holy Spirit.

HE TEACHES THROUGH A SERMON OR MESSAGE.

The Spirit's insight often comes while we listen to a message. When a teacher or preacher presents some point or series of truths that really hits home, we are tempted to think, *That person is the greatest preacher of all time.* Not so; it was really the Holy Spirit teaching us. In fact, the truths that just hit us between the eyes may not be the same ones the Spirit brought home for another person. The Spirit often uses the same spoken word to teach varying lessons to different people.

HE TEACHES US WHILE WE SPEAK OF CHRIST.

Have you ever been ministering to a fellow believer or sharing the gospel with an unbeliever when suddenly your mind started filling up with relevant verses and passages of Scripture that you didn't even know you knew? You were so good you wanted to take notes on yourself! At that moment, the Spirit brought those biblical insights to mind for a specific purpose. It's not that you suddenly got smarter or were able to communicate in a powerful way the message of a difficult passage; no, the Spirit worked through you to bring His wisdom to bear.

HE OPENS UP SCRIPTURE.

It is the ministry of the Holy Spirit to bring God's Word to our minds when we need it. No doubt this ranks among His greatest teaching ministries.

The Holy Spirit has the ability to open up passages in an incredible way. That is why we need to regularly spend time in Bible study, so the door remains open for the Holy Spirit to illuminate God's Word to us.

Let's be honest: certain passages can be difficult to grasp. But the good news is that the same Holy Spirit who inspired the Scripture can illuminate it for our benefit. He sheds more light on the original light.

Paul called the Bible "the sword of the Spirit" (Ephesians 6:17), so it stands to reason that without a good working knowledge of Scripture, we will surely become casualties in the spiritual battle.

May I ask what kind of shape *your* sword is in? Is it polished from daily use and sharpened on the anvil of experience? Or has it grown rusty from lack of preparation or dulled by disobedience?

Satan will do everything he can to keep you from the Bible, just as he did with Eve. First he questioned God's Word, then he distorted it, and finally added to it. Success or failure in the Christian life largely depends upon how much of the Bible we get into our lives and how much we obey God through it.

Every believer must make it a top priority to memorize the Word of God. We often forget what we ought to remember and remember what we ought to forget. To this day, some of my memory banks overflow with useless jingles and song lyrics I have heard over the years. We need to make a conscious effort to keep the Word of God at the forefront of our minds. Moses tells us to "lay up these words . . . in your heart" (Deuteronomy 11:18). Once Scripture gets stored in our memory, it will always be there for the Spirit to utilize. It will bring comfort to our hearts and needed strength in times of intense temptation. We ought to so saturate our minds with His Word so when we face crucial decisions or sharp temptations, we will automatically remember the Scriptures that relate to that particular situation.

While it is true that Jesus promised the Spirit will teach you all things and remind you of everything He said to you, we must remember that He will *not* necessarily remind us of something we have not learned.

So dig into the Word of God, friend, so that the Holy Spirit has some material to work with in your life!

CHAPTER **68**

Need Some Help?

*"I will pray the Father, and He will give you another
Helper, that He may abide with you forever."* John 14:16

The apostles knew they could depend upon Jesus. When they
needed His help, they had come to expect it. So it should have
surprised none of them when Jesus gave His disciples a big
promise of divine help.

"It's true that I'm going away and that where I'm going you
can't come right now," He said, in effect. "But I don't want you
to be worried! I'm going to prepare a place for you, and in time
I will come again and receive you unto myself. But in the
meantime, I will not leave you as orphans; I will not leave you
without any help. I will ask the Father and He will give you Another to come alongside and help you."

The word *helper* (verse 16) comes from the Greek term
parakletos, "one who is called alongside to help." While Jesus
walked the earth, He was present to help the disciples however
they might need Him. But on the day the Lord ascended into
heaven, He told His disciples (and all His followers, including
us) that from then on He would lead and guide and help them
in an entirely new way. He would be with them and help them
through the Holy Spirit.

To this day, the Holy Spirit is actively at work in the lives of
all Christians. He works in us throughout our lives, from our
conversion to our final journey to heaven.

The Spirit is the One who convicted us of our sins before we
accepted Christ. Then, after we believed, He gave us the inner
assurance that we belong to God. Paul wrote, "The Spirit Him-

self bears witness with our spirit that we are the children of God" (Romans 8:16). God marks us as His, forever. In the Bible's language, He seals us: "In Him you also trusted, after you heard the word of truth, the gospel of your salvation; in whom also, having believed, you were sealed with the Holy Spirit of promise, who is the guarantee of our inheritance until the redemption of the purchased possession, to the praise of His glory" (Ephesians 1:13-14).

When the ancients shipped goods from one place to another, they stamped the merchandise with a wax seal imprinted with a signet ring bearing a unique mark of ownership. Important documents—say, from a king—bore the same kind of seal. The royal letter was sealed in wax and imprinted with the official seal. No one but the addressee would dare open the note.

In the same way, God has put His royal seal on us through the presence and work of the Holy Spirit. When the devil comes to make havoc of our lives, the Spirit stops him cold. Satan sees God's seal of ownership and he respects it.

It works something like this. Let's say that as a thief prepares to rip off someone's bag, he sees an ID tag on it with the name "Tyson." That's Tyson, not as in the chicken dinner but as in Mike, the fighter. The thief would think twice because he doesn't want Iron Mike coming after him.

So the devil skulks around the planet, seeking to "steal, and to kill, and to destroy" (John 10:10). But when he sees an ID tag on us—"Property of Jesus Christ, sealed and insured by the Holy Spirit"—he backs off. He knows he's outgunned. That's help with a capital *H*!

But wait—there's more. The Bible also calls the Holy Spirit the deposit guaranteeing our inheritance (2 Corinthians 5:5). Suppose you put down cash to hold something at a store. Perhaps you see a gift you want to purchase and are told you must put a certain amount down to show good faith to hold the item until you make full payment. In the same way, God wants you to know that He is sincere about redeeming you. He intends to complete His transaction, and He won't back down or change His mind. So He gives you the deposit or down payment of the Holy Spirit to show you that He means business.

I am the purchased property of Jesus Christ. I was "bought at a price" (1 Corinthians 6:20). I like that idea, because it means I am under God's divine protection. But with that privilege comes responsibility.

I have two sons. They enjoy privileges appropriate to their status as my sons. They have a roof over their heads, food, clothes, skateboards, etc. They also have open and free access to me. If something happens to them, I am there to help. This all comes with relationship. I am their father; they are my sons. I love to help my sons however I can.

But with privilege comes responsibility. So I may say to one or both of them, "Take out the trash." Now, I wouldn't say to a stranger walking by, "Hey, you—take out my trash!" But I have the right to tell my sons what to do.

In the same way, God addresses us as His sons and daughters. "You have open access to My presence," He says. "You have My presence, My protection, and My help." Yet as our Father, He has the right to tell us to "take out the trash." We look to Him for help, and He looks to us for obedience.

CHAPTER 69

A Sure Thing

"If you abide in Me, and My words abide in you, you will ask what you desire, and it shall be done for you."
John 15:7

Has anyone ever handed you a blank check and given you the instruction, "Write in any amount you want. Whatever you mark down is what you'll get"?

Probably not. And yet, a blank check is exactly what Jesus gives us in John 15:7. Almost unbelievably, He says to us, "If you abide in Me, and My words abide in you, you will ask what you desire, and it shall be done for you." What is this but a blank check from the bank of heaven?

Immediately we gravitate toward the unlimited promise of such a verse: "Ask what you desire." In the original Greek, it's even more direct: "I command you to ask, at once, something for yourself, whatever your heart desires, and it will become yours."

How's that again? *Whatever* my heart desires? *All right!* Then give me a husband! Give me ten million dollars! Make me famous!

Or is there some catch? No, but thre is certainly a condition: "*If* you abide in Me." In other words, "He who maintains a living communion with Me, and in whom My words are at home, I direct *him* to ask. . . ." To abide in Christ is to spend regular time with Him in Bible study, prayer, and in fellowship with His people. It means to walk as He walked. If I'm doing all that, I will become more like Jesus—and then I will start wanting what He wants.

Does that sound like a catch more than a condition? It's

really not. When we realize how far superior His will is to our own and that His plans for us vastly outstrip our plans for ourselves, then it becomes progressively easier and more exciting to pray for what Jesus wants. "I know the thoughts that I think toward you, says the Lord, thoughts of peace and not of evil, to give you a future and a hope" (Jeremiah 29:11).

Unfortunately, any number of things may get in the way of our praying like this. All sorts of obstacles hinder us from receiving the "blank check" God really wants to give us. Consider five of the top barriers to answered prayer:

IF YOU CANNOT PRAY IN FAITH, IT WILL HINDER YOUR PRAYERS.

James tells us that those who pray without conviction should expect no answers to their prayers. "He who doubts is like a wave of the sea driven and tossed by the wind. For let not that man suppose that he will receive anything from the Lord; he is a double-minded man, unstable in all his ways" (James 1:6-8). When we pray, we must pray in faith—not as if we already know how God will answer but certain that our prayer pleases His holy heart.

IF YOU PRAY SELFISHLY, IT WILL HINDER YOUR PRAYERS.

Do you pray that God's Word will be honored, that His people will be blessed, and that His servants will be protected and sustained? Or do you pray that He might lavish on you the latest trinket or luxury item? James 4:2-3 tells us, "The reason you don't have what you want is that you don't ask God for it. And even when you do ask, you don't get it because your whole motive is wrong—you want only what will give you pleasure" (NLT).

IF YOU REFUSE TO FORGIVE, IT WILL HINDER YOUR PRAYERS.

Too many of God's children carry a huge spiritual chip on

their shoulders. Yet our Lord told us, "If you do not forgive men their trespasses, neither will your Father forgive your trespasses" (Matthew 6:15). Unforgiveness is simply unacceptable in God's family, and those who harbor it in their hearts will see their prayers go unanswered.

IF YOU NEGLECT YOUR WIFE'S NEEDS, IT WILL HINDER YOUR PRAYERS.

Not many men realize that the way they treat their wives carries immense spiritual consequences, but that's exactly what the Bible teaches. First Peter 3:7 says, "Husbands, . . . dwell with [your wives] with understanding, giving honor to the wife, as to the weaker vessel, and as being heirs together of the grace of life, that your prayers may not be hindered."

God wants you to have your home in proper spiritual order before you come to Him. To dwell with your wife does not just mean to live with her but rather to be aligned to her. Husband, let me ask you this: What are your wife's dreams? aspirations? concerns? God wants you to know and tend to her spiritual needs.

IF YOU HARBOR UNCONFESSED SIN, IT WILL HINDER YOUR PRAYERS.

God is under no obligation to hear the prayers of those who refuse to give up their pet sins. He never promises to hear the prayers of those who put their will above His or who cover their ears when they hear the still, small voice of the Spirit's conviction. In fact, He promises the very opposite: "But your iniquities have separated you from your God; and your sins have hidden His face from you, so that He will not hear" (Isaiah 59:2).

To those who abide in Christ, however, the news is just the opposite. A blank check awaits, backed up by the unlimited funds of paradise. Just make sure you read the contract and put those conditions into action.

CHAPTER **70**

Don't Give Up!

"So I say to you, ask, and it will be given to you; seek,
and you will find; knock, and it will be opened to you."

Luke 11:9

How many of us ask God for something once or twice, then immediately give up when we don't get the answer we want? We want the answer "Go!" or, barring that, at least a definite "No."

But sometimes God says to us, "Slow." When this is His answer, He is saying to us, "Not quite yet, but soon—so keep on asking!"

The Lord's language in Luke 11:9 is unusually compelling. He makes use of three strong verbs that indicate an ascending intensity of request. Jesus tells us, "Ask, and it will be given to you; seek, and you will find; knock, and it will be opened to you." Let's look a bit closer at these three verbs and what they can tell us about effective prayer.

ASK IMPLIES REQUESTING ASSISTANCE.

We begin prayer at this level, when we realize our need and ask God for help. The very fact that we ask implies that we do so humbly. We don't demand of God or insist that He answer according to our preconceived notions. Yet we ask because we know that what we want or need lies outside of our power.

SEEK DENOTES ASKING BUT IMPLIES ACTION.

The idea here is not merely to express our need but to get up and look around for help. Seeking involves effort. We do not passively sit by and hope that, just perhaps, our request might get noticed. Instead, we take decisive action to bring the desire of our heart to heaven's center stage. We invest ourselves in the prayer and actively seek out others to join us in the work.

KNOCK INCLUDES ASKING, ACTING, AND PERSEVERING. This last stage of prayer is like someone desperately pounding on a closed door. This is not a polite rapping or an occasional use of the door knocker; this is urgent, knuckle-pounding perseverance. Jesus asked,

> Which of you shall have a friend and go to him at mid-night and say to him, "Friend, lend me three loaves; for a friend of mine has come to me on his journey, and I have nothing to set before him"; and he will answer from within and say, "Do not trouble me; the door is now shut, and my children are with me in bed; I cannot rise and give to you"? I say to you, though he will not rise and give to him because he is his friend, yet because of his persis-tence he will rise and give him as many as he needs.
>
> Luke 11:5-8

The stacking of these three terms creates an extremely force-ful result. The text more literally reads, "*Keep on asking,* and it will be given to you; *keep on seeking,* and you will find it; *keep on knocking,* and the door will be opened." Jesus calls us to passionate, persistent prayer.

In the book of Acts we read how Jewish officials imprisoned Simon Peter. James had just been executed, and Peter seemed to be next. So what did the believers do? They prayed! But not just any old prayer: "Lord, would you (yawn) deliver Peter? Z-z-z-z-z." No indeed. They passionately, fervently prayed for Pe-ter's deliverance. "But constant prayer was offered to God for him by the church" (Acts 12:5).

The prayer that has power is offered continually. Constant prayer might be translated as "earnest prayer," or more liter-ally, "stretch-outwardly prayer." The same word is used of Jesus in Luke 22:44: "He prayed more earnestly. Then His sweat became like great drops of blood falling down to the ground." In other words, the prayer that prevails with God is the prayer into which we put our whole soul, stretching out toward God in intense and even agonizing desire.

Much of our prayer lacks power because it lacks heart. But if we put so little heart into our prayers, can we expect God to put much heart into answering them? God promises that His people will find Him when they search for Him with all their hearts (Jeremiah 29:13).

Believers who approach God in this way will never find Him too busy or too preoccupied with other requests. Aren't you glad that God doesn't have a computer phone system when you call on Him? Can you imagine facing an immediate crisis, calling out to God, and hearing this response?

"Hello. You have reached heaven. God is unavailable right now.

Push #1 if you need forgiveness.

Push #2 if you need healing.

Push #3 if you need to know the will of God.

Push #4 if you have another problem."

No, God never responds to passionate prayer with anything like this. Still, He may delay the answer to your prayer. Unconfessed sin always gums up the works of prayer. One way to clear the air is to pray, like the psalmist, "Search me, O God, and know my heart; test me and know my anxious thoughts. See if there is any offensive way in me, and lead me in the way everlasting" (Psalm 139:23, NIV).

The old Puritan Richard Baxter once wisely wrote, "Spend your time in nothing which you know must be repented of; in nothing on which you might not pray for the blessing of God; in nothing which you could not review with a quiet conscience on your dying bed; in nothing which you might not safely and properly be found doing if death should surprise you in the act."

Live like that, and you'll soon be praying with passion.

CHAPTER **71**

With God, Nothing Is Impossible

"If you have faith as a mustard seed, you can say to this mulberry tree, 'Be pulled up by the roots and be planted in the sea,' and it would obey you." Luke 17:6

Listen to some television preachers and you might get the idea that in order for God to listen to your prayers, you first have to develop a mountain-sized megafaith—the kind those preachers themselves supposedly possess and who then encourage you to send in your "gifts of faith."

But is this true? Does the Lord really reserve His best answers to prayer for the spiritual elite? If we want God to hear us, do we really have to aspire to be like those who have allegedly reached a higher spiritual plane than most mortals?

Not if Jesus is to be believed. For the Master promised His followers, "If you have faith as a mustard seed, you can say to this mulberry tree, 'Be pulled up by the roots and be planted in the sea,' and it would obey you."

And just how big is a mustard seed? Is it the size of a beach ball or maybe even as large as a weather balloon? Hardly. Elsewhere Jesus described it as "the smallest seed you plant in the ground" (Mark 4:31, NIV).

Such a seed may be small, but it's potent. It may seem insignificant next to walnuts or coconuts, but it has a remarkable capacity to grow into something much larger. Don't let its small size fool you. Jesus is saying to us, "You don't need a certain *quantity* of faith so much as the right *quality* of faith." It's not size but character that counts.

237

The great preacher G. Campbell Morgan once wrote of a re-markable tomb in Italy. The person who planned to be buried there purchased a huge block of granite to be placed on the top so that after he died, God would find it impossible to resurrect him.

But a funny thing happened between the time workers dug the hole for his casket and when the block of granite was placed over the top. A little bird apparently flew over the site and dropped an acorn into the hole. As the years passed, that little acorn grew into a massive tree that pushed up against the huge block of granite, eventually splitting it in two. When visitors see the grave today, they can see how the living power in the acorn split the massive granite slab right down the middle.

Looks like God won. And with a little acorn, no less!

Jesus says to us, in effect, "If you have faith as a grain of a mustard seed—if your faith has a living quality about it, if your faith is more than a dead orthodoxy, if your faith amounts to more than the mere acceptance of certain doctrinal state-ments and is instead a living thing that produces godly results in keeping with what you believe—then nothing will be impos-sible for you. Pray, and expect God to answer you."

What the angel Gabriel said to the virgin Mary, God says to everyone with a living, genuine faith: "For with God nothing will be impossible" (Luke 1:37).

Notice: This is *not* "faith in faith" but rather "faith in God." As Jesus said in another Gospel, "Have faith in God. For assur-edly, I say to you, whoever says to this mountain, 'Be removed and be cast into the sea,' and does not doubt in his heart, but believes that those things he says will be done, he will have whatever he says" (Mark 11:22-23).

Faith is not some mystical power that I unleash; it is trust in God Himself. To have faith in God means that I align myself with His perfect will as revealed in Scripture. "Now this is the confidence that we have in Him, that if we ask anything ac-cording to His will, He hears us," writes John. "And if we know that He hears us, whatever we ask, we know that we have the petitions that we have asked of Him" (1 John 5:14-15). Therefore to have faith in God does not mean that I will receive whatever *I want* but whatever *God wills* for me.

And how can we know God's will for us? Jesus made it quite simple. He said, "If you abide in Me, and My words abide in you, you will ask what you desire, and it shall be done for you" (John 15:7). The way to know God's will, Jesus taught, is to abide in Christ. Those who remain in close relationship with Him, who meditate on His words, and who put them into practice are the only ones capable of praying in God's will. And their prayers will always be answered.

On the other hand, there are prayers that *never* get answered. If you try to pray against some temptation even as you rush into a place of vulnerability, your prayers will have little or no effect. You are in essence thrusting your fingers into the fire while praying that they won't get burned. What makes resisting temptation difficult for many of us is that we don't want to discourage it completely. We want to be delivered from temptation but would like to keep in touch. And that is *not* the prayer of faith Jesus had in mind.

Nothing lies outside of the reach of prayer except that which lies outside the will of God. And who wants anything that God doesn't? I, for one, want nothing in my life that stands against the will of God. And I doubt that you do either.

CHAPTER 72

When Afraid, Dial 9-1-1

"Let not your heart be troubled; you believe in God, believe also in Me." John 14:1

Who among us can ever forget September 11, 2001? The tragedy prompted many Americans to make big changes in their personal lives as they were prodded by two lessons: Life is precious, and time is short.

Because of September 11, 64 percent of Americans admitted they cried. Seventy-nine percent told someone, "I love you." Seven in ten Americans said they felt depressed after the terrorist attacks, nearly half reported having trouble concentrating, and a third said they had trouble sleeping.[6]

Curtis McMillen, a professor of social work at Washington University in St. Louis, said, "We were all personally affected by this one. We were all traumatized." Associated Press reporter David Foster commented, "Suddenly it seemed as if everyone was turning forty, a collective mid-life crisis, that stirred smoldering dissatisfactions and awakened dormant dreams."[7]

And, of course, it's not over. We continue to hear threats of biological and even nuclear threats. We are warned of new terrorist attacks that could come at any time.

Newsweek magazine told of a meeting at the White House between the president and members of the clergy. "I have to alert the American people to the ongoing dangers without creating alarm and irrational fear," President Bush told his guests. "How do I walk that line? Another crisis could hit us, more terrible than this one. It could be more terrible—biological, chemical or plutonium."[8]

We want to know what is going to happen to us, as a nation and as individuals. That is why so many Americans spend millions every year consulting psychics. Will we get hit again? Will there be war? Will we prevail over the terrorists? Fear lies heavy in the air.

But as Christians, we don't have to be afraid because our future is as bright as the promises of God. No matter what happens, we know that God is in control of our lives. We are indestructible until God is done with us!

God appoints the day of our birth; He also has appointed the hour of our death. "You have decided the length of our lives. You know how many months we will live, and we are not given a minute longer" (Job 14:5, NLT). God determines this, not some terrorist or anyone else.

Still, we do get agitated. Just like the disciples.

Jesus unnerved His men in the upper room by prophesying that one of them would betray Him. He also predicted that Peter would deny Him three times. Jesus knew His men felt afraid. They feared what was coming. They knew of the powerful opposition organized against them in Jerusalem, of the bitter hatred of the Pharisees and their determination to eliminate Jesus and all His disciples. They knew they were in danger—and so they felt deeply troubled.

But more than the physical danger, they feared His words about leaving them. This had struck terror into their hearts. They feared that even though they might survive, they would have to go on living without Him—and that was a fate worse than death. It was the heaviest blow of all. Their whole world came crashing down and left them in a state of panic. *What will happen to us? What about the future? If someone as devoted as the outspoken Peter could deny Him, what about the rest of us? Will we also fall away?*

So Jesus comforted His men, "Let not your heart be troubled; you believe in God, believe also in Me." In the original Greek, this is a command. The disciples knew God could be trusted; now Jesus wanted them to trust *Him.* God wouldn't abandon them; neither would He.

For three years they had known Jesus and had every reason to trust Him. He had never let them down. Did Jesus know what He was doing? Yes! Could He be trusted? Absolutely!

Jesus spoke these words not only to some troubled disciples in the first century but to us in the twenty-first. "Believe in Me!" He says to us. "Believe that I know what I am doing. Your agitation results from not believing what God has said in the Scriptures. I see the big picture."

In the same way, we may hear repeated threats against our country and against our personal safety—but God is still seated on the throne. He will protect and preserve us, just as He promised.

With our memories full of 9-1-1, let's not forget another 9-1-1—Psalm 91:1, that is, and the following verses: "He who dwells in the secret place of the Most High shall abide under the shadow of the Almighty. I will say of the Lord, 'He is my refuge and my fortress; My God, in Him I will trust.'" So we shall "not be afraid of the terror by night, nor of the arrow that flies by day" (verse 5).

Although much in this world can cause us to feel troubled and afraid, we have even greater cause *not* to fear. We have Jesus' promise. That should be enough.

CHAPTER 73

Hearing His Voice

"My sheep hear My voice, and I know them, and they follow Me." John 10:27

Does God still speak to us today? Is He interested in what happens to us as individuals?

Does He indeed have a master plan for our lives? If so, how do we discover it? How do we know the will of God? How do we hear His voice?

Usually when someone says, "God has been speaking to me lately," we get a little suspicious (justly so, in many cases). Many who say God speaks to them are far too often what I would describe as a few clowns short of a circus.

Yet as our Good Shepherd, Jesus promises that we can hear and know His voice. This does not, however, have to be some mysterious, mystical process. In fact, you may be surprised to learn that God speaks to you quite often. I would venture to say He has spoken to you lately and may be speaking to you right now in some way.

You see, the Good Shepherd knows how to speak to you because He knows you by name (John 10:3). He knows not only your name, but your nature. The Bible not only compares God to a shepherd, but it compares us to sheep. And that certainly is fitting.

Each sheep has its own distinctive characteristics, and the loving Shepherd recognizes these traits. One sheep may be afraid of high places, another of dark shadows. I think in the same way of the dogs I've had over the years, each one with a unique personality. Some were loyal, others stupid, a couple were smart, and all were very entertaining.

Have you noticed how different the twelve apostles were from each other? Peter the Impulsive, Thomas the Skeptic, Andrew the People Person, and the twin Thunder Boys—James and John the Retributive, who wanted to call down fire on anyone who bothered them.

And not only does this Good Shepherd know our natures, He knows our needs. Don't forget that this Good Shepherd also knows what it is to be a sheep. John the Baptist described Him as "the Lamb of God who takes away the sin of the world" (John 1:29).

So as the Good Shepherd, Jesus speaks to His sheep. To some, like Moses, He spoke audibly. Though this is still possible today, it is highly unlikely. To others, like Elijah, He spoke quietly. First Kings 19:12 tells us that God spoke to the prophet in "a still small voice," nothing more than a gentle whisper.

Yes, God speaks—but we do not always like what He says. To Peter, warming himself at the fire of his enemies, Jesus could have asked, "What are you doing here?" To Samson, with his head in the lap of Delilah, the Lord could have asked, "What are you doing here?"

How do *we* react when God asks us gently, "What are you doing here?" Have you ever sensed the conviction of the Holy Spirit when you were in a relationship or a place you did not belong?

You're in a movie theater when a scene depicts characters laughing at your Lord.

You're in a parked car with someone when sexual passion spreads over you like wildfire.

You're at a party where people are getting drunk and high.

You're in a relationship that is spiritually draining you and dragging you down.

At times like those, God's Holy Spirit whispers in the stillness of your heart, "What are you doing here?"

How else can we know when God is speaking to us?

GOD SPEAKS TO US THROUGH HIS WORD.

God will never lead us contrary to His written Word. It is our litmus test, our bedrock, our absolute. If you had a personal note from God, would you wait until you had nothing else to do before you got around to reading it? "Your Word is a lamp to my feet and a light unto my path," said David (Psalm 119:105).

GOD SPEAKS TO US THROUGH CIRCUMSTANCES.

God often uses circumstances to speak to us, as He did to Gideon (Judges 6). Those circumstances can include failure. Jonah certainly heard God through his mistake. When we fail, God wants us to "fail forward"; perhaps our failure today can make us a success tomorrow. God may even speak to us through tragedy or hardship. C. S. Lewis wrote that, "God whispers to us in our pleasures, speaks in our conscience, but shouts in our pains. It is His megaphone to arouse a deaf world." God got the attention of Saul of Tarsus by knocking him to the ground (Acts 9). "Before I was afflicted I went astray, but now I keep Your Word," says David (Psalm 119:67).

GOD SPEAKS TO US THROUGH HIS PEACE.

When we live in God's will, we enjoy His peace. "Let the peace of Christ rule in your hearts, since as members of one body you were called to peace. And be thankful," Paul says (Colossians 3:15, NIV). More literally this could be translated, "Let the peace of God, as an umpire, settle with all finality all matters that arise in your hearts." Do you need God to make a crucial call in your life? Then listen for His peace.

And once we have heard God's voice, what should we do? We must follow. Jesus calls, we respond. He whispers, we move. We follow—and then we keep on listening.

CHAPTER **74**

Full Joy

"These things I have spoken to you, that My joy may remain in you, and that your joy may be full." John 15:11

In many ways, we live in bleak times. Millions feel disillusioned with life while millions more feel uncertain about the future—especially young people.

In a letter to a national magazine, a young woman named Brooke Davidoff writes,

> I am 17 years old and I am pessimistic about my future. The whole world is so messed up—just look at the news: You have parents beating kids. You have adults molesting and raping children. You have lots of kids on drugs and lots of depressed kids. Our whole generation, 'Generation X,' needs help. The 'X' is almost the end of the alphabet. Does that mean that we've come to the end and that we are the ones that will destroy everything? Yes, drug use and sexually active teens have always been around, but their numbers are rising. And now, middle school children are having sex. Middle school girls are having abortions. Something's gone wrong. Children are killing each other and themselves. Children are raping other children. Either these things have always existed but were never discussed or our whole generation was raised terribly wrong. About one-third of our generation doesn't care about anything. It's kind of like 'anything goes.' We feel like everything's changing and we have nothing to do with it, so we'll just sit back

*and let it happen. We have nothing to grasp. No one
to believe in. No one to trust in but ourselves.*

Yes, Brooke, in many ways your generation *was* raised terribly wrong. You are the victim of a great social experiment in which parents who never grew up cast aside time-honored moral values and, in the phrase of the 1960s, did their own thing.

Nevertheless, there *is* someone to believe in, something to grasp, and someone to trust. You need to go to the next letter in the alphabet after *X,* to *Y*—as in "*Why* do I exist? *Why* was I created? And what am I living for?"

According to Jesus, you were created for joy. "These things I have spoken to you," Jesus said, "that My *joy* may remain in you, and that your *joy* may be full."

The things Jesus spoke of were His teachings about bearing fruit. We were created to bear fruit for God, which essentially means to become like Jesus: His mind becomes our mind, His purpose becomes our purpose. Both His likes and dislikes become our own—and that's when we experience deep joy.

When we don't bear fruit, we cease to function as our Creator meant us to. A vine is of little use other than as a fruit bearer. One cannot build houses or make furniture with the wood of a vine. It is of little use even as fuel, for it flames up for a moment and then vanishes. A vine was intended for only one thing: to bear fruit.

While God intended Israel to bear fruit for Him before all the nations of the world, He sadly admitted, "Israel is an empty vine" (Hosea 10:1, KJV). How true this is of so many professing, joyless Christians! They seem far more interested in what God can do for them than in what they can do for God.

God wants us to bear fruit for Him—and when we do, *we* reap the benefits. Paul says, "The fruit of the Spirit is . . . joy" (Galatians 5:22). And there's only one way to produce such luscious fruit, according to Jesus: "Abide in Me" (John 15:4). This is the secret of spiritual growth and the key to overflowing joy.

To *abide* suggests permanence of position. It's not some flash-in-the-pan "try God" approach but a continuing commitment. It's staying in a given place, maintaining unbroken fellowship with God.

To abide means that I take time for God and His Word each day. To abide means that I spend regular time with the Lord in prayer—and I can do this anywhere, anytime! To abide is to take the time to be with God's people, "not forsaking the assembling of ourselves together, as is the manner of some" (Hebrews 10:25).

Abiding in Jesus takes time, and lots of it. Unfortunately, we live in a mobile and fast-paced society that just doesn't like to wait. We are used to getting our information fast and simplified. So if God has something to say, we expect it to be distilled to a ten-second sound bite. We clamor for the *Cliffs Notes Guide to Spirituality.*

Many freeways in southern California have fast-track lanes, but there exist no fast tracks on the narrow road that leads to life (or to joy). It takes time, and lots of it, to become more like Jesus and to bear the kind of fruit that pleases Him.

But what better way to spend life than in getting to know Him? And what better reward than fullness of joy?

If we want to grow spiritually and become more like Jesus, we must learn to abide in Him. This is essential if we desire to bring forth lasting fruit.

And don't forget the promised result: joy! This is a Jesus-sized joy, a joy that can be described only as full—and it's a joy that can be experienced only by those who abide in Him.

That's what Brooke's generation needs. In fact, that's what every generation needs. And if the Lord tarries, the generations to come will need that, too.

Are you bearing spiritual fruit?

CHAPTER 75

What Happens beyond the Grave?

"Most assuredly, I say to you, he who hears My word and believes in Him who sent Me has everlasting life, and shall not come into judgment, but has passed from death into life." John 5:24

Death!

Now, there's a subject that most of us find very uncomfortable. We don't want to face the fact that we are mortals, that our days are numbered. Yet everyone has to face it. British novelist William Boyd wrote, "We all want to be happy, and we're all going to die. . . . You might say these are the only two unchallengeably true facts that apply to every human being on this planet."[9]

Death is no respecter of persons. It matters not if you are a billionaire or the poorest of the poor, an old man or a very young woman. You may be a president, king, queen, movie star, or athlete. It makes no difference. Everyone dies.

Rock star Sting once weighed in with his view of death. "Without wishing to seem morbid," he said, "I'm trying to work out how to die well. I'm halfway through my life. Death's a taboo in our society, but let's think about it and work out a strategy. It's the most important thing we all face and it's kind of unavoidable. If you want to live well you must surely want to die well."

That's true. Death is unavoidable. Only those who are prepared to die are really prepared to live.

A tombstone in England features the words, "Pause now stranger, as you pass by. As you are now, so once was I. As I am now, so you will be. So prepare for death and follow me." Someone reading this scratched out his own response: "To follow you I'm not content, until I know which way you went."

In John 5, Jesus reveals four important truths about death:

DEATH IS NOT THE END OF EXISTENCE.

Four centuries before the birth of Christ, the condemned Greek philosopher Socrates drank poison hemlock and lay down to die. His friends asked, "Shall we live again?" The dying philosopher could only reply, "I hope so, but no man can know."

But Jesus *did* know, and He told us that plenty comes after this life on earth. Death does not end everything. We can enjoy everlasting life.

THERE WILL BE A FINAL JUDGMENT.

Scripture clearly teaches that there will be a final judgment. Paul told the Athenians, "God . . . now commands all men everywhere to repent, because He has appointed a day on which He will *judge the world* in righteousness by the Man whom He has ordained" (Acts 17:30, emphasis added; see also 2 Peter 2:9; Matthew 12:36).

The fact of a future judgment assures us that God is ultimately fair. It satisfies our need for justice in the world. We have all seen things that seem unjust, horrible, and wicked. And we say to God, "How can they get away with that?"

Know this: God is in control and He keeps very accurate records. "But he who does wrong will be repaid for what he has done, and there is no partiality" (Colossians 3:25). Every wrong in the universe will be paid for. Either it will have been paid for by Jesus Christ through His death on the cross (if the offender repents of his sins and puts his faith in Him), or it will be paid for at the final judgment (by those who do not trust in Jesus for salvation).

TWO FORMS OF EXISTENCE WAIT BEYOND THE GRAVE.
According to the Bible, there are two resurrections: the resurrection of the just and of the unjust (Revelation 20:4-6). All true believers will take part in the first resurrection. "We are confident, I say, and would prefer to be away from the body and at home with the Lord," wrote Paul. "So we make it our goal to please him, whether we are at home in the body or away from it" (2 Corinthians 5:8-9, NIV). The second resurrection is reserved for those who remain estranged from God; Scripture calls this the "second death" (Revelation 21:8).

**OUR DESTINY DEPENDS UPON
OUR RELATIONSHIP WITH JESUS.**
Jesus promises that whoever hears His words and believes them "has everlasting life, and shall not come into judgment, but has passed from death into life." Those who put their faith in Jesus Christ go immediately after death into the presence of Jesus Christ. There are no stopovers; it's a direct flight. As Jesus said to the thief on the cross, "*Today* you will be with Me in Paradise" (Luke 23:43, emphasis added).

This created something of a personal dilemma for the apostle Paul, for while he longed to be in heaven with Jesus, he knew he had work on earth to do. He spoke of wanting to "depart and be with Christ, which is far better" (Philippians 1:23). He did not say "depart for a few hundred or thousand years in a state of suspended animation" or "depart for purgatory."

At a memorial service for a deceased believer, a preacher wanted to say just the right thing. But instead of extolling the lady's virtues, he declared, "We have here only the shell. The nut is gone!"

The pastor might have confused his words, but he got the sentiment exactly right. Better to be a nut in heaven than anywhere else.

Which way are you going? And what about your friends and family?

CHAPTER **76**

Born Once,
Die Twice

> *"Do not marvel at this; for the hour is coming in which all who are in the graves will hear His voice and come forth . . . those who have done evil, to the resurrection of condemnation."* John 5:28-29

Timothy Leary, often called the "Messiah of LSD," died in 1996. Leary was a familiar fixture at love-ins and became an icon of the '60s. During his heyday, "Leary is God" buttons sprouted up on many college campuses.

In his final days, Leary made elaborate plans to turn his own death into a public event by committing suicide while logged on to the Internet. White haired and gaunt, he said he felt thrilled to learn he was dying. "Because that's the final party," he said in a March interview with the TV newsmagazine *Extra.* "I say dying is a team sport, like living is."

But Leary died before he got the chance to go through with the "ultimate dropout." And three weeks before he died, Leary abandoned his long-held plans to have his head frozen in cryonic suspension (he had hoped he could be thawed and re-vived in the future).

Even though Leary joked about death, "He is as afraid of dy-ing as any of us," said his friend. "Maybe more so, because he really doesn't believe there is anything that comes after this."

On his deathbed, Leary cried out, "Why?" A little later he added, "Why not?"

Most if not all of us ask Leary's first question. Why do we

have to die? And what of nonbelievers? What happens to them?

Jesus made it plain that just as surely as the Christian goes into the presence of God, the nonbeliever goes to a place of judgment. Jesus described this in vivid detail in the story of Lazarus and the rich man (see Luke 16:19-31).

One day, everyone without Christ will stand before God at the great white throne. Both small and great will appear before the Lord for judgment (Revelation 20:11-15). Jesus called this "the resurrection of condemnation."

But if the unbeliever is already condemned (John 3:18), then what purpose does the last judgment serve? This final confrontation between God and unredeemed humankind will clearly demonstrate why the unbeliever stands condemned.

John tells us that books will be opened (Revelation 20:12). Perhaps these books record all we ever said or did, "for every idle word men may speak, they will give account of it in the day of judgment," Jesus declared (Matthew 12:36). Perhaps one of the books will show how the lost failed to live up to their own standards (Romans 2:15). Another book might have a record of all the times these individuals heard the gospel. Yet another book might be the law with its righteous requirements, "that every mouth may be stopped, and all the world may become guilty before God" (Romans 3:19). The law condemns but does not convert. It challenges but does not change. It points the finger but does not give mercy. It makes all guilty.

Imagine the scene. The nail-scarred hand of Jesus runs over the lines in the Book of Life, but an individual's name cannot be found. The person begins to tremble. "Lord, Lord, did [I] not prophesy in your name, and in your name drive out demons and perform many miracles?" (Matthew 7:22, NIV).

"I never knew you," replies Jesus.

Never knew you!

Never knew you!

The awful words will ring in the condemned person's ears for all eternity.

No believer will be present for this terrible judgment. Why not? Perhaps because we would not be able to bear to hear a loved one turn to us and say, "Why didn't you warn me of this judgment and tell me about Jesus' forgiveness?"

Yes, death is coming. And all of us determine where we will spend eternity by our decision to follow or not follow Jesus Christ.

Are you ready?

Recently I read a tragic story about a man who did not realize how prophetic were the words he sang one night at the Metropolitan Opera. Tenor Richard Versalle, sixty-three years old, fell off a ladder during a scene and landed on the stage. Officials quickly declared an intermission and later canceled the performance. Versalle died without regaining consciousness, the victim of an apparent heart attack. His last words, sung from the stage of the Metropolitan Opera, were: "Too bad you can only live so long."

What if this were your last night on earth?

History tell us of the renowned French atheist Voltaire, one of Christianity's most aggressive antagonists. Speaking of Christ, he once said, "Curse the wretch!" He also boasted, "In twenty years, Christianity will be no more. My single hand will destroy the edifice it took twelve apostles to rear."

Yet on his deathbed, a nurse who attended him was reported to have said, "For all the wealth in Europe, I would not see another atheist die." The physician attending Voltaire at his death said that he cried out with utter desperation, "I am abandoned by God and man. I will give you half of what I am worth if you will give me six months of life. Then I shall go to hell and you will go with me. Oh Christ! Oh, Jesus Christ."

At the end, the Messiah of LSD, Timothy Leary, likewise felt afraid to die. "Why?" he cried. Death is a fearful thing for a nonbeliever—and there are no second chances at the second death.

Born once, die twice. Born twice, die once.

That is why we need to redouble our efforts to reach those who don't yet know Christ, people without the hope of life beyond the grave.

Pray that God would direct you to such a person today, and help him to change his eternal address.

CHAPTER **77**

Finish the Race
You've Started

*"Also I say to you, whoever confesses Me before men,
him the Son of Man also will confess before the angels
of God. But he who denies Me before men will be denied
before the angels of God."* Luke 12:8-9

On October 20, 1968, a dramatic moment took place at the
Mexico City Olympics. As the last of the marathon runners
stumbled across the finish line, a few thousand spectators remained in the almost-dark Olympic Stadium.

Finally the wail of police sirens ripped the air. As all eyes
turned to the gate, a lone runner wearing the colors of Tanza-
nia staggered into the stadium. John Stephen Akhwari was
the last contestant to finish the twenty-six-mile contest. He
had injured his leg in a fall and entered the track bloodied and
crudely bandaged. While he hobbled the final, lonely lap, spectators rose and applauded him as if he had won.

After the race, someone asked him why he had refused to
quit. "My country did not send me seven thousand miles to
start the race," he replied simply. "They sent me seven thousand miles to finish it."

To help us achieve a strong finish in our race of faith, Jesus
Christ gave us two strong promises, one positive and one negative. First the positive: "Whoever confesses Me before men,
him the Son of Man also will confess before the angels of
God." And then the negative: "But he who denies Me before
men will be denied before the angels of God."

The word *confess* means to affirm and agree with. It is not simply to recognize a truth, but to identify with it. Even the demons recognize that there is one God (James 2:19), but by no means do they *confess* God; in fact, they are His worst enemies. We do not confess Christ simply by acknowledging that He is Lord and Savior, but by acknowledging and receiving Him as *our* Lord and Savior. Outward confession with the mouth reflects genuine belief in the heart.

A true follower of Jesus Christ eagerly and openly identifies with Christ, whether before a fellowship of other believers, a group of serious inquirers, or a hostile crowd of unbelievers. "Whoever confesses that Jesus is the Son of God, God abides in him, and he in God" (1 John 4:15).

Of course, every one of us suffers lapses in this area. Who among us has spoken up for Jesus every time the opportunity arose? Even Peter denied the Lord, but after his denial he immediately went out into the night and wept bitterly. Though he denied the Lord, he felt deep remorse for his behavior and repented—and God made him into one of the true champions of the early church.

Any true child of God who lapses in this area will feel horrible about it, want to get right with God, and make sure not to repeat the incident. Contrast Peter's response to that of Judas Iscariot, who sold out Jesus, felt terrible regret for his awful deed—but then went out and hanged himself.

If you have failed to confess Jesus before others, don't despair. You may have stumbled, but you don't need to stay down. Ask the Lord for the courage and wisdom to represent Him boldly and effectively. And then prepare yourself for your next opportunity to confess Jesus. It's one thing to fall down. It's another thing to stay there.

But don't forget, people will treat us just as they treated our Lord. Some will love us; others will hate us. "If the world hates you, you know that it hated Me before it hated you," Jesus said. "If you were of the world, the world would love its own. Yet because you are not of the world, but I chose you out of the world, therefore the world hates you" (John 15:18-19). Let's just make sure we are persecuted for righteousness' sake. Frankly, far too often we Christians deserve the criticism that nonbelievers dish out. We have all seen people say and do harebrained things in the name of Christ, only to be mocked, rejected, or worse.

Then they console themselves by saying they were "persecuted for righteousness' sake," when in reality they were persecuted for being strange. It had nothing to do with righteousness or Jesus Christ. If we must face persecution, make sure it is for the right reasons, not the wrong ones.

The negative side of Jesus' promise ought to sober us: "But whoever denies Me before men, him I will also deny before My Father who is in heaven" (Matthew 10:33). This reminds us instantly of Jesus' prophecy concerning the end of time. "Not everyone who says to Me, 'Lord, Lord,' shall enter the kingdom of heaven, but he who does the will of My Father in heaven," He said. "Many will say to Me in that day, 'Lord, Lord, have we not prophesied in Your name, cast out demons in Your name, and done many wonders in Your name?' And then I will declare to them, 'I never knew you; depart from Me, you who practice lawlessness!'" (Matthew 7:21-23).

Are you confessing Christ before people or are you denying Him?

Jesus Christ is coming back, and it could be sooner than some of us think.

The Bible often compares the Christian life to running a race. Paul told the Ephesian believers that he wanted to finish the race and complete the task the Lord had given him (Acts 20:24). At the end of his life he could write, "I have fought the good fight, I have finished the race, I have kept the faith" (2 Timothy 4:7).

You too can finish the race well by eagerly confessing Christ before others. You too can have a testimony like that of

D. L. Moody, who on his deathbed said, "I see earth receding, and heaven is opening. God is calling me."

Remember: The goal is not simply to start the race but to finish it.

CHAPTER **78**

Bringing Others to Jesus

"Come, follow me," Jesus said, "and I will make you fishers of men." Matthew 4:19 NIV

It is worth noting that Jesus never deals with any two individuals in exactly the same way. Just as a physician varies his methods from patient to patient, so the Great Physician does the same.

Consider how differently Jesus captured the loyalties of four of His first disciples. Not everyone comes to faith in Jesus in exactly the same way!

The first disciple, Andrew, heard John the Baptist proclaim Jesus as "the Lamb of God," and as a result sought out Jesus for himself (John 1:35-40). Andrew was probably the cautious type, but he was also quite inquisitive. He would not do something just because someone told him to. Even though he had the greatest respect for John the Baptist, the prophet's endorsement of Jesus was not enough; he had to find out for himself. As Andrew cautiously followed Jesus, the Lord turned and asked him, "What do you seek?" In other words, "What are you really after here, son? What is it that you want? Please, Andrew, investigate for yourself. Nobody's trying to fool you here. Don't take John's word for it. Come and find out for yourself!"

Some people don't come to Jesus right away when they hear about Him. They want time to think over His claims and investigate the facts. But once convinced, like Andrew, they're *con-*

vinced! Andrew went out immediately to tell his brother, Simon.

How we need more Andrews today! Every time we read of him in Scripture, he's bringing someone to Jesus. It was Andrew who brought the little boy to Jesus, whose lunch the Lord multiplied and used to feed five thousand (John 6:8). When some Greeks came to Jerusalem wanting to see Jesus, once again it was Andrew who brought them to the Master (John 12:20-22). If we had more Andrews, we would have more Simon Peters—one person bringing another to Jesus. So simple. So effective. Yet so neglected.

God's primary way of reaching people is through people. Sadly, research tells us that only one in twenty Christians have ever shared the gospel, and only one in ten think they should. If fifty million true Christians live in America, that means about five million are sharing Christ, and most of them ineffectively. Did you know that only half the people sitting in our churches' pews can even articulate the gospel?

Andrew himself probably could not articulate the gospel, but he knew enough to bring his brother Peter to Jesus (John 1:41-42). The Lord dealt with Simon in a way completely different from Andrew. When John writes, "Jesus looked at him [Peter]" (verse 42), he uses a Greek word that means "he saw right through him." Peter gave Jesus no surprises. The Lord knew exactly what He was getting with Peter: he was quick-tempered, hot-headed, vacillating, impulsive. Jesus knew that Peter was full of doubt and uncertainty and that he had to be given hope. So Jesus said to him, "You shall be called Cephas" (verse 42), meaning "a rock."

A third disciple, Philip, had no believer to help him come to faith, no person who cared for his soul. Of him we read, "The following day Jesus wanted to go to Galilee, and He found Philip and said to him, 'Follow me'" (John 1:43). This is closer to my own story. No one invited me to church; I came on my own (drawn by the Holy Spirit, of course).

The last of the four, Nathanael, came to Jesus through the invitation of his newly converted brother, Philip. The text says, "Philip *found* Nathanael" (verse 45, emphasis added). Andrew *found* Peter; Jesus *found* Philip; and Philip *found* Nathanael. Sometimes we pray, "Lord, send someone in my life to whom I can preach the gospel." And though those occasions may come about every once in a while, God's standard mode of operation is for us to find people, not to wait for them to find us. Jesus did not say, "All the world should go to church," but rather that the church should "go into all the world" (Mark 16:15).

As we go into all the world to preach the gospel, we can begin by asking people the same question that Jesus asks the two disciples of John the Baptist in John 1:38: "What do you seek?"

We might phrase it differently. We might ask, "What do you want in life? What are you living for?" Then, when a person expresses an interest in knowing Jesus, we can say, "Come and see!"

Why did Jesus employ varying tactics? We don't necessarily know. Yet one lesson is clear: We should never talk to people about Jesus using some preprogrammed routine or spiel. If we have the luxury of time, it's always good to get to know the individual a bit. Certainly, tossing off trite religious clichés will not work; more likely, that will turn off most seekers.

Remember, different types of people come to faith in different ways. Some may have a tremendous emotional experience at conversion; others don't (I didn't). We all come to faith in Christ differently. The first disciple John describes found Jesus through a preacher's message. The second and the fourth came to Jesus as a result of the personal work of a believer. The third man came to faith without any human instrument (the exception rather than the rule).

So listen carefully and speak appropriately. Learn to fish for men in a way most appropriate to the fish swimming before you. That was always the apostle Paul's strategy in reaching people: "To the weak I became weak, to win the weak. I have become all things to all men so that by all possible means I might save some" (1 Corinthians 9:22, NIV).

And don't forget the most important lesson of all. When we get right down to it, we all come to Christ in different ways, but God does essentially the same thing for all of us. He tells us that we are separated from Him by sin, that we are all missing out on heaven, and that we must come to God through the cross of Jesus.

That message has never changed. And it never will.

CHAPTER 79
Exclusively Yours

Jesus said to him, "I am the way, the truth, and the life. No one comes to the Father except through Me."

John 14:6

You gotta love Thomas!

Thomas has been given the title "Doubting Thomas," but we really ought to consider him more of a skeptic. A doubter doubts even when the facts are clear. A skeptic looks carefully, wanting to see the truth for himself.

Thomas acquired this dubious handle probably because of what he said after he missed the appearance of Jesus in the upper room. "Unless I see in His hands the print of the nails, and put my finger into the print of the nails, and put my hand into His side, I will not believe," he declared (John 20:25). But when confronted with the risen Lord eight days later, his skepticism quickly gave way to belief. "My Lord and my God!" he exclaimed (verse 28).

Thomas never was one to let others do his thinking for him. When he didn't understand something, he said so. Earlier Jesus had told the Twelve that He was about to go away to a place they knew, in a way they knew. It was Thomas who replied, "Lord, we do not know where You are going, and how can we know the way?" (John 14:5). Jesus answered his puzzled disciple's question with a famous statement: "I am the way, the truth, and the life. No one comes to the Father except through Me."

Through this bold statement, the Master offers to us an implied promise: "If you go My way and believe My truth and accept My life, God will gladly welcome you into the very throne room of heaven."

Many feel comfortable with the concept of Jesus as a mild-mannered moral teacher, meekly spreading peace and love, with a lamb wrapped around His neck. But the Jesus of the Scriptures is far more than that. He is infinitely more than a prophet, a teacher, or a good man.

He is the God-Man!

So how is Jesus the Way? When the time came for Christ to be nailed to the cross, with one hand He took the hand of sinful humanity and with the other He took the hand of a holy God. He became the only bridge connecting a fallen humankind with a righteous heavenly Father. Man would rather try to build his own ladder to God, apart from Jesus—but as Scripture says, "There is a way that seems right to a man, but in the end it leads to death" (Proverbs 14:12, NIV).

Jesus is not only the Way, He is the Truth. He speaks the truth and only the truth, lovingly yet firmly.

Many people spend a lifetime asking the same question that Pontius Pilate put to Jesus: "What is truth?" (John 18:38). Today we have blurred the lines, calling wrong, right, and right, wrong. Nevertheless, there *is* absolute truth. All is not relative, as some would suggest. *Jesus* is the truth!

Certainly Jesus never shrank from making such a statement. Can you name the single phrase most often on the lips of Jesus during His earthly ministry? It's no contest. Almost *eighty times* in the Gospels, Jesus tells His audience, "I tell you the truth." Jesus never shied away from telling the truth, whether the crowds wanted to hear it or not. And He doesn't shrink from telling us the truth today, whether that truth comes in the form of the Holy Spirit's conviction or powerful encouragement.

Jesus is the Way. He is the Truth. And more than that, He is the Life.

Our Savior once told the crowds, "For as the Father has life in himself, so he has granted the Son to have life in himself" (John 5:26, NIV). Luke wrote about the Savior's resurrection from the dead, "It was *impossible* for death to keep its hold on him" (Acts 2:24, NIV, emphasis added).

And what does this fact have to do with us? Everything! John later wrote, "And this is the testimony: God has given us eternal life, and this life is in his Son. He who has the Son has life; he who does not have the Son of God does not have life. I write these things to you who believe in the name of the Son of God so that you may know that you have eternal life" (1 John 5:11-13, NIV).

The Bible insists that Jesus Christ is the only way to heaven. Scripture declares, "Without shedding of blood there is no remission" (Hebrews 9:22). Paul wrote, "For there is one God and one Mediator between God and man, the Man Christ Jesus" (1 Timothy 2:5). And Peter maintained, "Nor is there salvation in any other, for there is no other name under heaven given among men by which we must be saved" (Acts 4:12).

No one who wants life can find it anywhere outside of Jesus Christ.

Have you heard of the singing group The Smashing Pumpkins? At the height of their fame the band won seven MTV awards. Yet despite their success, several members of the band suffered major drug problems. Their drummer was charged with heroin possession, and backup player Jonathan Melvoin died of a heroin overdose.

Their song "Bullet with Butterfly Wings" speaks of the futility and emptiness of life. In the end, the singer equates his existence to that of a rat in a cage, and he sees himself as beyond salvation.

What could cause such hopelessness among a band with so much success? Especially since God Himself says, "Look to Me, and be saved, all you ends of the earth! For I am God, and there is no other" (Isaiah 45:22). No one lies beyond the forgiveness of God. Jesus promised, "The one who comes to Me I will by no means cast out [or turn away]" (John 6:37).

No one has to be a rat in a cage. You can become a child of God. If you are looking for Jesus, He is here for you, right now! He is the Way, the Truth, and the Life—and He is all of those things *for you.*

CHAPTER 80

The Fear Factor

"Do not fear, little flock, for it is your Father's good pleasure to give you the kingdom." Luke 12:32

Fear! We all know what it's like to be caught in its cold grip. Some fear the future. Others fear death. Most would probably agree with comedian Woody Allen, who said, "I'm not afraid to die. I just don't want to be there when it happens."

Jesus spoke often of fear. In one of the most tender passages of this sort, He commanded us, "Do not fear, little flock, for it is your Father's good pleasure to give you the kingdom." This verse suggests three kinds of delightful relationships with God:

- A Shepherd and His sheep ("Do not fear, little *flock*")
- A Father and His child ("your *Father's* good pleasure")
- A King and His subjects ("give you the *kingdom*")

A SHEPHERD AND HIS SHEEP

Jesus calls us His "little flock." In this context, the littleness seems affectionate. We often give our children nicknames to show our pleasure in them. Jesus is saying to us, "You are My little flock! You are dear to Me. Precious. Special." That's good, because sheep cannot take care of themselves. They need the shepherd's constant care and attention.

Jesus loved to describe Himself as the Good Shepherd and us as His sheep. "Most assuredly, I say to you, I am the door of the sheep," He said. "All who ever came before Me are thieves and robbers" (John 10:7-8). The high walls of ancient sheepfolds were designed to protect defenseless sheep. Often predators would circle the pen looking for an opening, but only one entrance existed: the door where the shepherd stayed to keep a careful eye on his flock.

God keeps a close watch on all His sheep. He knows everything about you—your hopes, fears, dreams, thoughts, sins, strengths, weaknesses. And still He loves you!

Jesus also said, "My sheep hear my voice, and I know them, and they follow me" (John 10:27). Sheep soon learn that when the shepherd calls, it's worth coming. He always calls for a specific purpose and with their best interests in mind; perhaps to give them fresh food or to lead them to a new stream or a new pasture. The word *follow* refers to "one who deliberately decides to comply with instructions." Followers decide not to go the way of the crowd but to stay as close to the Shepherd as possible as He leads the flock to green pastures and still waters.

A FATHER AND HIS CHILDREN

Jesus then shifts the imagery from a pastoral scene to a domestic one. We are not only Jesus' sheep, we are God's children. Most Jews considered it a radical concept to think of God as their Father. The Pharisees accused Jesus of blasphemy for referring to God as His Father—so they couldn't have felt overjoyed when He extended the image to include *us!*

To Mary after His resurrection, Jesus said, "Go to my brethren and say to them 'I am ascending to My Father and your Father'" (John 20:17). Jesus taught us to pray, "Our Father in heaven" (Matthew 6:9). John got the message, for he marveled, "Behold what manner of love the Father has bestowed on us, that we should be called children of God!" (1 John 3:1). As a Father, God always loves us—but He also will take whatever measures He needs to in order to keep us on track (see Hebrews 12:5-11).

A KING AND HIS SUBJECTS

Because Jesus is our Shepherd and God is our Father, the Lord makes us a tremendous promise: it gives God great pleasure to give us His kingdom. He wants to rule not only in our lives here on earth but also with us forever in His coming kingdom (Revelation 22:5).

No wonder we do not need to feel afraid! God wants us to relate to Him as Shepherd, Father, and King. "The Lord is my light and my salvation; whom shall I fear?" asked David. "The Lord is the strength of my life; of whom shall I be afraid?" (Psalm 27:1).

D. L. Moody had a favorite verse. He used to say, "You can travel to heaven first-class or second-class. First-class is, 'I will trust and not be afraid.' Second-class is, 'When I am afraid, I will trust in thee'" (Psalm 56:3-4, paraphrased).

God is your Shepherd, your Father, and your King. And to you, one in His little flock, He will give His kingdom. So do not fear, little flock!

That should take care of the fear factor for you.

CHAPTER 81

Time to Look Up

"Now when these things begin to happen, look up and lift up your heads, because your redemption draws near." Luke 21:28

You can hardly pick up a newspaper or turn on the news these days without learning of another terrorist attack in Israel. Is this a sign of the end times?

I believe it is.

Let's take a few moments to catch a bird's eye look at the future of the world. After all, it's your future and mine.

In Luke 21, Jesus describes a time known as the Great Tribulation, a seven-year period of horror that begins with the emergence of a wicked world leader called the Antichrist. In those seven years, God will pour out His wrath on an unrepentant humankind and lift Israel to worldwide prominence.

Jesus declared that in those days there will be "distress of nations, with perplexity" (verse 25). Much of this anxiety will focus on the city of Jerusalem. "But when you see Jerusalem surrounded by armies, then know that its desolation is near," Jesus said (verse 20). His prophecy reminds us of the words of God through the prophet Zechariah, uttered hundreds of years before: "I am going to make Jerusalem a cup that sends all the surrounding peoples reeling. Judah will be besieged as well as Jerusalem. On that day, when all the nations of the earth are gathered against her, I will make Jerusalem an immovable rock for all the nations. All who try to move it will injure themselves" (Zechariah 12:2-3, NIV).

Even now, Jerusalem finds herself surrounded by hostile nations whose armies keep themselves in a constant state of readiness for war. After the modern state of Israel came into existence in 1948, a war of independence left the city of Jerusalem divided, with Jordan retaining control over the Old City, including the Temple Mount and most of the historic sites. Finally, during the Six-Day War of 1967, Israeli forces captured the Old City and reunified Jerusalem. The entire city came under Jewish control for the first time in many centuries.

And there's the rub.

Jerusalem remains at the heart of the Israeli-Palestinian conflict, with many Arab leaders insisting that the Old City and the entire West Bank be ceded to the Palestinians as a condition of peace. The political situation remains so volatile that a literal gathering of armies against Jerusalem could happen within hours. The Palestinians want more than *part* of Jerusalem; they want *all* of it. Truth be told, they would like to see the Jews gone. But that is not going to happen.

Many Arab countries, including Iraq, Iran, Libya, and Syria, have long sponsored terrorism against the Jewish people and their allies. Just after the World Trade Center attacks, Osama bin Laden was shown on satellite television reciting an ode to Jerusalem at his son's wedding. "The wound of Jerusalem is making me boil," he said. "Its suffering is making me burn from within."[10]

The issue is much bigger than Osama bin Laden, Yasser Arafat, or Saddam Hussein (or whoever the leaders may be at any particular time). This conflict is not going away but ultimately will get worse. So, will the current crisis lead to the events we read about in Luke 21? Is this the end of the world as we know it?

Only God knows.

There may be a temptation in the days ahead to abandon Israel. But we must stand by her, for God promised Abraham, "I will bless those who bless you, and I will curse him who curses you" (Genesis 12:3). One reason God has blessed America is that this nation has faithfully supported Israel. Get out your history books and you will find that God ultimately cursed every nation that cursed Israel: Babylon, Imperial Rome, Nazi Germany. Ultimately the nations that call for holy war against Israel will see that *God* placed Isaac's descendants in the land. And He will be glorified.

So what should *we* do? How should current world conditions affect *us?* Jesus answered that question decisively. "Now when these things begin to happen," He said, "look up and lift up your heads, because your redemption draws near."

The current hostilities in the Middle East ought to remind us that Jesus is coming. So get ready to meet the Lord! Look up!

How quickly our values can change in times like these. Before the events of 9/11, the lead articles on TV and in the press highlighted the lives of so-called celebrities. In California we had a twenty-four-hour Gary Condit watch. The fall season of TV was upon us, along with a new football season. The day before the terrorist attacks, I read an article in *USA Today* headlined, "The dark side of age 25." A twenty-four-year-old from Austin, Texas, said, "I graduated when I was 21 with a political science degree. I thought because I was an honor student, everything would be fine and dandy, that I'd have this great job. I believed if I wasn't a dot-com millionaire, I was over the hill at 20."

Few remembered that story the day after 9/11. Our perspectives had changed radically. Suddenly some of us began to hear Jesus when He essentially declares, "Get a heavenly, eternal perspective on life. You don't know when your life will end or when I will come. So be ready."

As Christians, let's be looking up, ready for the return of the Lord. And let's follow Peter's good advice: "But we are looking forward to the new heavens and new earth he has promised, a world where everyone is right with God. And so, dear friends, while you are waiting for these things to happen, make every effort to live a pure and blameless life. And be at peace with God" (2 Peter 3:13-14, NLT).

CHAPTER **82**

"Let's Roll!"

"In My Father's house are many mansions; if it were not so, I would have told you. I go to prepare a place for you." John 14:2

What happens when we die? To many, this is life's ultimate mystery.

Some believe that we undergo repeated reincarnations, transmigrating from existence to existence. Others think that when we die, we cease to exist (that's what I used to believe).

But Jesus promised us a very different destiny, a reservation in a real place called heaven. As a Christian, I know that I am going to heaven when I die. "In My Father's house are many mansions," Jesus promised. "I go to prepare a place for you."

The word *mansions* does not describe palatial estates with neatly mowed lawns. *Mansions*—more literally, "dwelling places"—probably refers to our new, glorified bodies. "For we know that when this earthly tent we live in is taken down—when we die and leave these bodies—we will have a home in heaven, an eternal body made for us by God himself and not by human hands," wrote the apostle Paul (2 Corinthians 5:1, NLT).

When we're young, we have an abundance of energy, stamina, and strength. But as we grow older, strange things start happening. Type mysteriously starts getting smaller. People speak in lower and lower volumes. We feel and think young, but our bodies do not cooperate. We walk by a window, see our reflection and wonder, *Who's that old guy?* Kids start calling us "Mr." or "Mrs." or worse, "Gramps"!

The Bible reminds us that while our bodies will not live

forever, our souls will. We will eternally walk the streets of heaven in our glorified bodies. Yet even in our wildest dreams, it's virtually impossible to imagine the splendor, beauty, and awesomeness of heaven.

The Bible does not tell us much about heaven, probably because it lies so far beyond our comprehension. Paul, who personally saw it, said, "I was caught up into paradise and heard things so astounding that they cannot be told" (2 Corinthians 12:4, NLT). Try explaining the beauty of Hawaii to a three-month-old baby. He just sits there, propped up by some pillows, listening. Maybe he even smiles and we think, *Oh look, he smiled! He understands!* Hardly.

In the same way, we cannot grasp the glory of heaven any easier than a baby can grasp the beauty of Hawaii. There are, however, a few things the Bible tells us about heaven.

For starters, we know that heaven will never experience darkness of any kind, spiritual or physical. "There shall be no night there," John says. "They need no lamp nor light of the sun, for the Lord God gives them light" (Revelation 22:5). Even so, you won't have to worry about ultraviolet rays, so leave the sunscreen behind!

Fear will have no place in heaven. We won't need locks on the doors, bars on the windows, or alarm systems. God will eliminate everything that causes fear. We will have no concern for personal danger.

"God Himself will be with them and be their God," wrote John about heaven. "He will wipe away every tear from their eyes. There will be no more death or mourning or crying or pain, for the old order of things has passed away" (Revelation 21:3-4, NIV).

God will answer all our questions in heaven. Some will want to know, "God, if you are so good, why did You allow this or that to happen?" Or the big one we all want answered: "How do you stop '12:00' from blinking on the VCR?" Five seconds after you get to heaven, all your questions will be answered. "Now we see things imperfectly as in a poor mirror, but then we will see everything with perfect clarity. All that I know now is partial and incomplete, but then I will know everything completely, just as God knows me now" (1 Corinthians 13:12, NLT).

But better than new bodies, better than perpetual day, better than the absence of sorrow or pain or death, better than streets of gold and answered questions—will be the everlasting presence of Jesus. He has loved us, Paul exulted, "that in the ages to come He might show the exceeding riches of His grace in His kindness toward us in Christ Jesus" (Ephesians 2:7).

By now we've all heard the incredible story of United Flight 93 that left Newark, New Jersey, on the morning of September 11, 2001. One passenger, thirty-two-year-old Todd Beamer, called a GTE Airfone operator to report the hijacking. Convinced of the terrorists' plans, Todd cried out to God. He then asked the operator to recite the Lord's Prayer with him. His last words: "Help me, Jesus!" and then, "Let's roll!"

Although it is impossible to know exactly what happened next, evidence suggests that Todd and several other passengers stormed the cockpit and overpowered the terrorists. However, before they could gain control of the plane, it spiraled into the ground, killing everyone on board. It is generally believed that the passengers' heroic actions averted an attack on the U. S. Capitol dome or the White House.

Todd's wife, Lisa, later appeared on the *Oprah* show. "Life is bigger than what we see right here," she said. "Todd knew that and that is what enabled him to act rationally and calmly. He knew that whatever happened, he was going to end up in heaven that day. I know that same thing holds true for me. I'm going to see him again. . . . The hope I hold onto is that his death was not in vain. It was part of God's plan."

Jesus wants *you* to rest secure in His promise of heaven. God will keep you safe until the day He calls you home, and then He will give you the strength to bear the journey.

CHAPTER 83

Homesick for Heaven

> "And if I go and prepare a place for you, I will come again and receive you to Myself; that where I am, there you may be also." John 14:3

Have you ever felt really homesick? No matter how beautiful a place you visited and no matter how much you enjoyed the people there, as they say, there's no place like home.

I've always felt amazed at the homing instinct of many animals. Salmon return every year to spawn in the rivers of their birth (my family saw this happen in Seattle). Swallows return to the mission at San Juan Capistrano every year (although lately, more have been going to the local Kmart).

Believers, too, have a homing instinct. We have eternity in our hearts. "He has also set eternity in the hearts of men," writes Solomon (Ecclesiastes 3:11, NIV). We all have a sense, deep inside, that *something more* awaits us. The Bible tells us we have a home waiting for us that we all should desperately miss: heaven! Because of this, we will never feel fully satisfied in this life. Nothing will ever quite measure up.

Of course, we have all enjoyed those moments where everything seemed to be just perfect. That gorgeous sunset. That star-filled night. That special moment with someone you love. And you think, *I want it to be this way, always.*

But the moment always ends.

In a sense, in those few seconds you have received a glimpse of eternity, a taste of the bliss you will experience one day in glory. But until that day, you will always feel a bit homesick for heaven.

Your experience on this earth, no matter how great, pales in comparison to the Christian hope of heaven. "For our present troubles are quite small and won't last very long," wrote the apostle Paul. "Yet they produce for us an immeasurably great glory that will last forever! So we don't look at the troubles we can see right now; rather we look forward to what we have not yet seen. For the troubles we see will soon be over, but the joys to come will last forever" (2 Corinthians 4:17, NLT).

Not everyone has this great hope. A growing number of men and women have no idea what comes next.

But Jesus promises His followers a home in heaven.

You've probably heard about the New York City cab driver who approached the pearly gates. Next to him stood a well-known minister.

"Welcome!" Peter said to the cabbie. "I understand you were a New York City cab driver. Since I'm in charge of housing, I believe I have found the perfect place for you. See that mansion over the hilltop? It's yours."

The minister heard all this and began to stand a little taller. He said to himself, "If a cab driver gets a place like that, just think what *I'll* get!"

In a few moments the minister approached the gate. "Welcome!" Peter said to him. "I understand that you were a well-known minister. See that shack down in the valley? That's all yours."

Hardly had the words left Peter's mouth when the irate minister objected, "Hey, I was a minister! I preached the gospel! I helped teach people about God! Why does that cabbie get a mansion and I get a *shack?*"

"Well," Peter sadly responded, "it seems that when you preached, people *slept.* But when the cabbie drove, people *prayed!*"

It's virtually impossible for us, even in our wildest dreams, to imagine the splendor, beauty, and awesomeness of heaven. A young boy asked me the other day if he would recognize his grandma in heaven. I told him he would but that she would not look quite the same as she did on earth. For starters, she would not be old and wrinkled.

Do you know the best thing of all about heaven? We will be with Jesus! As He said, "Where I am, there you may be also." Quite frankly, I would be happy if heaven were a big Wal-Mart, so long as Jesus were there! You can be sure, however, that it will be infinitely better than any Wal-Mart. In fact, it will be far better than anything you have ever experienced. Take the most wonderful moment of your life, multiply it by a million times, and you will still have only a vague sense of the glories of heaven.

The Bible makes it clear that the Lord will not merely send for us, but He will come *in person* to escort us to the Father's house. "I will come again and receive you to Myself," He promised. Paul wrote, "The Lord Himself will descend from heaven with a shout, with the voice of the archangel, and with the trumpet of God. And the dead in Christ shall rise first. Then we who are alive and remain shall be caught up together with them in the clouds to meet the Lord in the air. And thus we shall always be with the Lord. Therefore comfort one another with these words" (1 Thessalonians 4:16-18).

Notice that Jesus does not say "*take* you" but "*receive* you." He will not take us against our will. He will return for those who are watching and waiting for Him. Sadly, many will be left behind. "One will be taken and the other left," Jesus warned (Matthew 24:40).

The promise of heaven is a promise only to the child of God who has received Christ. And for those who have received Him, heaven is a promise that lasts forever and ever and ever.

Some day in the not-too-distant future, Jesus will set His feet back on planet Earth and say, "I have returned." And it may be sooner than we think!

CHAPTER 84

At Home with Jesus

"Behold, I stand at the door and knock. If anyone hears My voice and opens the door, I will come in to him and dine with him, and he with Me." Revelation 3:20

Imagine that just as you sat down to dinner, you noticed someone standing at your door: the president of the United States! He tells you that he just happened to be in the neighborhood and thought he would stop by for a cup of coffee.

Even better than that, have you ever thought about how wonderful it would be to have *Jesus* come to your home for a visit? The truth is, He's already said that He'd accept the invitation: "Behold, I stand at the door and knock. If anyone hears My voice and opens the door, I will come in to him and dine with him, and he with Me."

The apostle Paul prays in Ephesians 3:17 that "Christ may dwell in your hearts through faith." Paul doesn't pray that Jesus would merely be allowed inside the house of our hearts but that He would feel at home there, settled down as a close family member. Paul prays that Christ may settle down and dwell in our affections, that Christ may dwell in our will, that Christ may be the dominating factor in the whole of our life.

Jesus Christ wants to be at the very heart of our hearts. He wants to be at the very center of our lives. The question is, do we want Him there?

In his excellent little book *My Heart—Christ's Home,* Robert Boyd Munger takes this concept and runs with it. He writes of

Jesus coming to his home and desiring to walk around in it. He and Jesus first look together at the study (something missing in most homes today; we're more likely to have surround-sound home theaters).

Munger writes, "He entered with me and looked around at all the books in the bookcase, the magazines on the table, the pictures on the walls. As I followed His gaze, I became uncomfortable. Strangely enough, I had not felt badly about this room before, but now that He was there with me looking at these things, I was embarrassed. There were some books on the shelves His eyes were too pure to look at. On the table were a few magazines a Christian has no business reading. As for the pictures on the walls—the imaginations and thoughts of my mind—some of these were shameful."[11]

Think about Jesus walking through your own home right now. What if He walked into your den or family room? What would He think of your video, CD, and DVD collections? Would you feel comfortable if Jesus took your remote control and checked out what cable channels you watched? What if He moved over to your personal computer and checked out the bookmarks on your favorite Web sites? Would that embarrass you?

Too many of us think of our homes as our castles, off-limits to everyone (including God) except by our consent. And so we think we can play around with sin in a private corner of our home with no one the wiser. But God warns us not to play games with sin. Sin usually starts out small, and then *whammo!* Far too often we underestimate its pull and power.

I recently read a book titled *Dumb, Dumber and Dumbest: True News of the World's Least Competent People.* The author told of an eighteen-year-old Englishman named Jordan Lazelle. The young man had to be hospitalized after his pet scorpion stung him on the tongue. When Lazelle tried to give Twiggy its usual good-night kiss, it grabbed his lip. When he opened his mouth in shock, he said the scorpion "jumped in and stung me on the tongue—it had never done that before."

If you're giving sin its little "good-night kiss," watch out! It's going to jump in and sting you.

We have to remember that we are not the hosts of our homes but the guests. Jesus is the owner of our lives; He purchased us at Calvary. "Do you not know that your body is the temple of the Holy Spirit who is in you, whom you have from God, and you are not your own?" asks Paul. "For you were bought at a price; therefore glorify God in your body and in your spirit, which are God's" (1 Corinthians 6:19-20).

How would our daily routines change if we lived as if we really believed God owned our bodies? Our churches would not be the same. Our nation would not be the same. I dare say the world would not be the same.

Jesus may be knocking on the door of your heart right now, telling you that He wants to come into your home. If Jesus were to walk into your home today, would He feel comfortable? I don't mean, would He find the couches comfy? I'm asking, would He feel *at home* there?

Take a moment and pretend that Jesus is walking in the door with you. Look around at what you hold dear—not just your house or apartment, but your heart. What pictures hang on those walls? What things signal your priorities?

Let Jesus do whatever spring cleaning He may find necessary. Sure, He may throw out a few things—maybe even a lot. But I can assure you, what He puts in their place will be so much better that you won't miss any of them. Not even a little.

NOTES

1. Alexander Maclaren, quoted in Steve Halliday and William Travis, *How Great Thou Art* (Sisters, Ore.: Multnomah Books, 1999).
2. Corrie ten Boom, *The Hiding Place* (New York: Bantam Books, 1974), 238.
3. Deanni Kizis, "The Kid's All Right," *Harper's Bazaar* (March 2000).
4. David G. Meyers, "Pursuing Happiness: Where to Look, Where Not to Look," *Psychology Today* (July/August 1993).
5. Merrill C. Tenney in *The Expositor's Bible Commentary*, vol. 9, ed. Frank E. Gaebelein (Grand Rapids, Mich.: Zondervan, 1981), 118.
6. "American Psyche Reeling from Terror Attacks," a survey report by The Pew Research Center (19 September 2001); <http://people-press.org/reports/display.php3?ReportID=3>.
7. David Foster, "Time Is Short: Attacks Prompt Soul-Searching, Big Life Changes," *SouthCoast Today* (20 September 2001); <http://www.s-t.com/daily/09-01/09-20-01/a02wn019.htm>.
8. Howard Fineman and Martha Brant, "Bush's Battle Cry," *Newsweek* (October 1, 2001).
9. William Boyd, *Stars and Bars* (New York: Morrow, 1984).
10. Bassem Mroue, "Bin Laden Cites 'Wound of Jerusalem,'" *The Associated Press*, New York (11 January 2001).
11. Robert Boyd Munger, *My Heart—Christ's Home* (Downers Grove, Ill.: InterVarsity Press, 1992).

Steps to Peace with God

 ## *Step 1* God's Purpose:
Peace and Life

God loves you and wants you to experience peace and
life—abundant and eternal.

The Bible Says . . .

**"We have peace with God through our Lord
Jesus Christ." Romans 5:1**

**"For God so loved the world that He gave His
only begotten Son, that whoever believes in Him
should not perish but have everlasting life."
John 3:16**

**"I have come that they may have life,
and that they may have it more abundantly."
John 10:10**

Since God planned for
us to have peace and
the abundant life right
now, why are most
people not having this
experience?

 ## *Step 2* Our Problem:
Separation

God created us in His own image to have an abundant
life. He did not make us as robots to automatically love
and obey Him, but gave us a will and a freedom of
choice.

We chose to disobey God and go our own willful way.
We still make this choice today. This results in separation from God.

Our choice results
in separation from
God.

The Bible Says . . .

**"For all have sinned and fall short of the glory
of God." Romans 3:23**

**"For the wages of sin is death, but the gift of
God is eternal life in Christ Jesus our Lord."
Romans 6:23**

People
(Sinful)

God
(Holy)

Our Attempts

There is only one remedy for this problem of separation.

Through the ages, individuals have tried in many ways to bridge this gap . . . without success . . .

The Bible Says . . .

"There is a way that seems right to a man, but in the end it leads to death." Proverbs 14:12, NIV

"But your iniquities have separated you from your God; and your sins have hidden His face from you, so that He will not hear." Isaiah 59:2

Step 3 God's Remedy: The Cross

Jesus Christ is the only answer to this problem. He died on the Cross and rose from the grave, paying the penalty for our sin and bridging the gap between God and people.

The Bible Says . . .

"For there is one God and one mediator between God and men, the man Christ Jesus." 1 Timothy 2:5, NIV

"For Christ also suffered once for sins, the just for the unjust, that He might bring us to God." 1 Peter 3:18

"But God demonstrates his own love for us in this: While we were still sinners, Christ died for us." Romans 5:8, NIV

God has provided the only way . . . we must make the choice . . .

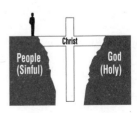

Step 4 Our Response: Receive Christ

We must trust Jesus Christ and receive Him by personal invitation.

The Bible Says . . .

"Behold, I stand at the door and knock. If anyone hears My voice and opens the door, I will come in to him and dine with him, and he with Me." Revelation 3:20

"But as many as received Him, to them He gave the right to become children of God, to those who believe in His name." John 1:12

"If you confess with your mouth the Lord Jesus and believe in your heart that God has raised Him from the dead, you will be saved." Romans 10:9

Are you here . . . or here?

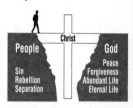

Is there any good reason why you cannot receive Jesus Christ right now?

How to receive Christ:

1. Admit your need (I am a sinner).
2. Be willing to turn from your sins (repent).
3. Believe that Jesus Christ died for you on the Cross and rose from the grave.
4. Through prayer, invite Jesus Christ to come in and control your life through the Holy Spirit. (Receive Him as Lord and Savior.)

What to Pray:

Dear Lord Jesus,

   I know that I am a sinner and need Your forgiveness. I believe that You died for my sins. I want to turn from my sins. I now invite You to come into my heart and life. I want to trust and follow You as Lord and Savior.

In Jesus' name. Amen.

_____   _____
          Date   Signature

God's Assurance: His Word

If you prayed this prayer,

The Bible Says...

"For 'whoever will call upon the name of the Lord will be saved.'" Romans 10:13, NASB

Did you sincerely ask Jesus Christ to come into your life? Where is He right now? What has He given you?

"For it is by grace you have been saved, through faith—and this not from yourselves, it is the gift of God—not by works, so that no one can boast." Ephesians 2:8,9, NIV

The Bible Says...

"He who has the Son has life; he who does not have the Son of God does not have life. These things I have written to you who believe in the name of the Son of God, that you may know that you have eternal life, and that you may continue to believe in the name of the Son of God." 1 John 5:12–13

Receiving Christ, we are born into God's family through the supernatural work of the Holy Spirit who indwells every believer. This is called regeneration or the "new birth."

This is just the beginning of a wonderful new life in Christ. To deepen this relationship you should:

1. Read your Bible every day to know Christ better.
2. Talk to God in prayer every day.
3. Tell others about Christ.
4. Worship, fellowship, and serve with other Christians in a church where Christ is preached.
5. As Christ's representative in a needy world, demonstrate your new life by your love and concern for others.

God bless you as you do.

Billy Graham

If you want further help in the decision you have made, write to:
Billy Graham Evangelistic Association, P.O. Box 1270, Charlotte, North Carolina 28201-1270

If you are committing your life to Christ, please let us know! We would like to send you Bible study materials and a complimentary six-month subscription to *Decision* magazine to help you grow in your faith.

The Billy Graham Evangelistic Association exists to support the evangelistic ministry and calling of Billy Graham to take the message of Christ to all we can by every prudent means available to us.

Our desire is to introduce as many as we can to the person of Jesus Christ, so that they might experience His love and forgiveness.

Your prayers are the most important way to support us in this ministry. We are grateful for the dedicated prayer support we receive. We are also grateful for those who support us with contributions.

Giving can be a rewarding experience for you and for us at the Billy Graham Evangelistic Association (BGEA). Your gift gives you the satisfaction of supporting an organization that is actively involved in evangelism. Also, it is encouraging to us because part of our ministry is devoted to helping people like you discover and enjoy the stewardship of giving wisely and effectively.

Billy Graham Evangelistic Association
P.O. Box 1270
Charlotte, North Carolina 28201-1270
www.billygraham.org

Billy Graham Evangelistic Association of Canada
Box 2276 Station M
Calgary, Alberta T2P 5M8
www.billygraham.ca

Toll free: 1-877-247-2426